THE SECRET CEMETERY

The Secret Cemetery

*A Guide to the Burial Ground
of the English Canonesses of the Holy Sepulchre
in the Parishes of Boreham and Springfield, Chelmsford*

Hannah Thomas

GRACEWING

First published in England in 2017
by
Gracewing
2 Southern Avenue
Leominster
Herefordshire HR6 0QF
United Kingdom
www.gracewing.co.uk

All rights reserved.
No part of this publication may be reproduced, stored in a
retrieval system, or transmitted in any form or by any means,
electronic, mechanical, photocopying, recording or otherwise,
without the written permission of the publisher.

© 2017 The Trustees of the Canonesses of the Holy Sepulchre

The right of Hannah Thomas to be identified as the author of this work
has been asserted in accordance with the Copyright, Designs and Patents Act 1988

ISBN 978 085244 910 3

Cover photograph taken by Pauline McAloone. Cover design by Mustard Creative.

Typeset by Word and Page, Chester, UK

CONTENTS

Foreword	vii
Acknowledgements	viii
Introduction	1
A History of the Convent Cemetery at New Hall	3
Liège, 1642–1794	3
Migration to England, 1794	16
Holme Hall and Dean House, 1794–1799	22
New Hall, 1799 onwards	30
The Cemetery	35
Cemetery Establishment and Early Burials	35
Cemetery Development: The Cemetery Wall	43
Burials: Community	48
Burials: Clergy	60
Burials: Lay People	68
Conclusion	80
Appendices	
Appendix 1. Memorial Inscriptions	83
Appendix 2. List of the Liège Community in 1794	122
Appendix 3. List of Clergy	123
Appendix 4. List of Lay People in the Original Cemetery	125
Bibliography and Further Reading	127
Index of Persons	133
Plan of Graves	*inside flap*

FOREWORD

In 1855, in writing *The Warden*, Anthony Trollope was minded to parody the anti-Roman Catholic sentiment of the country through reference to a 'Convent Custody Bill', clause 107 of which would allow 'the bodily searching of nuns for Jesuitical symbols by aged clergymen'. The jibe is a reminder of the very long-standing nature of anti-Roman Catholic, and specifically anti-nun, sentiment in England. This sentiment had by no means been resolved by the Catholic Emancipation Act of 1829. The Canonesses of the Holy Sepulture have been, for much of their history, a group of women under siege. Nevertheless, as much of their archive demonstrates, the Canonesses achieved a resilience to adversity. This book focuses on a very particular aspect of the Canonesses' lives: the way in which they strove to perform appropriate rituals at the time of death. This aspect has a material expression: a small burial ground, largely hidden in the trees surrounding New Hall School.

This burial ground is something of a gift to the unsuspecting visitor. The wall—several feet higher than it needs to be—hides a delicate and moving landscape of nineteenth-century tombstones recording the lives of past sisters and their servants, and of girls attending the school. The old section of the burial ground is small, with each grave marking the passing of an individual and valued member of the extended family of the Community. The later graveyard extension echoes the expansion of the Community beyond the school.

The site clearly has emotional significance, but it also carries religious political importance. Creating burial space in the grounds of the school was not just a pragmatic necessity. Hannah Thomas's history demonstrates that the Canonesses could not always be guaranteed a sympathetic reception to a request for burial space and tolerance to exercise their faith through funerary ritual. The burial ground is well hidden, and it is entirely possible that the wall represented a desire to hide burial practices, given a mid-nineteenth-century obsession with convent inspections.

Throughout the UK, the burial grounds of minority religious groups are being lost to urban development. This failure to protect the material culture of this aspect of our history is also a lost opportunity to recall past religious plurality and the shame of our past intolerances. The site remains important and distinctive. The Canonesses are to be congratulated for their determination to preserve the site intact, and to ensure that its history is accessible.

Julie Rugg,
Cemetery Research Group,
University of York

ACKNOWLEDGEMENTS

No research project is ever truly a solo venture, and this one would simply not have been possible without the help, support and encouragement of so many people. Firstly, to the team at the Centre for Catholic Studies, Durham University, who have made me so welcome since the project began. Particular thanks to Professor Paul Murray, Dr James Kelly and Dr Cormac Begadon for the support and encouragement, and to Tim Guinan and Andrew Harston for the hard work and fundraising that gave life to the project in the first place.

A number of scholars have kindly shared and discussed their own research with me and put up with my incessant questions about death, dying and all things related to convents: Caroline Bowden, Andrew Cichy, Douglas Davies, Peter Leech, Carmen Mangion, Emilie Murphy, Victoria Van Hyning and Maurice Whitehead. Special thanks to Julie Rugg, for encouraging the project to begin and for the never-failing willingness to discuss the minutiae of cemetery legislation, the support and the coffee, and for writing the foreword to this volume.

Scholars would be nothing without archivists and librarians, and thanks is also due to the staff at all of the archives, libraries and other repositories I have visited during the last three years, particularly the Bar Convent, Douai Abbey and Downside Abbey. Thanks to all at Ushaw College, especially Jonathan Bush and Claire Marsland.

Thanks must also go to my friends and family, who have always supported and encouraged me, my parents, Bernadette and Phillip, my brothers, Owen and Rhys, and my husband Richard, who have survived endless discussions about death, dying, burial and convents.

Finally, to the Canonesses of the Holy Sepulchre, whose project this is, so many thanks are due. Thank you for making me so welcome, for encouraging the project with such enthusiasm and willingness, and for making me a part of your wonderful family. Thanks to S. Mary Stephen for endless discussions about the wall. Particular thanks to S. Mary Magdalene and Pauline McAloone, without whom this book would never have been written.

INTRODUCTION

This book has been written to celebrate two significant occasions. The first is the conclusion of a three-year-long research project in association with the Centre for Catholic Studies, Durham University (2014–17). The second is that the work has been commissioned to preserve for posterity the importance of the Community cemetery at New Hall school, presenting a lasting record of this unique example of its place and period—physically, a small 'secret' corner of the school grounds, but spiritually and historically, so much more than that.

The Community cemetery in Chelmsford is, and always has been, an important part of Community spiritual and liturgical life. It represents a place of commemoration and remembrance for deceased members of the Community family, a focal point for current members of the Community and friends to gather together in celebration, and creates a continuous on-going link between the entire Community—yesterday, today and tomorrow.

Cemeteries are so much more than a place for burials, and are in fact richly varied examples of the Victorian culture of death and mourning.[1] This richness and variety is certainly evident in the cemetery of the English Canonesses of the Holy Sepulchre, which, as well as being special to the spiritual lives of the Community, is also historically significant. Cemeteries can be viewed as a microcosm of history, presenting the life and times of a cross-section of people, across a range of time periods, with a particular factor in common, whether that be geographical location or religious denomination. Cemeteries such as this one, deeply rooted within a particular group of people and a shared religious outlook, offer an opportunity to examine the wider context of the individuals buried within its walls, in this case the wider history of English Catholicism in the eighteenth and nineteenth centuries.

The cemetery is also special for other reasons. Created in 1799, it is likely to be the oldest Catholic cemetery in continuous use within the modern-day British Isles. It has been used by the Community continuously since the first burial in March 1799, with its most recent addition in September 2016 (at time of printing). Although it is predominantly for the use of the Canonesses, a special feature of the cemetery is that it has always been open to the wider Community family, particularly lay people and clergymen closely associated with them. This combination of priests, servants, school children and Community speaks to the great sense of family and togetherness felt by those who are associated with the Canonesses.

Approximately 325 people are memorialised in the cemetery. The original half, containing the entrance, is the final resting place of 227 people, buried between 1799 and 1956. This includes thirteen clergymen, forty lay people, and 174 members of the Community. The extension of the cemetery, which is entered from the opening in the wall at the rear of the original cemetery, includes, at the time of writing, a further ninety-three people, including one clergyman, fifty-four lay people, and forty-three members of the Community, laid to rest since 1956. In the interests of space, and out of respect to the families of the recently deceased, this book will focus predominantly on those buried in the original half of the cemetery, although the index of memorial inscriptions at the end of the volume includes the names of every person who has been buried in the cemetery up to the present day.

It is also important at this juncture to address exactly what is meant by a cemetery, as opposed to a burial ground, graveyard or any other type of burial space. What is it that defines a burial space as one or the other? The Community cemetery is more correctly identified as a burial ground, which is defined as 'a burial space intended to serve non-Anglicans, for example Roman Catholics or Quakers'.[2]

---

[1] See Sarah Rutherford, *The Victorian Cemetery* (Oxford: Shire Publications Ltd, 2008), pp. 5–7.
[2] See Glossary of terms relating to burial, as cited in Julie Rugg, *Churchyard and Cemetery: Tradition and Modernity in Rural North Yorkshire* (Manchester: Manchester University Press, 2015), pp. 380–5.

However, the burial ground at New Hall is referred to as 'the cemetery' by the Community, and its associates, and will therefore be described as such throughout this text.

The main sources for this text are preserved in the Community's own archive, currently housed at their base in Colchester.[3] The archive is substantial, and contains large amounts of material relating to their history. The material contained within the present volume has been drawn from sources such as the Community's account books and financial records; the Chantress's notebooks which function as the Community diary, as well as other manuscript records and chronicles; extensive burial registers and records of deaths; personnel files of individual members of the Community; school registers; the Book of Benefactors; and the Chapter Books, a record of the decisions discussed by the regular gathering of all members of the Community. There are also a number of letters sent to various members of the Community from their families and wider networks.

Please note, the cemetery is located within private ground, and as such is not open to the general public. Access is restricted to relatives or friends of those who are buried there, and to those with particular historical interests related to the cemetery.

---

[3] Archives of the Canonesses of the Holy Sepulchre, referred to throughout the text as ACHS.

A HISTORY OF THE CONVENT CEMETERY AT NEW HALL

Liège, 1642–1794

Before the Reformation and the dissolution of the monasteries in Britain in the 1530s, religious communities had been a key part of medieval life in England and Wales, providing care for the sick, religious guidance, centres for art and culture, centres of prayer and spirituality, and education for local children. After the Reformation, when it was illegal to practise Catholicism in England and Wales, and all nine hundred monasteries, abbeys and convents had been destroyed; religious orders were no longer able to provide any of these essential services.[1] By the end of the sixteenth century, further legal changes implemented under Elizabeth I (r. 1558–1603) meant that the practice of Catholicism was treasonous activity, seen as expressing an allegiance to a foreign head of state, rather than to England's appointed sovereign.[2] Many English Catholics chose to live in exile in continental Catholic Europe, rather than in the dangerous conditions of a now-Protestant England. Religious orders also established 'convents in exile' on the continent, where those with religious vocations could receive training, and English Catholic children could be sent to receive the Catholic education that they were no longer able to get at home.

The cemetery at New Hall is the Community cemetery of the English Canonesses of the Holy Sepulchre, founded in Liège in 1642 by Susan Hawley (1622–1706).[3] Hawley had known she wanted to found a religious house for English women in Flanders since she was a teenager, and, shortly after being clothed in 1641 with the name in religion of Mary of the Conception, she and Frances Cary, S. Francis (1619–59), established an English house of the Canonesses of the Holy Sepulchre in Liège, the only English branch of this international order. Gradually others joined them, until after seven years there were twenty-two sisters in total, and Hawley was elected the first prioress in 1652, when there were enough members to hold an election. The Community also established a school for English Catholic girls in Liège, and it became one of the most sought-after educational establishments of its time.

The Sepulchrines flourished in Liège for over 150 years, a location that was deliberately chosen by Hawley for close proximity to the English Jesuit College in the same city. Indeed, the very process of locating the Community convent in Liège in the first place had been negotiated with much assistance

---

[1] See for example Barry Collett (ed.), *Female Monastic Life in Early Tudor England* (Farnham: Ashgate, 2002); Edward Alexander Jones and Alexandra Walsham, *Syon Abbey and its Books: Reading Writing and Religion, c. 1400–1700* (Woodbridge: Boydell & Brewer, 2010); and J. H. Bettey, 'The Suppression of the Benedictine Nunnery at Shaftesbury in 1539', *Hatcher Review*, 4:34 (1992), pp. 3–11. A comprehensive bibliography of literature relating to the dissolution of English and Welsh female religious houses can be found on the History of Women Religious of Britain and Ireland website, at https://historyofwomenreligious.org/women-religious-bibliography, hereafter HWRBI.

[2] Studies of the various reactions to these changes are wide-ranging, and far beyond the scope of the present volume. As a starting point, see Peter Marshall, *The Oxford Illustrated History of the Reformation* (Oxford: Oxford University Press, 2015). For more on the reaction of the English Catholic community to these changes, see, for example, John Bossy, *The English Catholic Community 1570–1850* (London: Darton, Longman & Todd, 1979); Christopher Haigh, *English Reformations: Religion, Politics and Society under the Tudors* (Oxford: Clarendon Press, 1993); Eamon Duffy, *The Stripping of the Altars: Traditional Religion in England, c.1400–c.1580* (London: Yale University Press, 2005); and Alexandra Walsham, *Catholic Reformation in Protestant Britain* (London: Ashgate, 2014).

[3] Caroline M. K. Bowden, 'Hawley, Susan (1622–1706)', *Oxford Dictionary of National Biography* [ODNB], online edition.

An English Canoness of the Holy Sepulchre.
Image courtesy of the Canonesses of the Holy Sepulchre.

from Joseph Simons, *vere* Emmanuel Lobb (1594–1671), a Jesuit based at the English College there.[4] Simons helped the Community in negotiations to obtain the permission of the Prince Bishop, Ferdinand of Bavaria (r. 1612–50), and in the difficult process of establishing an English convent in a Flemish city.

The Community were based at three sites within the city during this period. Initially based at a small house in the north of the city, in the parish of St Hubert, once the Community had grown sufficiently in numbers, they moved to a large plot in the gentrified suburbs outside the city on Rue Pierreuse overlooking the town, in the parish of Saint-Servain. The Community moved in on Christmas Day 1644, after attending Midnight Mass at the Church in the English Jesuit College. Later that morning they were joined at their new convent by Simons, who heard their confessions, said Mass in the new convent chapel, gave them communion, and delivered a short sermon. The Canonesses stayed at

---

[4] Thomas M. McCoog, SJ, *English and Welsh Jesuits Part 2: G–Z* (Southampton: Catholic Record Society, 1995), p. 295, hereafter *Jesuits*. Simons/Lobb was also an important dramatist: see Maurice Whitehead, *English Jesuit Education: Expulsion, Suppression, Survival and Restoration, 1762–1803* (Farnham: Ashgate, 2013), pp. 34–5.

Liège, 1642–1794

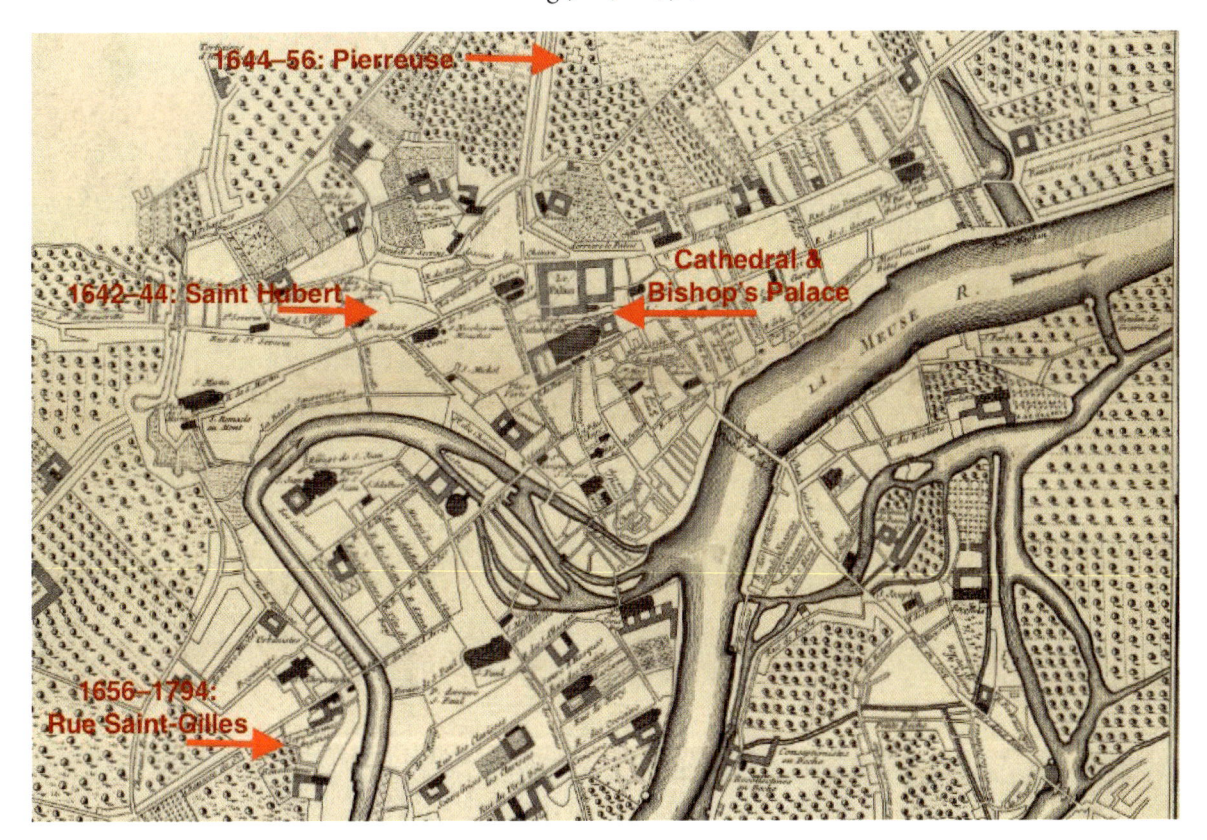

Sites in Liège at which the English Canonesses of the Holy Sepulchre were based.
(Map: Hannah Thomas, from the map drawn by Christopher Maire SJ, 1720)

this location for eleven years, but by 1655, the development of the nearby citadel or barracks on Rue Pierreuse had made it unsafe as a location for a convent. In fact the barracks shared a land boundary with the convent, making it extremely dangerous for the Community to remain where they were. They were also under pressure from the Prince Bishop, Maximilian Henry of Bavaria (r. 1650–88) to find new premises, as the land on Pierreuse was in a prime location, in the gentrified rural suburbs of the city, but only a short walk from the centres of power at the Cathedral and the Bishop's Palace. The Bishop wanted to give this valuable estate to one of his trusted advisers, but needed to offer the Community somewhere more suitable first, as alternative accommodation.

On the other side of town on the Faubourg D'Avroy, on Rue Saint-Gilles, just outside the city centre in the parish of Saint-Christophe, was an old monastery in the possession of a community of Coquin Brothers. The men were an unruly group, and had let the house fall into serious disrepair. The Prince-Bishop was able to solve several problems at once by evicting the Coquins and offering the Coquin monastery to the Sepulchrine Community.[5]

The Sepulchrines moved in to the old monastery in May 1656, and after some extensive repairs and building work, their new convent was completed in 1660. Numbers expanded rapidly. The new site on Rue Saint-Gilles was on the banks of the River Meuse, in a much safer location and was nearer to the Jesuit College than their previous residence had been. It was also within close proximity of several other convents and monasteries, all of which were very modern, and had been established since the 1620s. There was also several older convents and monasteries located on the opposite bank of the river, within the city walls, dating back several hundred years.

---

[5] The Coquins were evicted in such haste that they left behind many of their books and manuscripts. These were carefully looked after by the Sepulchrines, and even reused in some cases. They were brought to England in 1794 and remained with the Community until the 1950s when they were sold to the John Rylands Library in Manchester. Much more research is needed into these manuscripts and the order to whom they originally belonged.

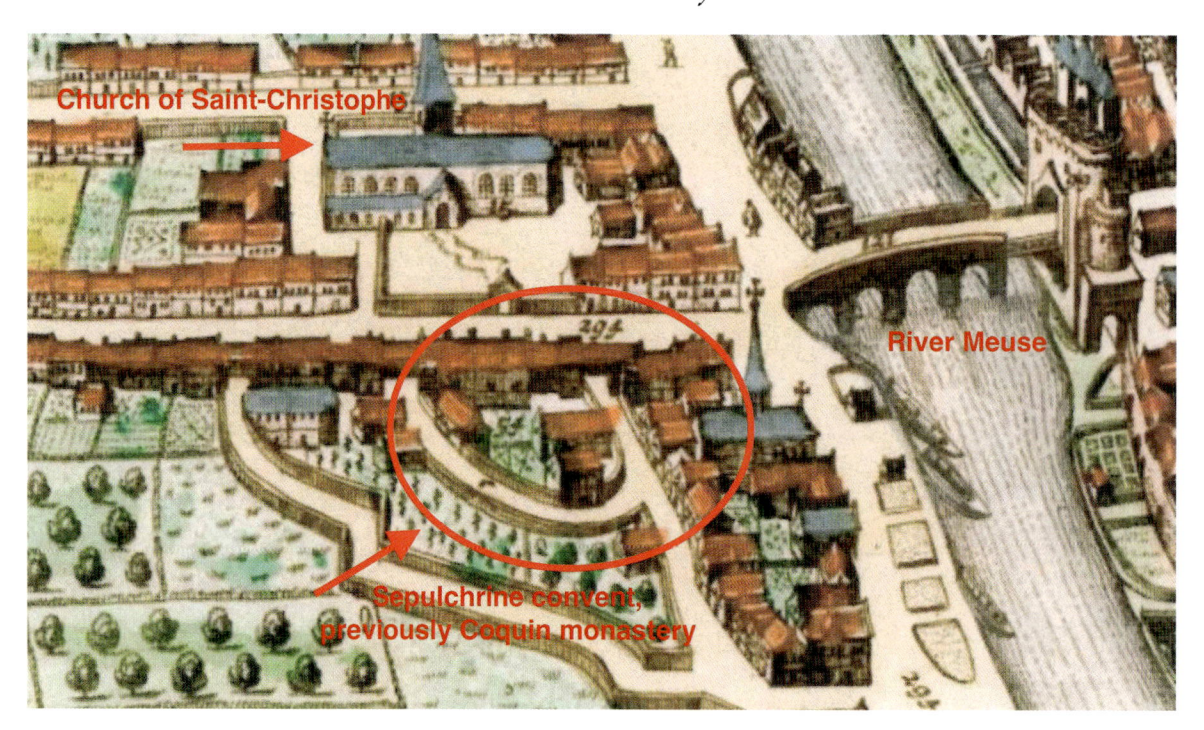

The third and final site in Liège at which the Community were based, on Rue Saint-Gilles.
Note the proximity to the river bank, and the nearby church of Saint-Christophe.
(Map: Hannah Thomas, from the map drawn by Julius Milheuser, 1649).

The Community remained in their new home for just less than 140 years, until 1794. The school was developed and much improved at this location, under the guidance of the sixth prioress, Mary Dennett, S. Mary Christina (1730–81).[6] Prior to 1770, when she was elected prioress, the school had been very small, with no more than six pupils, but under Dennett's encouragement and vision it soon flourished to over forty pupils, and continued flourishing such that a second school building was required by 1776. For Dennett, the proper education of English Catholic girls was a true expression of religious fervour and vocation.[7] She also improved the Community's finances and introduced new levels of spiritual discipline. Dennett was much beloved within the Community, and is referred to in Community records as a second foundress, such was her religious zeal and effectiveness during her time as prioress.

Although very little trace remains of the convent buildings in Liège, documentary evidence allows some sense of Community life in this period to be established. In 1652, shortly after her official election as the first prioress of the Community, Susan Hawley published *A Brief Relation of the Order and Institute of the English Religious Women at Liège*, in which she aimed to introduce her order to England:

> [this] Institute is so exceedingly agreeable and suitable to our English natures that many
> by the knowledge of it may be invited to serve God in it, who otherwise in the world
> may perish most miserably.

The booklet was small and easily portable, consisting of only fifty-six pages. This was particularly important in making sure that it reached its intended audience of English Catholics: Catholic literature, and its potential influence on the Catholic community, was deemed extremely dangerous by the English state authorities. Such literature was outlawed in England, and had to be carefully smuggled in past watchful port authorities. Anyone caught in possession of such works, or attempting to bring them in to the country, could be fined or even imprisoned.[8]

---

[6] Caroline M. K. Bowden, 'Dennett, Mary (1730–1781)', *ODNB*. A manuscript biography of Christina Dennett was written by a member of the Community approximately eleven years after Dennett's death: see p. 65 below.

[7] See *History of the New Hall Community of Canonesses Regular of the Holy Sepulchre* (Roehampton: Manresa Press, 1899), pp. 48–67, hereafter *History of the Community*; and Whitehead, *English Jesuit Education*, pp. 127–30.

[8] An Act to Prevent and avoid Dangers which may grow by Popish Recusants was passed in 1606. The act laid out

Liège, 1642–1794

Mary Dennett, S. Christina (1730–81), 6th prioress of the Holy Sepulchre, Liège.
Image courtesy of the Canonesses of the Holy Sepulchre.

As well as emphasising the advantages of joining the Community, the text also gave practical information, such as the routine of day to day life at the convent in Liège. After rising at 4am, and following half an hour of private meditation, the Community processed to the chapel for the morning Offices of Matins, Lauds and Prime. At 6am, the day's work began, accompanied by a prayer and appropriate readings. The Canonesses returned to their chambers for more private meditation at 7.30am, before processing to the chapel for the Offices of Terce, Sext and None, as well as daily Mass. Work and prayer continued until 10.45am, when it was time for dinner. After dinner, private meditation and communal work continued until 3pm, when the Community gathered together for Vespers, followed by further prayer and communal work until Compline at 5pm. Supper was served at 6pm, and after further prayers, an examination of conscience and private spiritual readings, the Community retired to bed at 8.30pm. Other practical information contained within the text included directions for travelling to Liège, noting that 'the best and shortest way from England to Liège is by Holland to Rotterdam, thence to Boiseduc, then to Maestricht, so to Liège'.[9]

specific restrictions on the buying or selling of Catholic books, which were seen as potentially so dangerous that those caught importing, printing, buying or selling 'popish' books were to be seized, and the perpetrator fined forty shillings per book. See 3 Jac 1 cap. 5: An Act to Prevent and avoid Dangers which may grow by Popish Recusants 1606, as cited in *The Laws against Papists and Popish Recusants, Nonconformists and Nonjurors* (London: Printed for W. Bickerton, 1744), pp. 40–51.

[9] Compiled from information given in Susan Hawley, *A Brief Relation of the Order and Institute of the English Religious Women at Liège* (Liège, 1652), pp. 40–5.

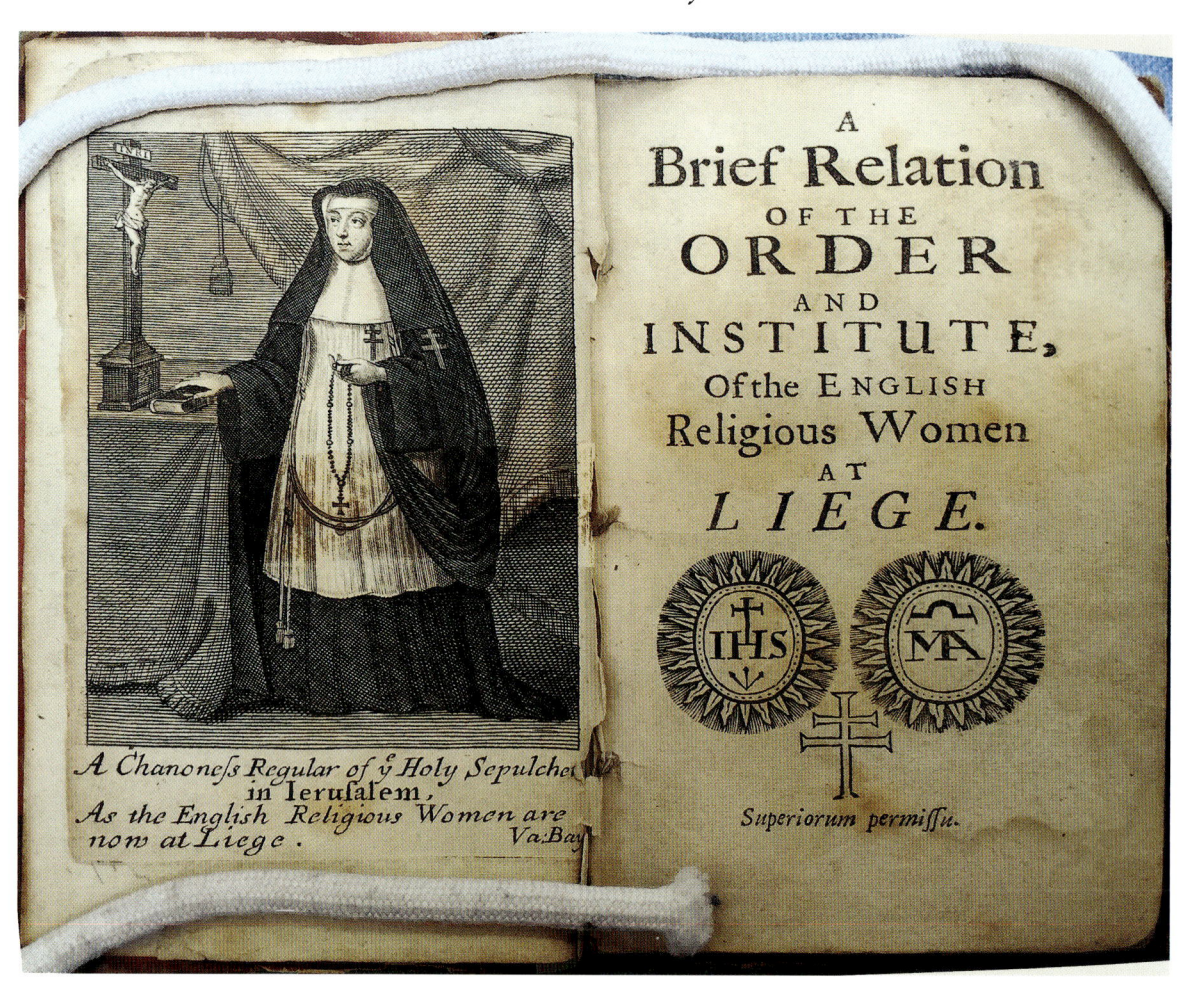

A Brief Relation of the Order and Institute of the English Religious Women at Liège (Liège: 1652).
Image courtesy of the Canonesses of the Holy Sepulchre.

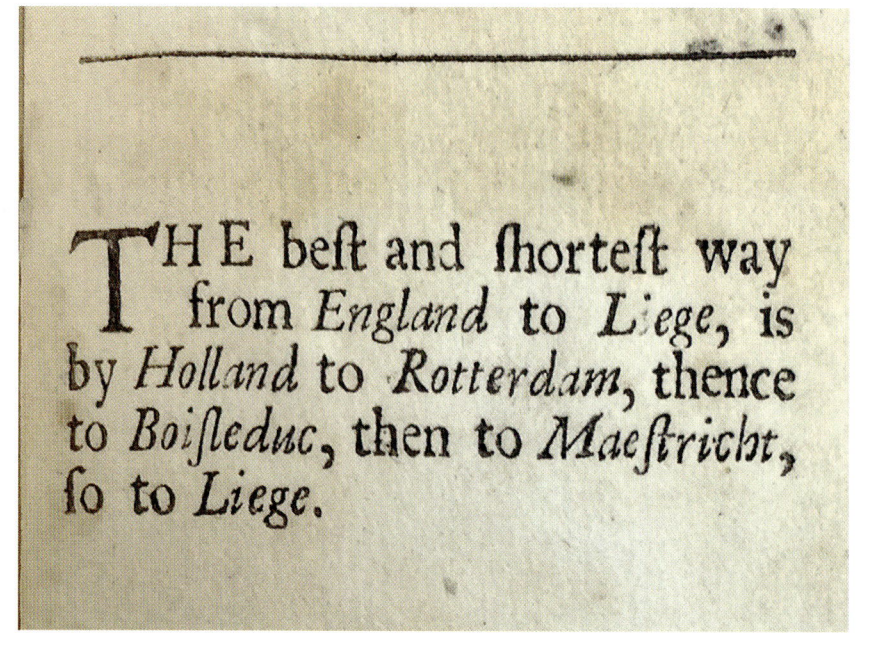

Travel advice to get from England to Liège,
especially useful for parents of prospective pupils
and those who felt called to join the Community (1652).
Image courtesy of the Canonesses of the Holy Sepulchre.

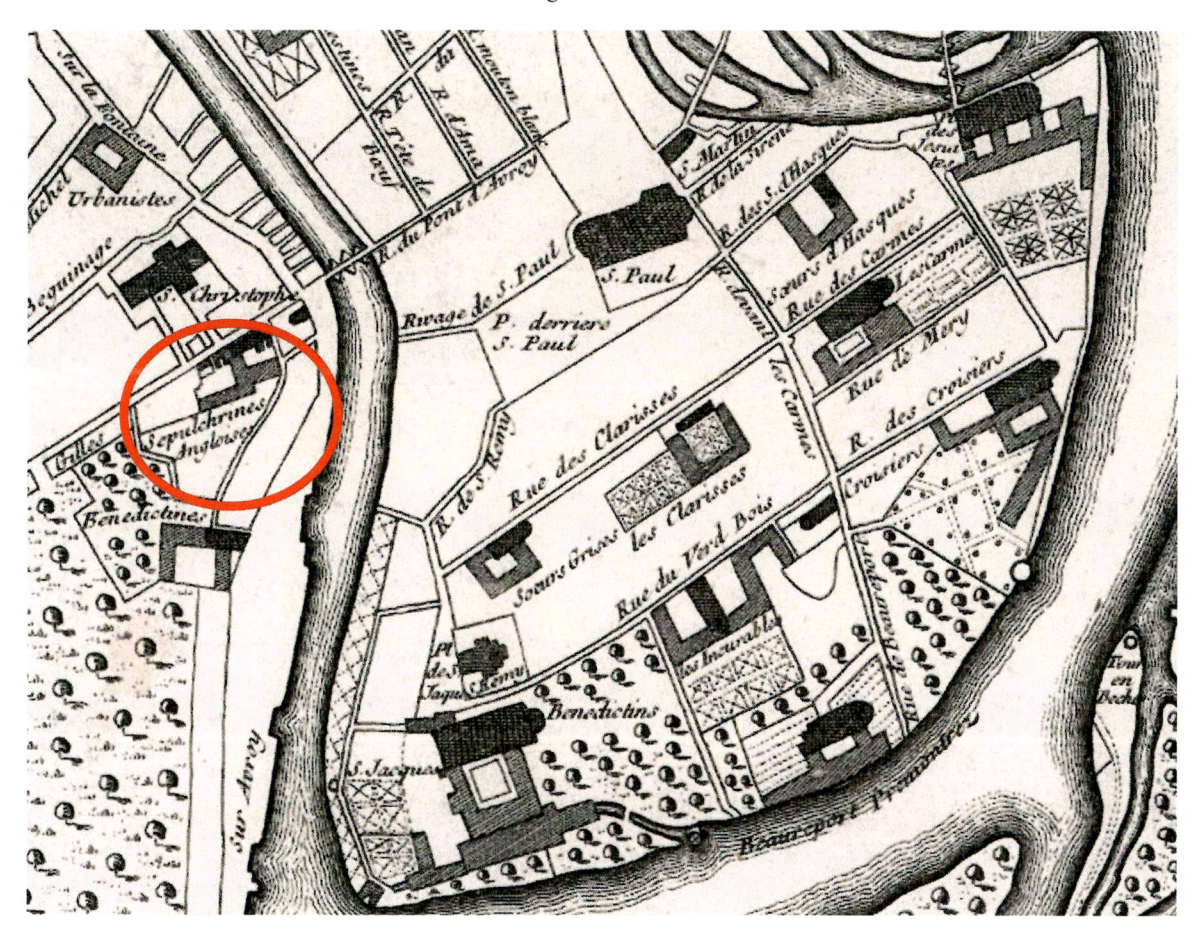

Location of English Canonesses of the Holy Sepulchre and church of Saint-Christophe.
(Map: Hannah Thomas, from the map drawn by Christopher Maire SJ, 1720)

In Liège itself, very little physical evidence remains of the convent buildings on Rue Saint-Gilles, as most of the city was destroyed as a result of the revolutionary wars. The river near the convent was diverted and built over in the nineteenth century, and many of the current buildings on the street, and indeed in the surrounding area, were erected at around the same time. Historic maps reveal that the convent was in a large parcel of land, surrounded by an enclosure wall that marked its boundary. It was also in close proximity to the parish church of Saint-Christophe, and therefore in the very heart of the parish. The Community began to compile a Book of Benefactors in 1662, and this text indicates that the outside of the convent buildings were painted white, and frequently refreshed. Entries for the application of new whitening appear in 1682, 1728, 1753, 1760 and 1765 as a result of donations from various benefactors and sponsors. A large donation from Lady Frances Talbot, Duchess of Tyrconnel (c. 1648–1731), was used to fund the painting of a number of religious images on the wall around the entrance gate in 1706, making the convent a noticeable part of the city landscape.[10]

The enclosure wall was not finished until 1735, and was only completed thanks to the generosity of another wealthy donor, Lady Dorothy Goring, née Plowden (1669–1737). Lady Goring had retired to the convent shortly after the death of her husband, Sir William Goring (1659–1724). She was a generous benefactor to both the Sepulchrine Community, and the nearby English Jesuits. Four of her brothers were Jesuits, and all served at the English College in Liège during this time. Her brother Edmund Plowden (1665–1740), *alias* Simons, was Rector of the English College between 1731 and 1734, which would have further enhanced links between the Canonesses and the English Jesuits within Liège.[11]

---

[10] ACHS/Benefactors Book 1662–1871/August 1706. Entries are not paginated, but are arranged chronologically.
[11] Geoffrey Holt, SJ, *The English Jesuits 1650–1829: A Biographical Dictionary* (Southampton: Catholic Record Society, 1984), p. 196.

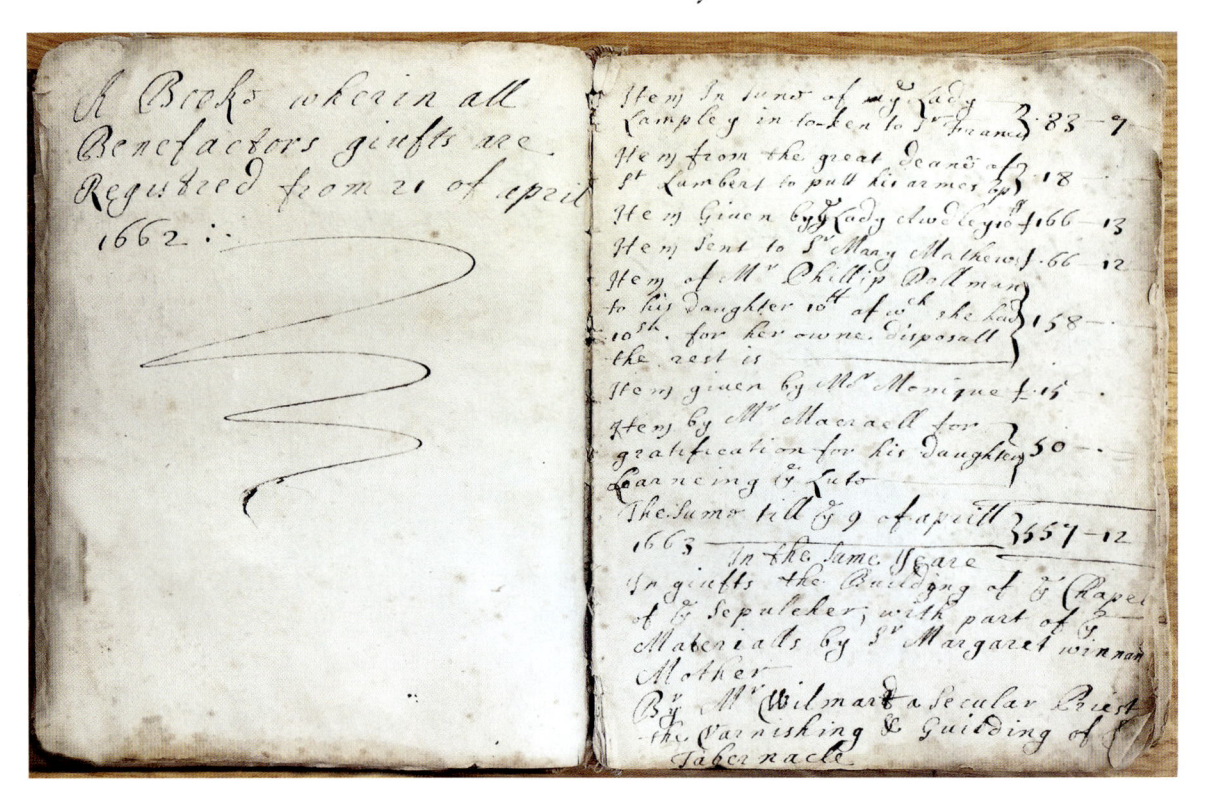

Book of Benefactors (1662).
Image courtesy of the Canonesses of the Holy Sepulchre.

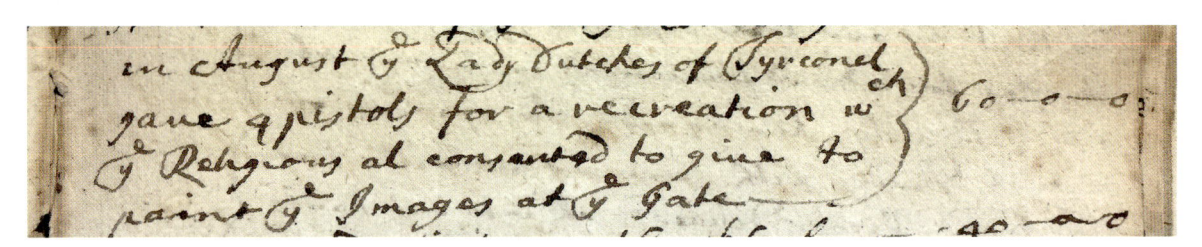

A donation from Lady Frances Talbot, Duchess of Tyrconnel (1648–1731) in August 1706, used to paint religious images on the wall around the gate of the convent.
Image courtesy of the Canonesses of the Holy Sepulchre.

Lady Goring donated money, vestments, and other liturgical objects regularly from 1724 until her death in 1737. For example, in 1728, she gave money towards the sealing and whitening of the house; and in 1735, she paid for the building of a covered passageway to the privies, which were located at the far end of the garden. In the same year, she also gave money towards to the completion of the wall around the boundary. Community records describe the existing boundary wall before this date as 'so low as to expose us often to great inconvenience', noting that the cost of remedying this were beyond their financial means. With this in mind, in 1735, Lady Goring,

> at a very great expense, raised the wall for a respectable and proper inclosure [sic] height: much against her will, an inscription on a large stone in the wall bore testimony to her benevolent charity & our gratitude.[12]

This 'large stone', along with several others from the enclosure wall, was saved when the convent was demolished in the nineteenth century, and can be found embedded in the wall of the university building that now occupies the former site of the convent.

[12] ACHS/D4 'Mss Notes on the Traditions of our Community, given to me by Reverend Mother' (December 1889). This anonymous scrapbook is a compilation of older notes, memories, documents and traditions; many of which have not survived elsewhere.

> In the year 1735 Lady Goring built the other part of the wall, quite round ye enclosure, her Lp also gave us a black suit for the Church trim'd with gold galloon, and two paire of silver flower pots.
>
> In the year 1736 Lady Goring gave us 28ll to repaire the old houses which we burnt by casuall fire on ye 22th of yare 1736, her Lp also gave 14 paire of silver flower pots, and guilded two ciboriums, and one patten, she also gave us two brass sconces which hang before the Alter, and 7 paire of single ones to hang about.
>
> Lady Goring our speciall benefactor dyed on ye 8th of January 1737 she left us 22l for the use of the Church, of which was made a silver holy water kettle, she also left us all her furniture and beds, beding, liting &c.

Generous donations from Lady Dorothy Goring (1669–1737) allowed the enclosure wall to be finished in 1735. The Benefactor's Book notes the Community's grief at her death in 1737.

Memorial tablet recording the Community's gratitude for Lady Goring's assistance. The inscription reads 'Built by the famous Lady Dorothy Goring in the year 1734. Pray for her'. (Photograph: Hannah Thomas)

Several memorial tablets were saved from the enclosure wall, and are now embedded in the wall of a university building, built on Rue Saint-Gilles in the nineteenth century. (Photograph: Hannah Thomas)

The convent church, which had been built by the Community soon after they moved in, was dedicated to St Helen, and included several side chapels, one of which was dedicated to St Cecilia, and another to the Holy Sepulchre. Further evidence from the Book of Benefactors indicates that the church was richly decorated. It included a gilded tabernacle, a silver crucifix mounted on a pedestal, silver candlesticks and vases, beautiful red and gold fabrics hanging around the church, and brass sconces mounted on the walls. Several wall paintings and images were also displayed in the main body of the church and in the side chapels, and most of the windows included decorated glass, or the coats of arms of donors and benefactors.[13]

Although very little information about Community burial practices during their time in Liège has survived, it is quite likely that the Community had its own cemetery or burial ground within the convent grounds, and there is certainly evidence of burials taking place inside the convent church itself.

Lady Goring's will, proved shortly after her death in 1737, casts some light on burial practice. She requested that her body 'be decently and privately buried in the Church of the English Sepulchrines

---

[13] Compiled from entries in ACHS/Benefactors Book.

Liège, 1642–1794

Here Lies
The Rd. Mr. John Howard
Last Rector of the College of English
Jesuits at Liège
First President

Of the Anglo-Bavarian Academy, erected ten
years since in the same City, for the Education of
youth, whom He loved wth the tenderness of a Father,
whose improvement in Virtue & Science were the
Chief object of his Care.

A solid piety, an ardent Zeal for the Salvation of Souls,
a Fortitude & greatness of Soul, superior to the rudest
Shocks of Adversity, profound Science, the most amiable
meekness & Consummate prudence Characterised this
true Religious.

A Director of Souls no less Zealous than Prudent
twenty years he made Piety & Virtue flourish in this
House, where he piously departed this Life the 16th Octr.
1783.

Penetrated with grief & gratitude his Spiritual Child-
=ren Consecrate this Monument to the Memory of
the tenderest & best of Fathers.

Requiescat in Pace.

Sketch of memorial tablet to Fr John Howard SJ, believed to have been laid in the floor of the convent chapel (1783).
Image courtesy of the Canonesses of the Holy Sepulchre.

Mr Mary Angela Stourton
died on ye 29th July 1777

Mr Frances Borgia Burnett died on ye 30th December 1777

Mr Mary Longina Hogan died on ye 26 Jan: 1778

Mr Mary Agnes Butler died on ye 25th Aug: 1778

General Plunkett, Governor of Antwerp, died in ye Parish of St Thomas on the 20 of January 1779 and was buried in our Church on the 22d

Miss Anne Ferral died on ye 28th Janr 1779

Sr Mary Clare Charnley died on ye 23d Feb: 1779

Sister Mary Lucy Merrick died on ye 1st Nov: 1779

Mr Thadous Madden an Irish Austin Friar of Paris died on ye 20th of March 1780 he is buried in our Church Thomas was put on his grave stone by mistake

The Rd Mother Mary Christina Denny died on ye 12th July 1781

Mr Frances Borgia Howse died on ye 7th Janr 1782

Mr F. Xaveria Burke died on ye 7th May 1783

Sister Mary Regis Lynche died on ye 11th 7bre 1783

Mr Mary Felix Sharples died ye 8th October 1783

Rd Father John Steward our Confessor died on ye 16th October 1783

Mr Mary Agnes Tanner died on ye 22d Janr 1784

The Rd Mr James Stuart an exjesuit died on ye 1st March 1784

Sr Ann Teresa Kennard died on ye 23d March 1784

The Rt Honble Lady Ann Barnes died on ye 2d May 1784, she was buried in the Vaults

Mrs Elizabeth Hill died on ye 27th Xbre 1784, she was buried in the Vault

375

These lists show burials that took place in the convent church between 1777 and 1790.
Note that some are 'buried in the vaults' and others are 'buried in the church'.
Image courtesy of the Canonesses of the Holy Sepulchre.

376

Mrs Mary Holtz a Dame donnè, died on ye 20th March 1785 she was buried in the Vault —

Sr Mary Winifrid Thornborough died on ye 25th March 1785

Sr Mary Agnes Meade Novice died on ye 19th of November 1785 —

Mr James Darrell an ex-Jesuit died ye 18th May 1786 was buried in our Church

Rd Mother Mary Austin Westby died on ye 3d of March 1786 —

Mor Mary Benedict Berrington died on ye 6th Nov 1786

Mor Mary Felicitas Corcoran died on ye 25th Janry 1787 —

Mor Mary Bernard Plowden Died on the 12 Xbre 1787 —

Miss Victoria Plunkett died upon the 25 Novr 1788 —

Mor Monica Emmott died upon the 29 Xbre 1788

Mr Scarisbrick an ex-Jesuit Died the 16 July 1789 & was buried in our Church — — —

Mor Bridget Dawtrey died on the 17 August 1789 —

Mor Mary Xaveria Clough Died on the 24 May 1790 —

at Liège'.¹⁴ Earlier entries from the Book of Benefactors suggest other similar requests. In April 1681, one Mrs Blanchfield had given money for 'a poore Irish gentlewoman to be buryed in our church', and in 1687, the Community received money by way of compensation for costs incurred for burial, after a visitor from Charleville had died unexpectedly earlier in the year.¹⁵ Similarly, in May 1702, one Mr Horney had left money in his will to allow him 'to be buried in our church'.¹⁶

Later records suggest that the Community had an underground burial facility, as well as the option to bury people within the church. A list of burials between 1777 and 1790 records that in May 1784, one Lady Ann Bartres died and 'was buried in the vaults'. The same burial place is recorded for Mrs Elizabeth Hills, who died in December 1784, and Mrs Mary Kelly, who died in March 1785. The list also includes three ex-Jesuits from the English College: John Howard (1718–83); James Darrell (1707–85) and Francis Scarisbrick (1703–89), all of whom had died during the period of the suppression of the Society, and were buried in the convent church.¹⁷

According to the parish records of Saint-Christophe, none of the English Sepulchrines were buried in the church there, or indeed at the parish church of Saint-Servain in their former base on Rue Pierreuse. Approximately 145 members of the Community died during the Liège period, 140 of whom died between 1656 and 1794, while the Community was at Rue Saint-Gilles. It seems unlikely that this number of deaths would have been missed by the parish clerks in both parishes, and it seems far more probable that the Community had their own private burial facility, within the enclosure wall. Documentary evidence, such as entries from the Book of Benefactors, suggests that this burial facility was also available to select lay people. Although no physical evidence remains of the burial space used by the Community during their time in Liège, examples can be found of many other similar conventual cemeteries, in locations such as Paris, Toulouse and Saint-Étienne.¹⁸

Migration to England, 1794

The revolutionary fever which took hold in France in the late 1780s soon reached Liège, after which time the fortunes of the city fluctuated as the Revolutionary war progressed. The city was seized and declared a republic in September 1789. By 1791, Imperial troops had entered and successfully recaptured the city, and restored the Prince Bishop. Less than twelve months later, in 1792, French Revolutionary troops had defeated the Imperial forces and occupied the city, forcing the Prince Bishop into exile. Many religious houses were compelled in Liège to provide billeting for soldiers. By March 1793, the

14 The National Archives, London [TNA]/PROB 11/683/336, Will of Dame Dorothy Goring, 2 July 1729 (proved 8 June 1737).
15 ACHS/Benefactors Book/April 1681 and November 1687 respectively. The 'visitor from Charleville' was probably a member of the French Sepulchrine Community, founded there in 1622. The Constitutions followed by the Liège Community were printed at Charleville in 1631, and all Sepulchrine communities that used these Constitutions were encouraged to stay in close communication with each other. See S. Mary Simon Metcalf OSSJ, 'The Holy Sepulchre: A study of its position in the spirituality of the Canonical Order of the Holy Sepulchre, with special reference to the English sources' (unpublished thesis, Pontificum Institutum Regina Mundi, Rome, 1960), pp. 10–12.
16 ACHS/Benefactors Book/ May 1702.
17 List of burials as written in ACHS/Account Book 07/S: Pensioners 1777–1859 etc., pp. 375–6.
18 See Vanessa Harding, *The Dead and the Living in Paris and London, 1500–1670* (Cambridge: Cambridge University Press, 2002), pp. 120, 125–7, 136–7 and 165; and Phillippe Aries, *The Hour of Our Death* (New York: Alfred A. Knopf, 1981), pp. 73–4 and 82–92. See also Peter Marshall, 'Confessionalisation and Community in the Burial of English Catholics, c. 1570–1700', in Nadine Lewycky and Adam Morton (eds), *Getting Along? Religious Identities and Confessional Relations in Early Modern England—Essays in Honour of Professor W. J. Sheils* (Farnham: Ashgate, 2012), pp. 57–75.

situation had changed again: Imperial troops had recaptured the city, the Prince Bishop had been re-restored to his throne, and the French soldiers had left the city. The restoration of peace was temporary, and by May 1794, French military successes in the surrounding areas suggested that a further assault on Liège was inevitable.[19]

This was a difficult and dangerous time for the Community, particularly as the likelihood of a war with England drew nearer. The Canonesses managed the situation with a characteristic pious pragmatism, carefully negotiating their own survival as a group of unprotected English ladies caught in the midst of a continental civil war. The Community cleverly used their 'Englishness' to escape some of the more extreme consequences of the various military occupations, noting that 'we made it a principle to remain neutral being religious people and strangers we did not look upon it our business to enterfere [sic] in any shape'. In June 1790, the newly installed republican authorities demanded 'donations' from all religious institutions in Liège. These demands were repeatedly ignored by the Community, on account of their 'being strangers' and therefore not obliged to pay.[20]

When the Imperial troops arrived in 1791, the Community chronicle piously notes that 'by a special providence of God we received not the least damage', a more understandable escape when it is noted later on in the same account that the Community had taken

> great care [that] they [*i.e. the troops*] should be duly informed of the particulars and sensible of the advantage our convent was to the country on account of the considerable sums of money which we annually brought into the town.[21]

However in November 1792, at least sixty French Revolutionary soldiers were quartered at the convent, adding a great deal of strain to Community resources and patience. The chronicle notes a sense of relief at being able to use their Englishness as a form of protection under these difficult circumstances:

> Dreading the consequences, which we had reason to expect from their hatred of religious persons would ensue, our only hope was that being English and as England had not yet declared war with them that might afford us some kind of protection.[22]

France declared war with England on 1 February 1793, and by 1794, the situation had become so dangerous that Liège was no longer safe for a Community of English women religious.[23] In May 1794, the decision was taken to leave and seek refuge in England. Although no evidence survives of the actual discussion to leave, it is clear that this momentous decision was approached in a very pragmatic and sensible way. Organised, forward-thinking plans made the process relatively straightforward, which was remarkable considering that many of the members of the Community fleeing Liège rarely set foot outside their convent walls.

Records in the archive also suggest that although plans to leave *were* put in place, the decision to put them into action and evacuate Liège in May 1794 was something of a last resort. Major building work to extend the convent chapel was undertaken from September 1792 onwards, and candidates were being accepted for the noviceship as late as January 1794. From the beginning of that year, and as the political situation worsened, emergency transport out of Liège was arranged to be on standby

---

[19] See Whitehead, *English Jesuit Education*, pp. 165–72 and Hubert Chadwick, SJ, *St Omers to Stonyhurst: A History of Two Centuries* (London: Burns & Oates, 1962), pp. 360–83.

[20] Other communities of English women religious in exile used similar techniques for survival. For a detailed exploration of three English communities in Paris during the 1790s, see Carmen M Mangion, 'Avoiding "rash and imprudent measures": English Nuns in Revolutionary Paris, 1789–1801', in Caroline Bowden and James E. Kelly (eds), *The English Convents in Exile, 1600–1800: Communities, Culture and Identity* (Farnham: Ashgate, 2013), pp. 247–63.

[21] ACHS/D2 S. Mary Joseph Smith, 'A Short Account of Some Particulars which Happen'd during the Revolutions at Liège and of our Journey from thence to England', pp. 10–12. See p. 65 below.

[22] Smith, 'A Short Account', p. 15.

[23] Britain was the only power to remain at war with France throughout the 1790s, engaging in battles from 1793 to 1795, and in 1799. For a more detailed chronology, see Colin Jones, *The Longman Companion to the French Revolution* (New York: Longman, 1990), pp. 26–32, 42–52 and 131–2.

An entry from the Chapter Book, commissioning major building works
to extend the convent chapel, September 1792.
Image courtesy of the Canonesses of the Holy Sepulchre.

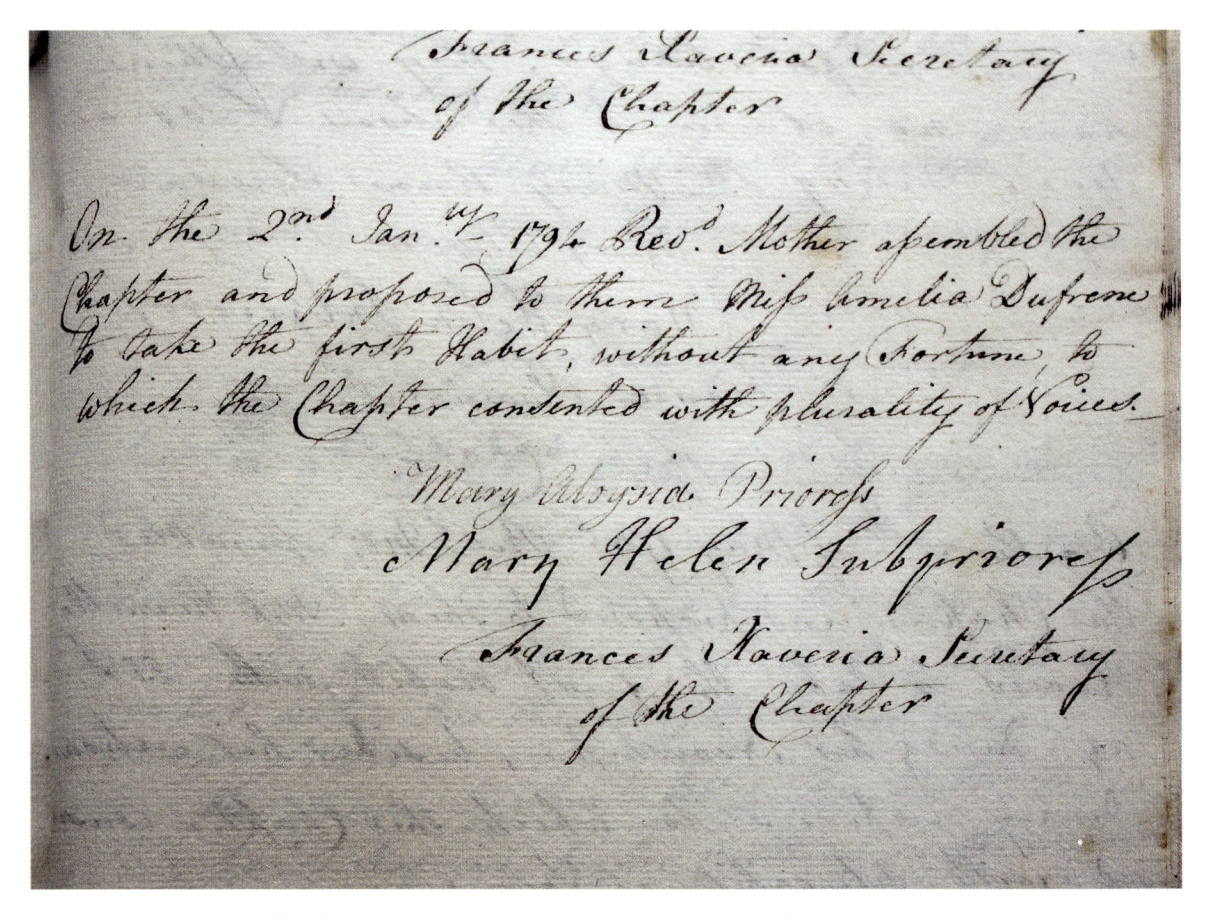

An entry from the Chapter Book, accepting Amelia Dufrene to the noviceship in January 1794.
Image courtesy of the Canonesses of the Holy Sepulchre.

Migration to England, 1794

Small wooden chests, commissioned by the Community in 1794 and still in use today.

from this time. A house was leased in nearby Maastricht to regroup and prepare for the journey ahead, and several hundred portable wooden chests were commissioned from a local carpenter for the easy transportation of books, archives and other precious items.[24] It is notable that a few of these chests survive, and are still used by the Community: the chests are a variety of sizes, but very portable, being no taller than knee height, and approximately arms-width.

The Prince Bishop of Liège, François Antoine Marie Constantin de Méan et de Beaurieux (r. 1792–4) was also petitioned for permission to leave if the situation necessitated it. This was an essential requirement that took several months to obtain, and was only granted on the condition that evacuation was done discreetly and without causing panic to the remaining residents. All the arrangements, such as the hiring of transport and houses, were made on temporary rolling terms of a few months at a time, to allow for cancellation if the situation got any better, extension if the situation remained unclear, or called into use if necessary. In order to avoid causing panic, the Community left their convent at Rue Saint-Gilles in the middle of the night, at 3am, on 29 May 1794, silently processing through the convent grounds to the procured coal barges, which were the only vessels big enough that were still available within the city.

Artist's impression of the coal barges used to transport the Community out of Liège in May 1794. Drawn by S. Mary Stephen CRSS.

A Jesuit at the nearby English College, Francis Clifton (d. 1813), was of great help to the Community at this time, and acted as their agent in securing the transport and accommodation. His own Community of English Jesuits, led by rector Marmaduke Stone (1748–1834), stoutly refused to consider evacuation as an option. Eventually forced to leave the city in July 1794, two months after the Community had left, some of the Jesuits' important goods and valuable books were dispatched to a safe house, and the men also commissioned wooden chests from a local carpenter. However, these were not as carefully planned as the portable chests used by the Sepulchrines, partly due to the by-then urgent need to leave the city. The wooden chests commissioned by the Jesuits were far too large and bulky to be transported, particularly when filled with heavy items such as books, relics, vestments and archive documents. The chests were so heavy, that their weight combined with the weight of the fleeing Jesuits caused the barges to sink into the mud of the river. The chests and other luggage had to be removed and piled up on the quayside, where an impromptu auction was quickly held with the help of the town crier.[25]

Clifton is listed amongst the large number of people that left the Liège convent, which included forty-nine Community, thirteen pupils and three elderly ladies who were in the care of the Community, as well as just two servants to look after everyone. Three Canonesses supervised this momentous operation—Bridget Clough, S. Mary Aloysia (1739–1816), Prioress 1786–1816; Elizabeth Talbot, S. Mary Helen Aloysia (1738–1808), Sub-Prioress 1793–8 and 1803–8; and Sarah Trant, S. Frances Xaveria (1764–1807), Procuratrix 1792–7 and 1802–7.

Seventeen other English convents were forced to flee the continent and seek refuge in England, a country where Catholicism was still illegal:

[24] The actual number varies in different records, but is thought to have been between 500 and 800. Approximately fifteen survive today.
[25] Whitehead, *English Jesuit Education*, p. 173.

Migration to England, 1794

Miniature portrait of Fr Francis Clifton SJ (d. 1813).
By permission of the Governors of Stonyhurst College.

1. English Augustinians, Bruges: left Bruges 1794; based in London, then Hengrave Hall until 1803; returned to Bruges, where they still remain.
2. English Augustinians, Louvain: left Louvain 1794; based at Amesbury until 1800; settled Spetisbury until 1860.
3. English Benedictines, Brussels: left Brussels 1794; based at Winchester until 1857; then settled at Haslemere in East Bergholt from 1857 onwards.
4. English Benedictines, Cambrai: convent seized 1793; left Cambrai 1795; Woolton until 1807; settled at Stanbrook Abbey in 1838.
5. English Benedictines, Dunkirk: evicted from convent 1793; imprisoned with Poor Clares from Dunirk and Gravelines; released and travelled to England 1795; based at Hammersmith until 1863; settled at Teignmouth 1863 onwards.
6. English Benedictines, Ghent: left Ghent 1795; based at Preston until 1811; settled at Oulton 1811 onwards.
7. English Benedictines, Paris: convent raided 1793; imprisoned 1794; released and travelled to England 1795; based at Dorset; settled at Colwich.
8. English Poor Clares, Aire: evicted 1795; based at Yorkshire from 1807; settled at Darlington 1857 onwards. Moved to Much Birch, Herefordshire, 2007.
9. English Poor Clares, Dunkirk: imprisoned 1793–5; settled in England with Aire community.
10. English Poor Clares, Gravelines: convent seized and nuns imprisoned 1793; released and travelled to England 1795; based in Essex until 1814; returned to Gravelines until 1838; returned to England 1838 onwards.
11. English Poor Clares, Rouen: convent seized and nuns imprisoned 1794; released and travelled to England 1795; based at London and Northumberland; settled at Yorkshire 1807 onwards.
12. English Carmelites, Antwerp: evicted 1794; based at London; settled at Lanherne.

13. English Carmelites, Hoogstraten: left Hoogstraten 1794; based at Dorset until 1825; based at Normandy until 1870; settled at Chichester 1870 onwards.
14. English Carmelites, Lierre: evicted 1794; based at County Durham until 1804; settled at Darlington.
15. English Dominicans, Brussels: left Brussels 1794; settled at Gloucester 1794 until 1839.
16. English Franciscans, Brussels: left Brussels 1794; based at Winchester until 1808; settled at Taunton 1808 onwards.
17. English Conceptionists, Paris (known as the Blue Nuns): convent seized 1793; imprisoned 1794; released and travelled to England 1795; based at Norfolk; settled at Norwich 1800; order dispersed by 1806.[26]

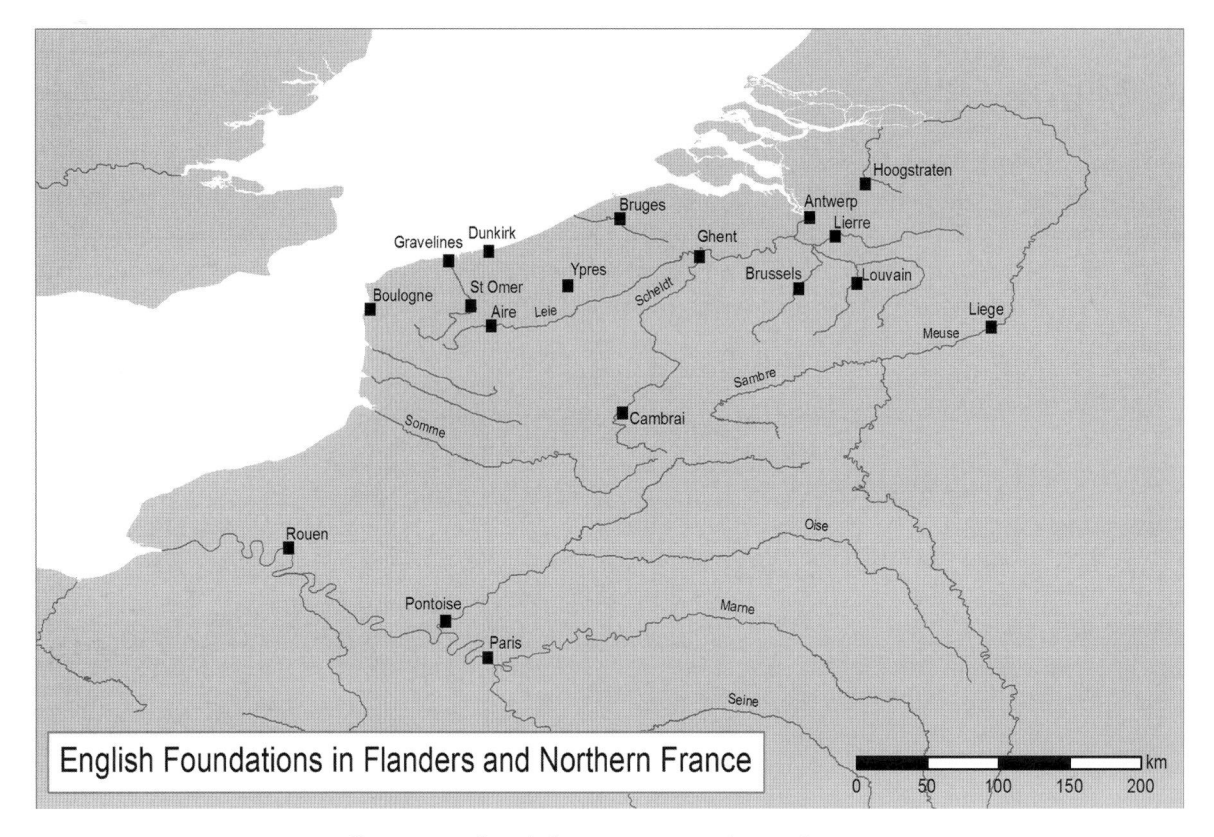

Map of locations of English convents in exile, northern Europe.
Courtesy of Dr Caroline Bowden and Dr James E. Kelly.

Holme Hall and Dean House, 1794–1799

After enduring a long journey of nearly three months, the Canonesses finally arrived in Gravesend on 16 August 1794, but remained on board their ship for several days as, initially, no pilot could be found to guide them safely up the treacherous waters of the Thames Estuary and enable them to travel onwards to London. After the barges were inspected by English Commissaries, a pilot was provided and the ship was allowed to continue, docking at Greenwich on 18 August. The Community, dressed in lay clothing so as to avoid attracting attention, disembarked very early the next morning, and made their way to two separate dwellings at Burlington Street and Dover Street, both houses far too small for such large groups of people. Here they stayed for ten days, until more suitable accommodation could be found.

[26] Drawn from 'Convent Notes' as cited on *Who were the Nuns?* database, https://wwtn.history.qmul.ac.uk/about/convent-notes/, hereafter *WWTN*.

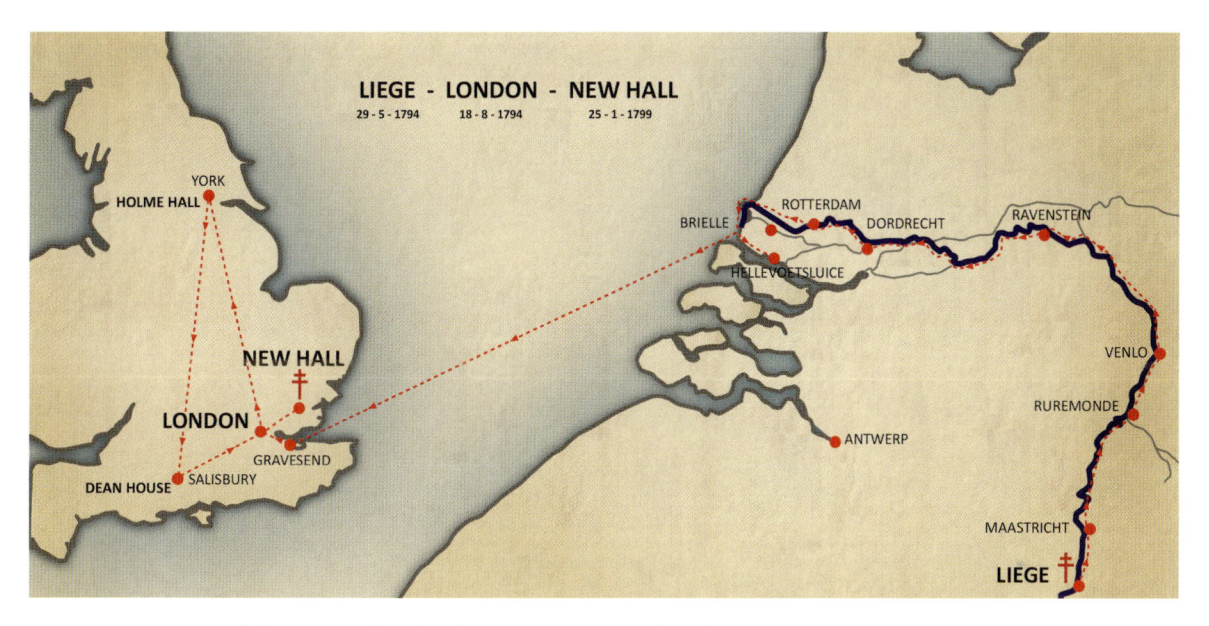

Map of the route taken by the Canonesses as they fled from Liège to England, 1794.
Image courtesy of the Canonesses of the Holy Sepulchre.

England at this time was very hostile to Catholicism, and although conditions were generally more tolerant than they had been a century earlier, Catholicism was still illegal, and those who practised the faith had to be very cautious and avoid drawing attention to themselves. In 1794, it was illegal for Catholics to sit in Parliament, or vote in elections, and Catholics had only been allowed to own or inherit property, or to join the army, since 1778. Catholics also had to publicly swear an oath before a Justice of the Peace, at the Quarter Sessions:

> I hereby do sincerely promise and swear that I will be faithful and bear true allegiance to his Majesty King George the Third, and will defend to the utmost of my power against all conspiracies and attempts whatever that shall be made against his person, crown or dignity. I will do my utmost endeavour to disclose and make known to his majesty, his heirs, and successors all treasons and traitorous conspiracies which may be formed against him or them. And I do faithfully promise to maintain, support, and defend to the utmost of my power the succession of the crown, and stand committed to the Duchess Dowager of Hanover and the heirs of her body, being Protestant, hereby utterly renouncing and abjuring any obedience or allegiance unto any other person claiming or pretending a right to the crown of these realms.
>
> I do swear that I do reject and detest as an unchristian and impious position that it is lawful to murder or destroy any person or persons whatsoever for or under pretence of their being hereticks or infidels, and also that unchristian and impious principle that faith is not to be kept with hereticks or infidels. And I do further declare that it is not an article of my Faith, and that I do renounce, reject and abjure the opinion that princes excommunicated by the pope and council or any authority of the See of Rome, or by any authority whatsoever, may be deposed or murdered by their subjects or any person whatsoever. And I do promise that I will not hold maintain or abet any such opinion or any other opinions contrary to what is expressed in this declaration.
>
> And I do declare that I do not believe that the pope of Rome, or any other foreign prince, prelate, state or potentate, hath or ought to have any temporal or civil jurisdiction, power, superiority or pre-eminence, directly or indirectly, within this Realm.
>
> And I do solemnly, in the presence of God, profess, testify and declare that I do make this declaration, and every part thereof in the plain and ordinary sense of the words of this oath without any evasion, equivocation or mental reservation whatever and without any dispensation already granted by the pope or any authority of the See of Rome...[27]

---

[27]   Essex Record Office [ERO], Q/RRo 1/43/2, Quarter Sessions Papists Roll, 1792–1815.

1. May 1794 - leaving Liège by coal boat. "Confusion and distress ... all crying bitterly".
2. Maestricht: full of singing birds.
3. Ruremonde: fleas.
4. Rotterdam: public curiosity, decision to change out of habits.
5. Rotterdam: Nun overboard while transporting effects to ship. Rescued by captain.
6. Ship stuck on sands. trying to leave Briel.
7. 15th August: put off religious habits.
8. Fire on the ship.
9. Collision between ships.
10. London: Separation of the Community in 2 houses. Burlington Streen & Dover Street.
11. Reunification of the Community at Bruton Street: Community suffering from great expense, lack of air and exercise.
12. Death of M.Teresa Dennett "We were all of us much hurt not to be able to bury her ... in her religious habit."
13. Move to Holme Hall - mistaken for French soldiers dressed as women.
14. April '95: School had to be sent home.
15. Sept. '96: Decision to rent Dean House - large and in proper situation for a school.
16. Nov. '96: Community move to Dean House.
17. 1797: Community put on habits at desire of Bishop Walmesley.
18. 1797: Oct. - oath of allegiance in order to open a school.
19. Mr.McEvoy offered to buy the Community a house.
20. Friends wanted the Community to buy Clarence House.
21. Community informed of New Hall.
22. 5th Nov.'98: Rev.Mother proposed to the Chapter the purchase of New Hall.
23. 25th Jan.'99: First four nuns arrive at New Hall.
24. 3rd March '99: the whole Community "safe arrived at New Hall".
25. First Mass in completed Chapel at New Hall on the Assumption 1799.

Highlights of the long journey from Liège to England, May–August 1794.
Image courtesy of the Canonesses of the Holy Sepulchre.

1794

Augt

The Ladys of Leige

To Thos: Christopher

To Petition of Surveyors For 800 Packages of Baggage Furniture & Stores By the Smallbridge Captain Symes from Rotterdam		2 ..
To Lighterage & Officer	16	10 ..
To Wharfage	10	..
To Landing & Housing	20	..
To Unhousing & Loading	10	..
To Watching & Beer	10	6
To Attendance & Clearing Ditto	5..5	..
	£62..7..6	
To Fees	45	..
	£107..7..6	

Settled By Cash Oct. 18th 1794

Witness   Francis Clifton

Bill of Carriage for 'The Ladys of Liège', which was settled by Francis Clifton on 18 October 1794, only a few days before the Community moved to Holme Hall. Image courtesy of the Canonesses of the Holy Sepulchre.

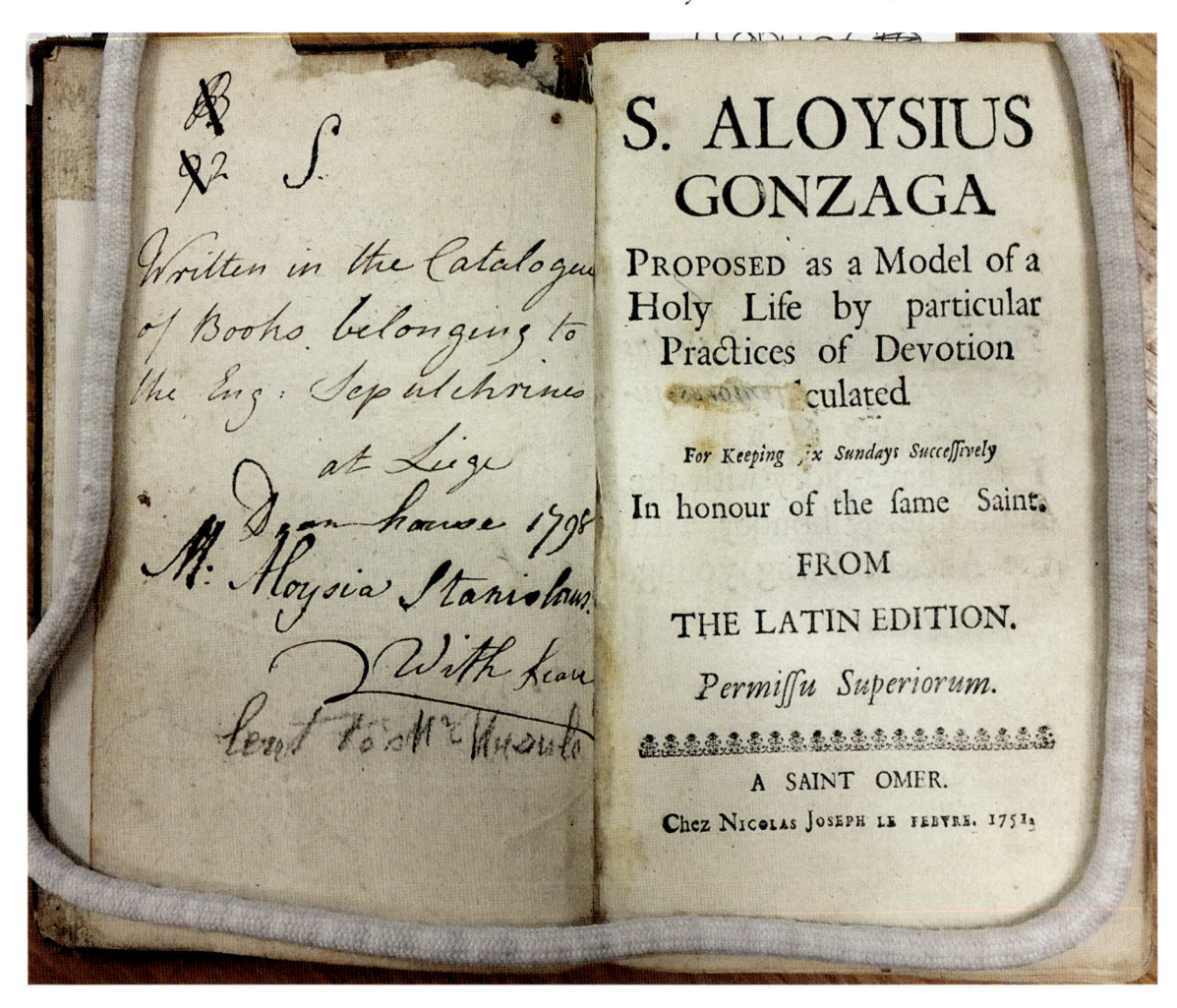

The Community took stock of their books once they had arrived at Dean House, producing a now-lost catalogue of the several hundred volumes in their possession. Image courtesy of the Canonesses of the Holy Sepulchre.

The oath was phrased in such a way so as to allow no flexibility for those taking it, and had to be sworn publicly to ensure compliance. The text of the Oath is particularly revealing of the government's fear and concerns for the potential trouble that Catholics could cause, perhaps in a Jacobite Restoration. The final phrase allowed for no equivocation whatsoever, covering all possibilities for those who may take the Oath but privately feel that they were not legally obliged to uphold it. The Community had to publicly swear this oath on more than one occasion, which will be explored in more detail below.

Soon after the Community arrived in London, Lord Charles Clifford, sixth baron Clifford of Chudleigh (1759–1831), an influential English Catholic gentleman and brother of Charlotte Clifford, S. Anne Teresa (1773–1801), offered them the use of his house on Bruton Street in Mayfair.[28] This house was cramped, but sufficiently large for the whole Community to be together again. They were also able to attend daily Mass, using Lord Clifford's private chapel at the top of the house.

The search for a more suitable premises took several weeks, and was solved with the help of Lord Charles Stourton, seventeenth baron Stourton (1752–1816), another influential English Catholic gentleman. Stourton also had family connections with the Canonesses: his sisters Catherine, S. Mary Agatha (d. 1768), and Charlotte, S. Mary Anne (1751–75), had been professed members of the Community during their time in Liège.[29] Stourton offered them the use of his Yorkshire property, Holme Hall, in the parish of Holme upon Spalding Moor in the East Riding of Yorkshire.

---

[28] Clifford family tree, as cited on *WWTN*. See also pp. 50, 52 and 66 below.
[29] Stourton family tree, as cited on *WWTN*. See p. 66 below.

Both Stourton and Clifford were members of a committee of prominent Catholic laymen, elected in 1782 with the aim of working towards a greater emancipation and improved legal position of Catholics in England and Wales, and thus ideally placed to assist the refugee communities of English women religious in the 1790s. Clifford, Stourton, and the other members of the committee, were part of a network of prominent English Catholics, liaising with English government on behalf of the convents, and finding suitable accommodation for them at various unused properties around the country.[30]

The Canonesses moved to Holme Hall on 23 October 1794, and stayed there for two years. The property was also rather small for their needs, particularly when combined with the number of young ladies in residence for their education. Larger accommodation was secured at Dean House in Wiltshire, in the parish of West Dean. The arduous task of moving began in October 1796, where they remained until transferring to New Hall, near Chelmsford, in March 1799.

During this long migration from 1794 to 1799, since leaving Liège nearly five years earlier, many of the records in the Community archive show that convent life continued virtually uninterrupted throughout this turbulent time. Meetings continued to happen regularly and novices were accepted and professed without any discernible break. The school was temporarily resumed at Holme Hall with ten pupils, but had to be closed due to the cramped conditions. It was firmly re-established at Dean House with the arrival of three new pupils in the summer of 1797, and by the time of the move to New Hall in 1799, there were fifteen pupils in total.

One thing that brought the Community's new, and somewhat perilous, existence into sharp relief during this period was the question of what to do when one of their Community died. Previously, at Liège, the Community responded to the death of a member through a fixed set of ritual activities, which all took place within the enclosure walls. The body was dressed in a habit and placed in a coffin, the relevant requiem Masses were sung, prayers were said over the coffin in the chapel, before being carried to the final resting place, accompanied by her sisters in procession. In England in the 1790s, these rituals were more difficult to perform.

This was particularly highlighted by the first death after leaving Liège, which occurred less than a month after the Community had arrived in London. Helen Dennett, S. Mary Teresa (1725–94), an elderly nun who had been ill for some years, and elder sister of S. Christina Dennett, died on 16 September 1794:

> We strove to pay all the funeral duties in our power to our deceased Sister, not a little affected by this first obit since we left Liège, and under such a variety of distressing circumstances … Though we were crowded even to painfulness, we recited together the whole Office of the Dead … The funeral was respectable and neat, but as private as possible. We were all of us much hurt not to be able to bury her, according to our holy rule, in her religious habit, and not to attend her Corpse to the burial place.[31]

Dennett was buried in the churchyard of St Pancras, an ancient church that, although Anglican, was also a burying place for Roman Catholics who died in London. In 1791, a specific portion of the churchyard had been allotted for Catholic interments, as a result of the large number of refugees arriving from France and Belgium at that time. The location of Dennett's grave has not been recorded, and physical evidence has not survived, but it is quite likely that she was laid to rest in this Catholic part of the churchyard. St Pancras was at the heart of a busy parish on the outskirts of London: some 389 burials took place there in 1794 alone.[32]

---

[30] See Geoffrey Scott, 'Catholic Committee (*act.* 1782–1792)', *ODNB*; Mark Bence-Jones, *The Catholic Families* (London: Constable & Co. Ltd, 1992), pp. 66–84; Hugh Clifford, *The House of Clifford from before the Conquest* (Chichester: Phillimore & Co. Ltd, 1987), pp. 169–73; ACHS/Clifford correspondence and Westminster Diocesan Archives [WDA]/A66 IX (1).

[31] Smith, 'A Short Account', p. 29.

[32] See Samuel Palmer, *St Pancras, being Antiquarian, Topographical and Biographical Memoranda relating to the Extensive Metropolitan Parish of St Pancras, Middlesex* (London: Field & Tuer, 1870), pp. 26–7; and Charles E. Lee, *St Pancras Church and Parish* (London: privately printed, 1955), pp. 35 and 44–7.

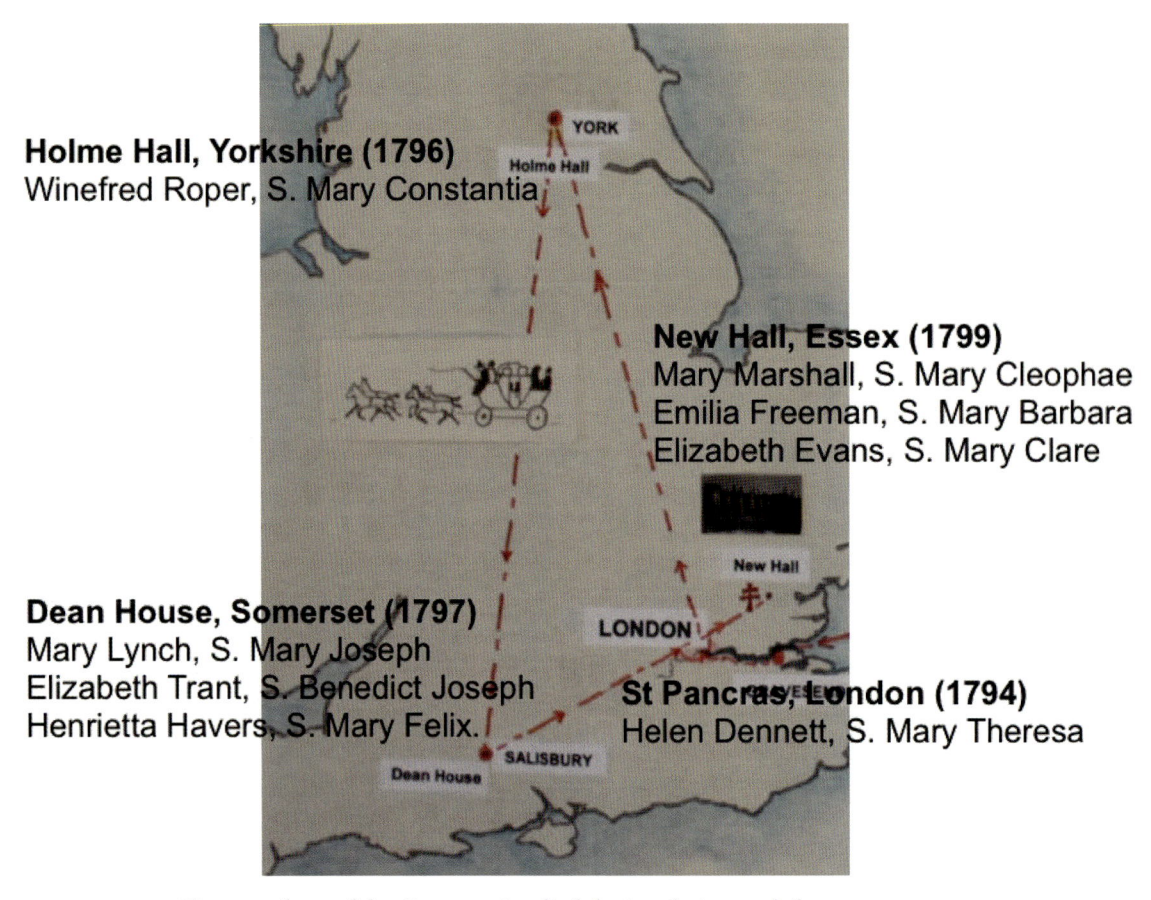

Holme Hall, Yorkshire (1796)
Winefred Roper, S. Mary Constantia

New Hall, Essex (1799)
Mary Marshall, S. Mary Cleophae
Emilia Freeman, S. Mary Barbara
Elizabeth Evans, S. Mary Clare

Dean House, Somerset (1797)
Mary Lynch, S. Mary Joseph
Elizabeth Trant, S. Benedict Joseph
Henrietta Havers, S. Mary Felix.

St Pancras, London (1794)
Helen Dennett, S. Mary Theresa

Five members of the Community died during their search for a permanent residence in England, and were buried in three separate locations.

One member of the Community also died during their time at Holme Hall. Winefred Roper, S. Mary Constantia (1743–96) died on 1 June 1796, and had to be buried at All Saints, the local Anglican church, for lack of other options. Attitudes towards Catholicism were sufficiently tolerant in Yorkshire, where at least 200 of every 1,000 households were known to be Catholic.[33] Through the patronage of Holme's previous owners, the Langdale family, the house itself had been something of a centre of Catholicism since the late seventeenth century, and was an English Benedictine mission from 1743 until 1864.[34] This meant some semblance of normality was able to be resumed, as far as the burial services were concerned, although the Community still had to be discreet. Roper was allowed to be buried in her habit, and a small number of her sisters were allowed to accompany the coffin to the grave.[35]

During their time at Dean House, a further three members of the Community died: Mary Lynch, S. Mary Joseph (1757–97); Elizabeth Trant, S. Benedict Joseph (1767–97); and Henrietta Havers, S. Mary Felix (1774–97).[36] All three had to be buried in the local Anglican church of St Mary the Virgin, as had been the case previously in London and Yorkshire. However, Wiltshire had a much smaller number of Catholic residents, less than 50 of every 1,000 households.[37] In West Dean, the somewhat

[33] Distribution of Catholics in 1767, as cited in Bossy, *English Catholic Community*, pp. 408–9.

[34] See Henry Houston-Ball and Joseph S. Hansom (eds), 'Catholic Registers of Holme-on-Spalding Moor, East Riding of Yorkshire, 1744–1840', as printed in *Miscellanea IV* (London: Catholic Record Society, 1907), pp. 272–318. See also Geoffrey Scott, OSB, *Gothic Rage Undone: English Monks in the Age of Enlightenment* (Bath: Downside Abbey, 1992), pp. 87–91, 109 and 280.

[35] When the Community arrived in 1794, the Benedictine mission at Holme was in decline, and was being managed by John Storey OSB (d. 1799), an elderly man described as 'very infirm'. There is no record of his involvement with Roper's burial service.

[36] Henrietta Havers had not been with the Community in Liège, but had entered the noviciate at Holme Hall in May 1795.

[37] Distribution of Catholics in 1767, as cited in Bossy, *English Catholic Community*, pp. 408–9.

hostile local population complained to the vicar, Edward Dawkins (d. 1816), about the presence of the Community. Archive documents note

> Very different was the reception that awaited the Community [in West Dean], from that which they had met with in Yorkshire ... an unpleasant neighbourhood and a troublesome landlord completed the catalogue of inconveniences which rendered Dean House a most undesirable residence.[38]

This hostility and suspicion is visible through recourse to the legal mechanisms that existed to require Catholics to identify themselves, which had not been enforced during their time in Yorkshire. On 17 October 1797, one Bridget Clough appeared before the General Quarter Sessions for the county of Wiltshire, and publicly 'did take, make and subscribe the Declaration and Oath appointed to be taken, made and subscribed by persons professing the Roman Catholic religion.'[39] Although the official documents fail to mention her religious vocation, other evidence from the convent archives confirms her identity as S. Mary Aloysia, eighth prioress of the Community.

Oath of Allegiance publicly declared by Bridget Clough before the quarterly County Assizes Court on 17 October 1797. Image courtesy of the Canonesses of the Holy Sepulchre.

Twelve months later, in October 1798, three members of the Community had to publicly swear the oath again, at the county Quarter Sessions. As well as Clough, this declaration was also sworn by the Sub-Prioress, Elizabeth Talbot, S. Mary Helen Aloysia; and the Procuratrix, Sarah Trant, S. Frances Xaveria. On both occasions, the Community members had to travel into Salisbury in order to fulfil their obligations, a seven-mile journey in each direction.

---

[38] Smith, 'A Short Account', p. 53.
[39] ACHS/D1a/Certificate of taking Oath of Allegiance, 17 October 1797.

In this context of hostility, traditional Community practices had to be set aside, in favour of local Anglican practices, in order to allow any burial to take place at all. Lynch, Trant and Havers were refused burial in the main body of the churchyard, but were grudgingly given burial space against the far west wall, physically as far away from the church as possible, whilst still remaining on consecrated ground. The corpses had to be dressed in a shroud rather than their habits, and had to be carried into the churchyard by local men. None of the sisters were permitted to accompany the coffin to the burial, and the coffin was not allowed to be taken into the church at any point. It was clear that Wiltshire was not the best location for the Community, and that an alternative location would have to be found.

The headstone of Henrietta Havers, S. Mary Felix (1774–97) at St Mary the Virgin, West Dean. Image courtesy of the Canonesses of the Holy Sepulchre.

New Hall, 1799 onwards

On 5 November 1798, the Revd Mother Clough proposed to the Chapter the purchase of New Hall in the county of Essex, a large mansion in several acres of land, at a cost of £6,000 (approximately £193,000 in modern terms).[40] The house was located far enough away from the nearby town of Chelmsford to allow complete privacy for the Community, but near enough to allow them access to the relevant facilities and amenities. The building was very old, and in need of some serious repair, but the Community opted to move in straight away, whilst the building work was ongoing.

The Community were encouraged to purchase New Hall by a generous donation of £4,000 (approximately £130,000), given to them by a wealthy English Catholic gentleman, Mr Michael McEvoy (fl.1798–1816), who was keen that the Community should purchase more suitable premises as soon as possible. On 19 September 1798, McEvoy wrote to the Revd Mother Clough:

> I agree to pay to Mrs Clough or her order the sum of four thousand pounds to be employed in the purchase of Mortlake or any place she may hereafter wish to purchase for which I entail no kind of obligation for myself of family—except as that of being consider'd as a founder for the general good of the Community & of Religion. NB Mrs Clough and Community will be attentive in a little way to the wants of my sister with respect to her [duration].[41]

---

[40] ACHS/Chapter Book 1642–1800/5 November 1798. Entries are not paginated, but are arranged chronologically.

[41] ACHS/McEvoy correspondence/Letter to Mrs Clough, 19 September 1798.

New Hall, 1799 onwards

New Hall in the eighteenth century. Image courtesy of the Canonesses of the Holy Sepulchre.

'A View of the Front of the Palace of Beaulieu commonly call'd NEW HALL in Essex'.
Image courtesy of the Canonesses of the Holy Sepulchre.

Similarly to previous benefactors, McEvoy had something of a vested interest in the welfare of the Community, as he was the brother of Ann McEvoy, S. Aloysia Stanislaus (1768–1836). Ann had joined the Community in Liège in 1784, and had endured the hardships of the migration to England in 1794, as well as the hunt for a suitable property that had taken nearly six years. Perhaps her brother simply wanted to ensure she had somewhere safe and suitable to live, along with the rest of her Community.

New Hall had an illustrious past prior to 1799, as one of the now-lost palaces of King Henry VIII (r. 1509–47). It was later the home of other notable residents, such as Henry's daughter, Mary Tudor (r. 1553–8); Thomas Radclyffe, Earl of Sussex (1525–83); George Villiers, Duke of Buckingham (1592–1628) and Oliver Cromwell (r. 1653–8). The house was purchased in 1737 by John Olmius, Baron Waltham (1711–62), who demolished and rebuilt much of the Tudor palace. The north wing of Henry's palace survives, and forms the main part of the school building today.

After purchasing the house, the Community undertook an extensive programme of building and repair. Buildings were added to make the property suitable for use as a convent, including a chapel and cells. The chapel was completed on 14 August 1799, celebrated with a Mass on the feast of the Assumption, and the rest of the building work was completed by 29 May 1800, six years to the day since they had left Liège.[42]

The Community remained at New Hall until 2005, at which point they handed the school over to a lay trust. They remained in the diocese of Brentwood, serving their local community in new ways. Members of the Community continue to be buried in the cemetery, which at the time of publication remains in their ownership.[43]

---

[42] For more on the history of New Hall, see Tony Tuckwell, *New Hall and its School: 'A True School of Virtuous Demeanour'* (King's Lynn: Free Range Publishing, 2006).

[43] For more information on the post-New Hall life of the Community, see their website at www.canonesses.co.uk

New Hall, 1799 onwards

Ann McEvoy, S. Aloysia Stanislaus (1768–1836).
Image courtesy of the Canonesses of the Holy Sepulchre.

The chapel at New Hall, built by the Community soon after their arrival in 1799.
Image courtesy of the Canonesses of the Holy Sepulchre.

THE CEMETERY

The Establishment of the Cemetery and Early Burials

The Community arrived at New Hall on 3 March 1799, and the practicalities of a cemetery or burial space had to be addressed within a few weeks. Mary Marshall, S. Mary Cleophae (1723–99), died on 14 March 1799, and the decision was made to find a final resting place for her within the grounds of their newly acquired estate.[1] There were few other options in the local area. Building work did not begin on the first Catholic church in Chelmsford, Our Lady Immaculate, until 1845, nearly fifty years after the Community had arrived at New Hall. In the cities, urban cemeteries were being built from the 1820s but the municipal cemetery in Chelmsford would not be opened for another ninety years, in 1887.

Headstone of Mary Marsall, S. Mary Cleophae, the first person to be buried in the cemetery in March 1799. The stone is now very weathered, but it is still possible to make out the inscription which reads 'Mrs Mary Marshall, died the 14th of March 1799'.

The nearest Anglican church, St Andrews in the parish of Boreham, was nearly two miles away from the convent; and in the opposite direction, All Saints, the parish church of Springfield, was equally far away. Use of the Anglican parish churches for burial at Holme Hall and Dean House had not been ideal, and had been the only option for the Community in their temporary situation. Their new location at New Hall was a long term home, and more permanent plans could now be made.

The only decision that had to be made was exactly whereabouts in the extensive grounds the burial site should be located. A small plot in the south-west corner of the ground, known as the wilderness, was chosen. The plot was soon required again, as a further two members of the Community died in June of the same year: Emilia Dufrene, *alias* Freeman, S. Mary Barbara (1776–99), who died on 13 June, aged 24; and Elizabeth Evens, S. Mary Clare (1734–99), who died a few days later on 25 June, aged 57.[2]

---

1 A location reference will be given for each burial, in the form of Side Row/Grave Number. Burials in the original half are preceded by 'O', and those in the extension by 'E'. For example, Mary Marshall is at O/RA/22, which indicates the original half of the cemetery, in the row labelled 'A' on the right-hand side as you enter. See the plan of the cemetery for more information, and Appendix 1. Memorial Inscriptions.
2 O/RA/20–1. See Appendix 2. The Liège Community in 1794.

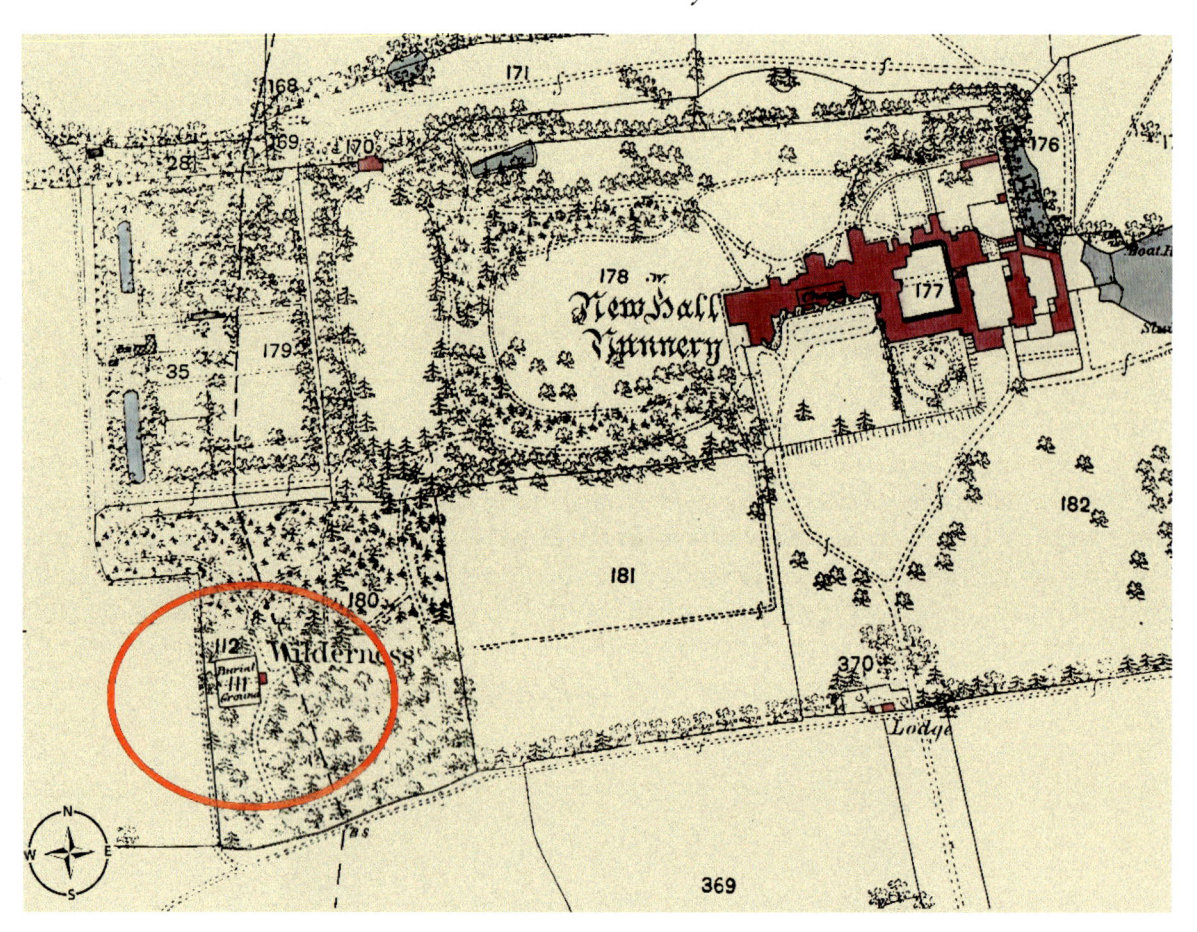

Detail of cemetery location, 1875, showing cemetery wall and entrance porch.
(Map: Hannah Thomas, from the Ordnance Survey map surveyed in 1875)

Although there is no surviving record of the discussion and decision of location for the cemetery, it was not by chance that a 'secret' corner was chosen in a distant and overgrown part of the grounds. Specifically Catholic burial grounds were only legally allowed after 1847, whether as part of a churchyard, or as a separate facility, and the Community had to keep their new cemetery relatively hidden from public view.[3]

The cemetery is also located very close to the boundary that divides the parishes of Boreham and Springfield, which runs vertically through the estate, from the north-east corner at an angle down towards the south of the estate, running parallel with the avenue. This was another clever tactic employed by the Community which enabled them to remain relatively undetected during this period, and is something that had been used by the English Catholic Community throughout the sixteenth and seventeenth centuries in order to maintain secrecy. Until the 1830s, law enforcement was organised according to geographical boundaries such as parishes and counties, and the borders between these areas were somewhat confusing when it came to deciding who had jurisdiction there. These 'grey areas' of administration functioned as a uniquely Catholic insurance policy of sorts, providing administrative and legal delays that would have allowed extra time for the removal or hiding of any illegal and necessarily secretive Catholic activity.[4]

---

[3] 10 and 11 Victoria cap. 65: Cemeteries Clauses Act 1847.

[4] County borders were utilized by the Catholic community in many similar locations in England and Wales. Stonor Park, within striking distance of the Oxfordshire, Buckinghamshire and Berkshire county borders, had been home to the recusant Stonor family since 1349: it operated as a missionary headquarters for both Edmund Campion, SJ, and Robert Parsons, SJ, in the early years of the Jesuit English mission. See Bede Camm, *Forgotten Shrines: An Account of Some Old Catholic Halls and Families in England and of Relics and Memorials of the English Martyrs* (Burns, Oates & Washbourne: London, 1936), pp. 97–103.

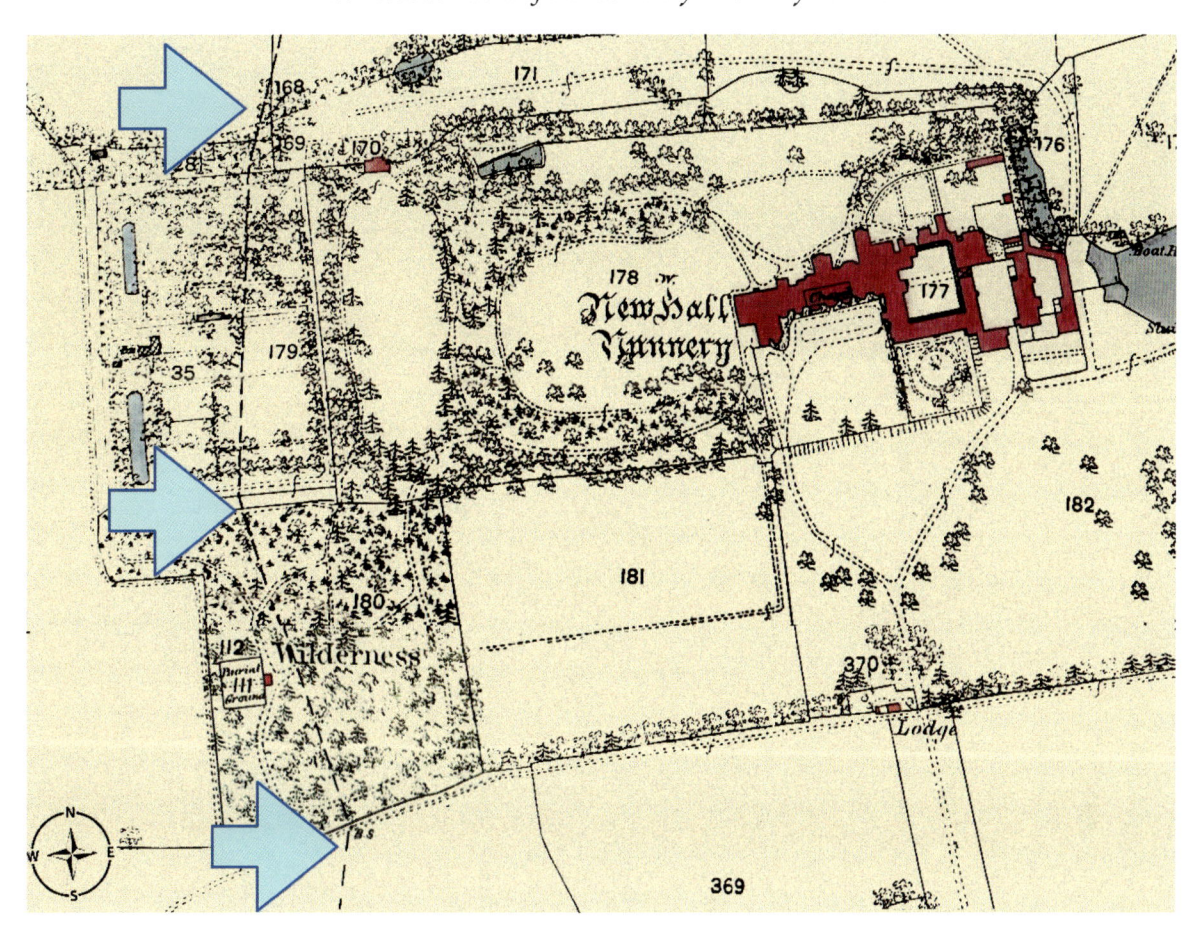

The Establishment of the Cemetery and Early Burials

A map of the site, marking the parish boundary between the parishes of Boreham and Springfield.
(Map: Hannah Thomas, from the Ordnance Survey map surveyed in 1875)

This caution is reflected in the administrative records of the Community. The burial register, which was started in May 1803, carefully notes that the deceased 'departed this life at New Hall, within the parish of Boreham … and was interred in the burial ground within the premises of New Hall, appropriated for the private use of the same mansion, being within the parish of Springfield'. Similarly, members of the Community who were professed at New Hall took their vows to 'the parishes of Boreham and Springfield'.[5]

In 1799, it was also still illegal to build a Catholic church. If the occupants of a building required a chapel, such as the Community at New Hall, that chapel had to be built very discretely, and was usually at the centre of the building so as not to be obvious from the outside. Sometimes even the builders themselves did not know what type of room they were constructing: the rooms could be round in shape or architecturally very simple, and builders might be told they were constructing a ballroom or entertainment space, which every well-to-do mansion would have needed in the eighteenth century.

The location of the cemetery in a relatively secret corner of the grounds was therefore a prudent and practical choice that allowed the Community to resume something like normal practice, as had been the case in Liège. They now had a chapel, convent and burial ground all within the enclosure walls again for the first time since 1794.

---

[5] ACHS/J1.11/Burial Register 1803–1979. The first entry is dated May 1803, but it is likely that the register was retrospectively compiled some time after 1812, in line with the Parochial Registers Act that required registers to be kept of public and private baptisms, marriages and burials (52 Geo 3 cap. 146). Although this legislation only legally applied to Anglican churches, the entries in the Community's Register are written in the same formulaic arrangement given by the act, suggesting that the wording had been copied from this source. See J. Brook Little, *The Law of Burial: including all the burial acts and official regulations, with notes and cases* (London: Shaw and Sons, 1902), pp. 373–81.

Burial Register

R.I.P.

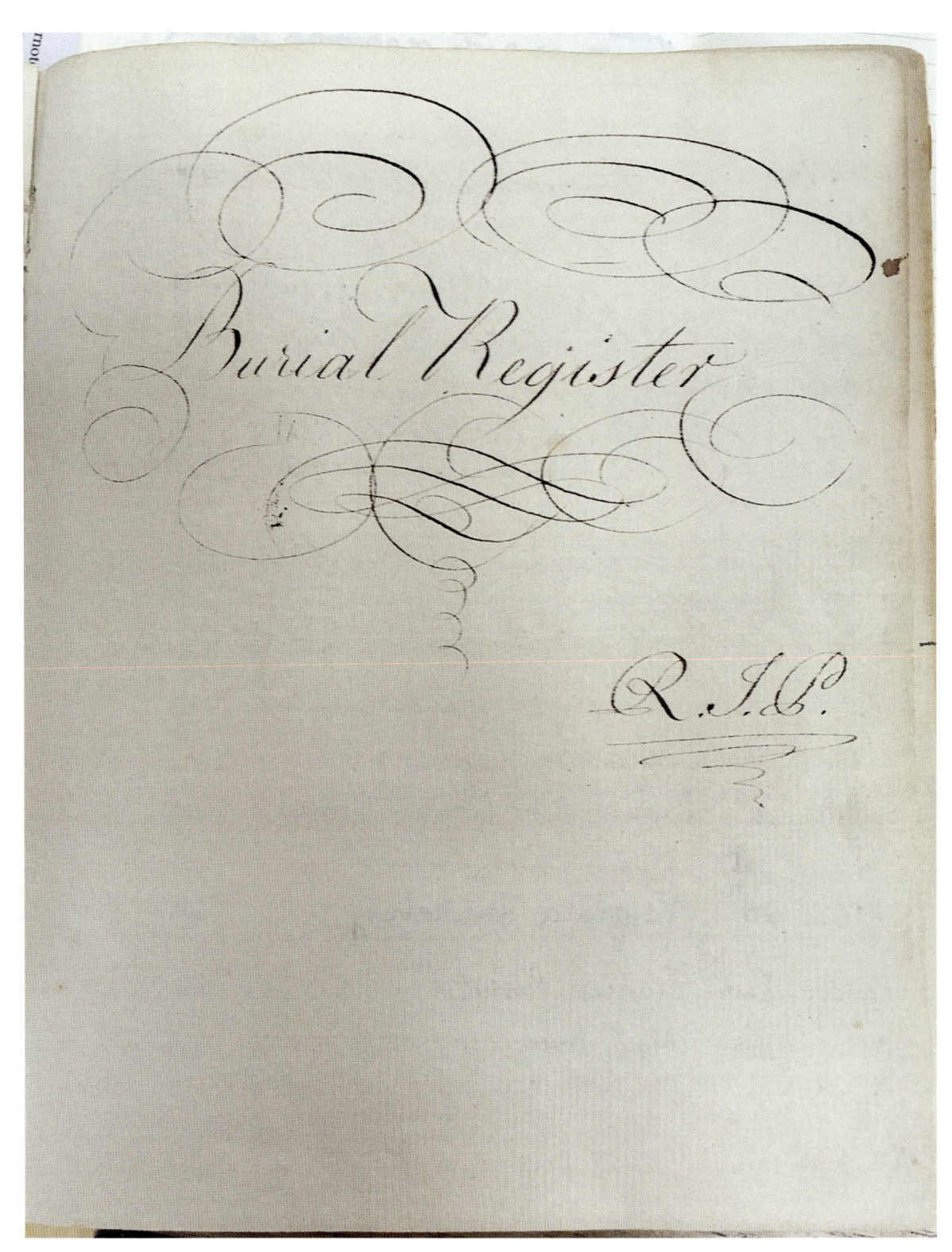

The Community's Burial Register, which was begun in 1803.
Image courtesy of the Canonesses of the Holy Sepulchre.

1803 I hereby certify that Mary Seymour of the County of Dorset, departed this life at New Hall, within the parish of Boreham, in the County of Essex, the third of May, One thousand eight hundred & three: and was interred by me, on the fifth of the same month: in the burial ground, within the premises of New Hall appropriated for the private use of the same mansion, such burying Ground being within the parish of Springfield. Stephen Chaffon

The opening page of the Burial Register.
Image courtesy of the Canonesses of the Holy Sepulchre.

Interestingly, the issue of Catholic cemeteries was still causing friction nearly a century after the creation of the Community cemetery in 1799. As late as 1887, Sr Mary Rudolph, Mother Superior of the convent of Notre Dame in Southend, wrote to the local Board of Health to ask for permission to create 'a small cemetery in the convent grounds, to use exclusively for our Community'. As was required by law at that time, the proposals were advertised, and several local residents responded by writing to the Board to complain about the potential convent cemetery. It was claimed that the cemetery would have an adverse effect on property prices in the area, it was too close to residential water supplies, and that there were two public burial grounds within close proximity to the convent that 'allotted a portion to the Catholics', therefore deeming a convent cemetery to be unnecessary: permission was refused.[6]

It is uncertain if many of the other English religious communities returning from exile risked creating their own cemetery or burial ground in the early years of their return, and, where burial practice has been recorded, there are very few examples that are comparable with the cemetery at New Hall. Amongst the other returning communities of English women religious, some simply continued to use local Anglican churchyards, with the necessary discretion. The English Carmelite Community from Antwerp settled at Lanherne in Cornwall by October 1794. Deceased members of the Community were buried in the chapel of our Blessed Lady in the nearby parish church of St Mawgan's until the 1830s, when the decision was made to create a Community cemetery within the convent walls.[7]

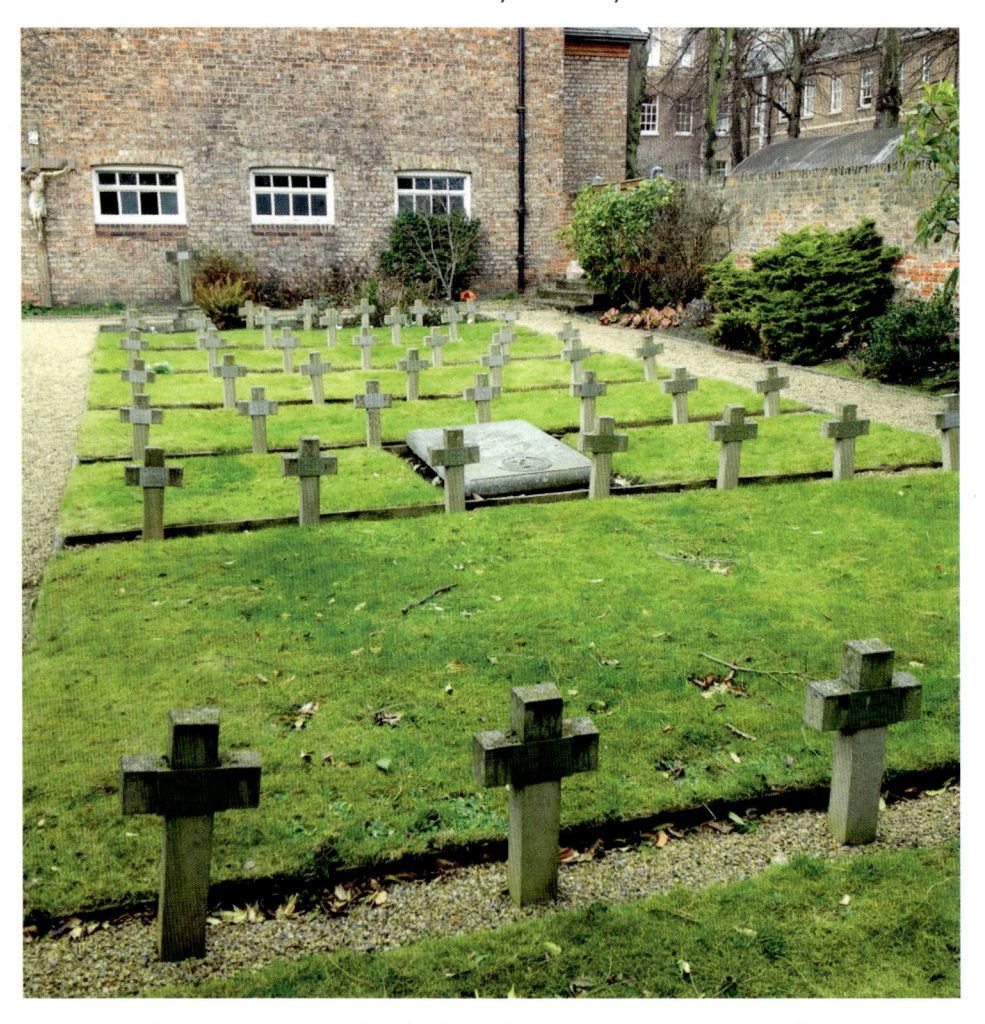

Cemetery at the Bar Convent, York, which was begin in 1825. The grave markers are modern.
(Photograph: Hannah Thomas)

[6] ERO D/HS/45 Bundle of documents from Southend Board of Health regarding application from Sr Mary Rudolph to convert ground into burial ground, 1887.
[7] Douai Abbey [DAR] CA/1/C/2 Registry of deaths of the community of Lanherne

The Establishment of the Cemetery and Early Burials

At the Bar Convent in York, where the Mary Ward sisters had been based since 1686, it was not until 1825 that the Community were able to create their own burial ground within the convent walls.[8] The chronicle of the convent records a detailed account of the process leading to this event:

> For many years Rev. Mother Coyney [1759–1826] had set her heart upon securing a place of burial within the Convent grounds; and her desire grew stronger when the practice of the 'Resurrection men' gave friends and relatives every reason to fear that the bodies of those they loved might be disinterred and made over to the surgeons for the purpose of dissection. It was with considerable difficulty—for the land required was let to a tenant on a long lease- that the coveted ground was obtained in 1825. Mr. Newsham, the Chaplain, with his own hands laid it out and planted its yew trees. The first to find a grave within its precincts was a little child, one of three orphaned sisters whose education and maintenance Mother Coyney had undertaken to provide for. The first among the religious laid to rest there was Mother Coyney herself.[9]

Several of the other English communities had broadly positive experiences upon their arrival in England, and encountered generally sympathetic local populations, willing to be somewhat flexible when it came to the practicalities of arranging burials. However, even in these more tolerant surroundings, very few communities were able to replicate the situation at New Hall and create a distinct convent cemetery within their enclosure walls.

Both the English Benedictine Community from Brussels and the English Augustinian Community from Bruges, who settled in Winchester and Hengrave respectively, found themselves in towns that had already had existing Catholic populations, and as such, were more tolerant of the spiritual and practical needs of the communities.[10] This meant that some semblance of normality was able to be resumed as far as burial services were concerned, as had been experienced by the Sepulchrines during their time at Holme Hall. In Winchester, the issue of burial did not have to be addressed until the death of Mary Stapleton, S. Mary Christina (1714–97), on 14 January 1797. Their manuscript chronicle notes that, at this time, 'there was no possibility of having a cemetery attached to the convent', and the Community were given a corner of the nearby cemetery in the parish of St James to use for their burials. An additional note, added by a later chronicler, explains that this was a corner of the churchyard specifically for Catholic burials, situated about a mile from Winchester.[11] Similarly, at Hengrave Hall, Community records note the outpouring of generosity and support from the local population, both Catholic and Protestant. Mr Carter, vicar of Flempton-cum-Hengrave, promised not to interfere with the funerals of any members of the Community, and the Community's own chaplain Andrew Oliver (*fl.* 1784–1812), who had travelled with them from Bruges, was even able to officiate at a burial in 1796. Even in this tolerant atmosphere, caution was still required. Community burial services were held

---

[8] See 'Convent Notes', *WWTN*. The complex history of the Mary Ward Institute in the seventeenth and eighteenth centuries means that the sources and the data relating to the members of the Institute are very different from the other convents, and it has been treated as a separate example of an English religious community to those listed above. The sisters were not enclosed and their religious life was based on the model of the Society of Jesus. They were suppressed in 1631 but managed to survive through their educational work in the schools they established at St Omer, Liège, Munich and other cities across Europe. They were the first women religious to establish themselves permanently in England: they opened a school in Hammersmith in 1669 which survived until the end of the eighteenth century and in 1686 founded the Bar Convent in York.

[9] Henry James Coleridge (ed.), *St. Mary's Convent, Micklegate Bar York, 1686–1887* (London: Burns & Oates, 1887), pp. 182–3.

[10] Distribution of Catholics in 1767, as cited in Bossy, *English Catholic Community*, pp. 408–9.

[11] Downside Abbey Archives [DAA]/Haslemere accounts 1794–1853: *Annals of the Community of the Glorious Assumption of the Blessed Virgin Mary*, Volume II, p. 83. See also Dom Aidan Bellenger, 'The Brussels Nuns at Winchester 1794–1897', *English Benedictine Congregation History Commission Symposium*, 1999 and John Thornhill, *History of the Parish of Hampshire Downs* (published online, url: http://www.hampshiredowns-winchester.org/wp-content/uploads/2013/11/Hampshire-Downs-Parish-history-timeline.pdf, 2013), p. 3. The burial ground and church are no longer in existence. I am grateful to Dr Roberta Anderson for her assistance with these sources.

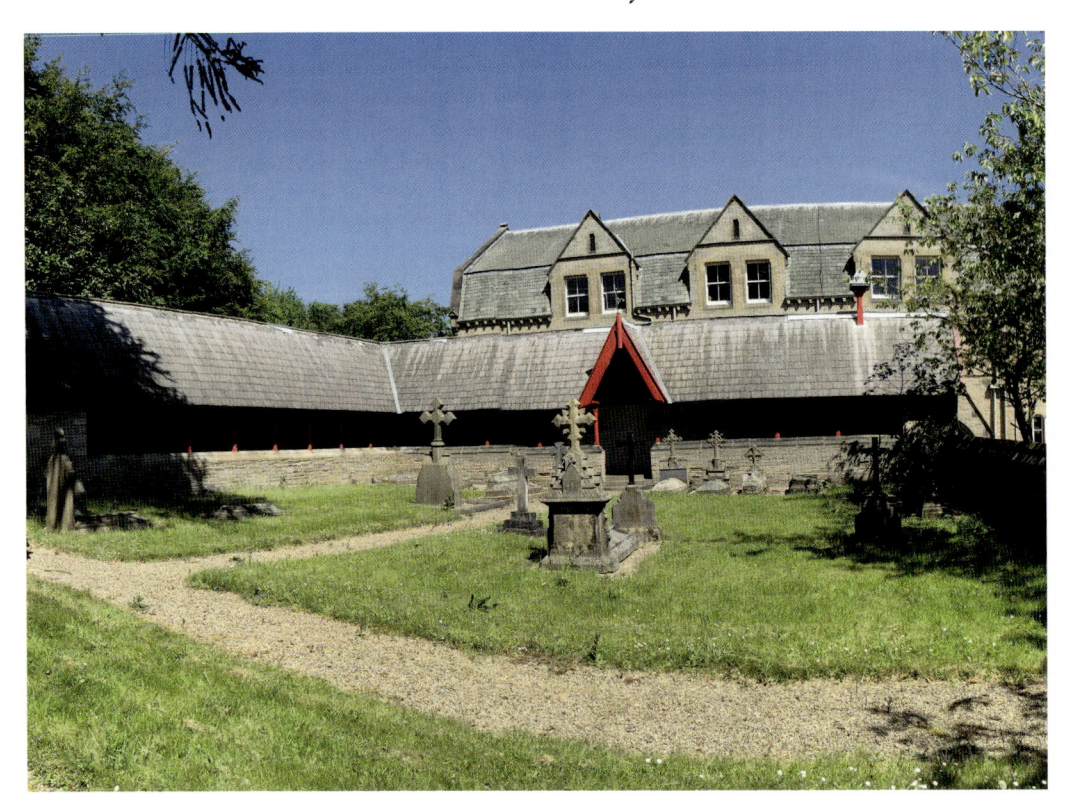

Cemetery at Ushaw College, near Durham, which was begun in 1809.
(Photograph: Hannah Thomas)

at very early dawn, and were kept a secret from the Community's Protestant servants. The deceased sisters still had to buried in a discrete corner of the parish churchyard, and were not able to be buried in their habits, as had been the custom in Bruges.[12]

Similar patterns of burial practices can be detected in the several communities of English male religious that were also forced to migrate to England from the 1790s onwards. Some members of the English secular college at Douai, in northern France, settled at Ushaw College near Durham in 1808.[13] Five students died in a typhoid epidemic in January 1809, and the decision was taken, in the wake of that tragedy, to create a College cemetery 'formed within a clearing in the wood away to the west side of the College'. The College chronicle acknowledged the potential legal difficulties that this could cause, commenting 'apparently the new cemetery was made in defiance of the law which forbade burial other than in the churchyard of the parish to those who had not taken the oath of supremacy'.[14] Similarly, the English Jesuit College at Stonyhurst, new home of the Academie Anglaise at Liège, established a small cemetery within the College grounds soon after their arrival.[15] The Benedictine Community at St Gregory's in Douai settled at Downside Abbey near Bath in 1814, and established a small cemetery there by 1827.[16]

[12] See Francis Young, 'Mother Mary More and the Exile of the Augustinian Canonesses of Bruges in England 1794–1802', *Recusant History* 27 (2004), pp. 86–102, especially p. 93. I am grateful to Dr Young for his assistance with my research. Six members of the Community died between 1794 and 1802, and were buried in the churchyard attached to the parish church.

[13] Others settled at St Edmund's College at Ware in Hertfordshire.

[14] See David Milburn, *A History of Ushaw College* (Ushaw College: Ushaw College, Durham 1964), pp. 110–13 and 'Junior', 'Praeterita I', *Ushaw Magazine* (1920), pp. 89–98. See also Ushaw College [UC]/H 297a—List of those Buried in the Cemetery in Chronological Order, Jan 1809–May 1893 and UC/H 297a—List of those Buried in the Cemetery by Month, 1809–93.

[15] The first burial was made on 1 May 1795—see p. 63 below.

[16] See Dom Aidan Bellenger, Gerald Brine and Frances Daniels, *St Benedict's, Stratton on the Fosse, Somerset: A History* (Radstock: Downside Abbey Press, 2014); and DAA/*Fasti Gregoriani* 1793–1932.

Cemetery at Stonyhurst College, Lancashire, which was begun in May 1795 and used until the 1990s.
Eventually, the left-hand side of the church, shown here, was used for lay burials.
(Photograph: Hannah Thomas)

It is clear from these examples that the Community's decision to establish a cemetery so soon after their arrival at New Hall in 1799 was indeed unusual, particularly amongst contemporary communities of English women religious. Many of their contemporaries were not in a position to do the same for several decades, and others had to rely on the toleration and understanding of nearby Anglican parishes and parish churches to allow any burial to take place at all.

Cemetery Development: The Cemetery Wall

An important aspect in the history of Community cemetery is the large brick wall that encloses it. The date of construction of the wall gives a clear indication of when the Community first considered this to be a distinct cemetery, rather than the burial ground in the corner of the garden. Evidence from seventeenth-century maps and other records shows that the Community did not simply repurpose an existing walled garden dating from before they moved in. This is supported by physical evidence on site, such as the seventeenth-century walls around the tennis court, in which the bricks are a noticeably different shape, size and construction from those in the cemetery wall.

The wall surrounding the cemetery,
which is noticeably different in construction from the earlier walls on the premises.
(Photograph: Hannah Thomas)

Other evidence from the Community archives suggests that the wall was built some time after 1845. The perimeter wall, which ran around the entire premises, was built in 1845 under the watchful guidance of the eleventh prioress, Anna Maria Blount, S. Mary Teresa Joseph (1791–1879), who had been elected only a year earlier in 1844.[17] This wall, which can still be seen opposite the entrance gate of the cemetery, and through which you enter the newer half of the cemetery, seems to have been completed before the cemetery wall was added later on.

Physical evidence within the cemetery itself would seem to support this theory, as evidenced by the join between the enclosure wall and the cemetery wall in the far right and far left corners of the original half of the cemetery. The two walls are clearly constructed separately from each other, built to different heights, and both are finished with totally different coping stones.[18] The first edition map of the Ordnance Survey map, which surveyed the Chelmsford area in 1875, shows the cemetery marked in the area labelled 'the wilderness'.

In the national context, cemetery walls were a topic of much discussion in both the secular and the sacred environment. After the Catholic Emancipation Act 1829, the English Catholic Church had to re-establish rules, guidelines and structures for day-to-day management as a legally recognised religion in

[17] Community records refer to this as the enclosure wall, but strictly speaking, 'enclosure' is applied to the section of a convent where only the Community may enter, unless specific permission has been given by the relevant bishop.

[18] Although it is most likely that the enclosure wall was built before the cemetery wall, it is also possible that the cemetery initially had a boundary wall that was constructed before the enclosure wall was finished, which finished a few feet short of the existing wall. The Ordnance Survey map of 1875 shows the back wall of the cemetery to be a few feet away from the boundary, and burials within this gap date to after 1875, suggesting that the space had not been available before that date.

> Boundary wall, on right hand side of entrance to extension
>
> Cemetery wall, on right hand side of cemetery

Close up of the boundary wall (on the left) and the cemetery wall (on the right) showing the different heights and coping stones of each. (Photograph: Hannah Thomas)

England and Wales. One particularly important question was how the treatment of deceased Catholics should be different from, or indeed similar to, that of deceased Anglicans, or members of other faiths. The matter was considered of such importance to the liturgical lives of English Catholics that it was debated by the newly re-established Catholic hierarchy at a synod in Westminster in 1855.[19] At the synod, implications for the afterlife were considered, as well as questions of consecration, and the right to use an exclusively dedicated physical space for the burying of the dead of one particular denomination. Eventually a decision was reached in Rome that forbade the consecration of a cemetery in which the Catholics were not 'separated by a wall from the corpses of heretics'. This was interpreted literally by the English Catholic Community, and had serious implications for consecration. In a letter to Canon John Maddocks (1801–65) in June 1856, who had written on behalf of the Sisters of Mercy in Liverpool about their convent cemetery, Bishop Alexander Goss (1814–72) explained

> You are probably aware that the Cemetery cannot be consecrated or rather solemnly bless unless it be separated by a wall from all unconsecrated ground … One thing only I know, that the laws of the Church are so severe on the subject of burials and burial grounds that I dare not lend myself to their transgression, though the good sisters will hardly credit me.[20]

Bishops of other dioceses were similarly concerned to get these important details correctly recorded. In December 1859, Bishop Thomas Brown of Newport and Menevia (1796–1880), also wrote to Bishop Goss, asking him to explain 'if a [cemetery] wall be required, what must be its height?'[21]

This was also a time of great change in terms of the national development of the cemetery in England. From 1852, a series of Burial Acts allowed the creation of municipal cemeteries, which were to be managed by Burial Boards made up of elected ratepayers. The newly created cemeteries had to be

---

[19] See WDA/E5603/AFS II—Provincial Synod 1855; and WDA/Ma 2/36/1—Manning correspondence 1858–86.
[20] Lancashire Record Office, Preston, RCLv Box 14, 5/1/253, Letter to Canon Maddocks, 4 June 1856. As transcribed in Peter Doyle (ed.), *The Correspondence of Alexander Goss, Bishop of Liverpool, 1856–1872* (Woodbridge: Catholic Record Society, 2014), p. 74.
[21] UC/P42/301, Letter from Chepstow, 24 December 1859.

Detail of cemetery location, 1875, showing cemetery wall and entrance porch.
(Map: Hannah Thomas, from the Ordnance Survey map surveyed in 1875)

marked with a boundary wall on at least two sides. The municipal cemetery at nearby Colchester, opened in 1854 and managed by a conglomerate of eleven parish councils, was marked by a tall brick boundary wall on both the south and west sides, which is stylistically quite similar to the wall at the Community cemetery.

Other evidence allows some of the remaining gaps to be filled, and provides 1875 as the last date by which the cemetery wall was constructed. Ordnance Survey maps from this date show the cemetery wall marked. It is even possible to make out the original entrance porch, which was demolished ten years later in 1885, when the current gateway was erected. An entry in the Community Chapter Book records that 'on 11 May 1885 ... Reverend Mother proposed to rebuild the porch to the burial ground and appropriate to this purpose a legacy of £100'.[22]

Combining these pieces of evidence together therefore gives a likely construction date for the wall as some time between 1845 and 1875, a period within which the Community considered the cemetery as a distinct space in its own right. These snippets of information help to identify four major phases in the development of the cemetery in its first ninety years:

1. **1799–1809**: first deaths at New Hall, burial in remote and discreet corner of the grounds. Twenty-one graves within first decade, all grouped around the first three burials in 1799.[23]
2. **1810–44**: more burials added to same part of grounds; extra space required. A handful of graves have been dug to the left of the original group and the whole area is developing into a more distinct cemetery.[24] Seventy-nine graves in total by 1844, sixty-seven of which are situated around the first three burials, which is now the right-hand side of the cemetery.

---

[22] ACHS/Chapter Book 1800–1976/11 May 1885.
[23] O/RA/20-2.
[24] O/LE/19-29, LD/25-9.

The Community's Chapter Book records that 'on 11 May 1885 … Reverend Mother proposed to rebuild the porch to the burial ground and appropriate to this purpose a legacy of £100'.
Image courtesy of the Canonesses of the Holy Sepulchre.

3. **1845–75**: enclosure wall built around grounds, cemetery wall added soon afterwards with small entrance porch, landscaping developments such as creation of a path between two sides of cemetery. By 1875, there were a further forty-four burials. All burials in this period are in the newly developed left-hand side of the cemetery.[25]
4. **1876–85**: porch and entrance wall demolished, arched gateway and wall erected (with blue brick detailing). An additional eighteen burials took place in this period, ten on the right-hand side and eight on the left. The burials on the right-hand side are clustered together near the enclosure wall suggesting a deliberate policy of using up all available spaces in what is now the 'original half' of the cemetery.[26] 141 graves in total by 1885, neatly arranged on either side of a landscaped path, and enclosed by a tall brick wall that abutted the enclosure wall.

Several more burials took place over the following decades, and by the 1930s it became evident that a larger cemetery space would be needed in the near future. The Community purchased a small part of the field directly behind the enclosure wall in November 1930,[27] which allowed the farmer, Mr Hodge, to square off his field, and gave the Community the option to extend the cemetery as and when required. Additional spaces were found in between existing graves and around the wall of the cemetery for another two decades, until 1956, when the enclosure wall was knocked through and the cemetery extended into the field beyond.[28] All new burials have taken place in the new half since that date, and the new half is divided into Community members on the left, and lay people on the right-hand side.

---

[25] That is O/LC/11–29 and LB/9–25.
[26] O/RC/3–7; RB/1–5; RA/1–7.
[27] ACHS/List of Repairs 1868–73 and 1889–1941. Entries are not paginated, but are recorded chronologically.
[28] My sincere and grateful thanks to Moira Metcalf, previously S. Mary Simon, for sharing her detailed knowledge with me.

The entrance to the new half of the cemetery.
Image courtesy of the Canonesses of the Holy Sepulchre.

The cemetery late nineteenth century, before the enclosure wall was knocked through.
Image courtesy of the Canonesses of the Holy Sepulchre.

Burials: Community

The cemetery is the final resting place of all the Canonesses who have died since 1799, providing an important and special link between the past and present Community. This accounts for approximately three-quarters of the burials in the cemetery, and includes prioresses, as well as choir and lay sisters. A total of 174 members of the Community were laid to rest between 1799 and 1956 in the original half of the cemetery, and a more detailed exploration of the people whose names are now preserved on headstones has much to reveal about the history of the Community itself.

Burials: Community

The three Canonesses who oversaw the migration of the Community from Liège to New Hall died between 1807 and 1816, and all are buried in the cemetery.[29] Sarah Trant, S. Frances Xaveria, died 7 February 1807, aged 43, having served as procuratrix of the Community throughout the migration, from 1792 until 1797, and again from 1802 until her death in 1807.[30] Her job would have included making sure sufficient funds were available for the various expenses of the journey, as well as managing the day to day expenses of the convent, and ensuring that currency was correctly exchanged between English sterling and Flemish florins. Her younger sister Elizabeth, S. Benedict Joseph, had also been amongst the group which left Liège, and had died during the Community's time at Dean House in Wiltshire.

Elizabeth Talbot, S. Mary Helen Aloysia, died soon afterwards, on 20 April 1808, aged 50. She served the Community as Sub-Prioress, from 1793 until 1798, and again from 1803 until her death in 1808, providing valuable and vital assistance to the Prioress.[31]

Headstone of Bridget Clough, S. Mary Aloysia, 8th prioress of the Community. She organised and led the migration from Liège to England in 1794. Image courtesy of the Canonesses of the Holy Sepulchre.

Bridget Clough, S. Mary Aloysia, who had served as eighth prioress of the Community since 1786, died on 6 July 1816, aged 79. Her death left a deep mark on the Community, and it is clear that she was revered and loved by everyone. Her headstone conveys something of the grief felt by her death, noting that she 'for more than 30 years governed those committed to her charge with uncommon indications of heavenly wisdom, fortitude and sweetness'.[32] Records from the Community archives

---

[29] See Appendix 2. The Liège Community in 1794.
[30] O/RC/17.
[31] O/RC/13.
[32] O/RD/18.

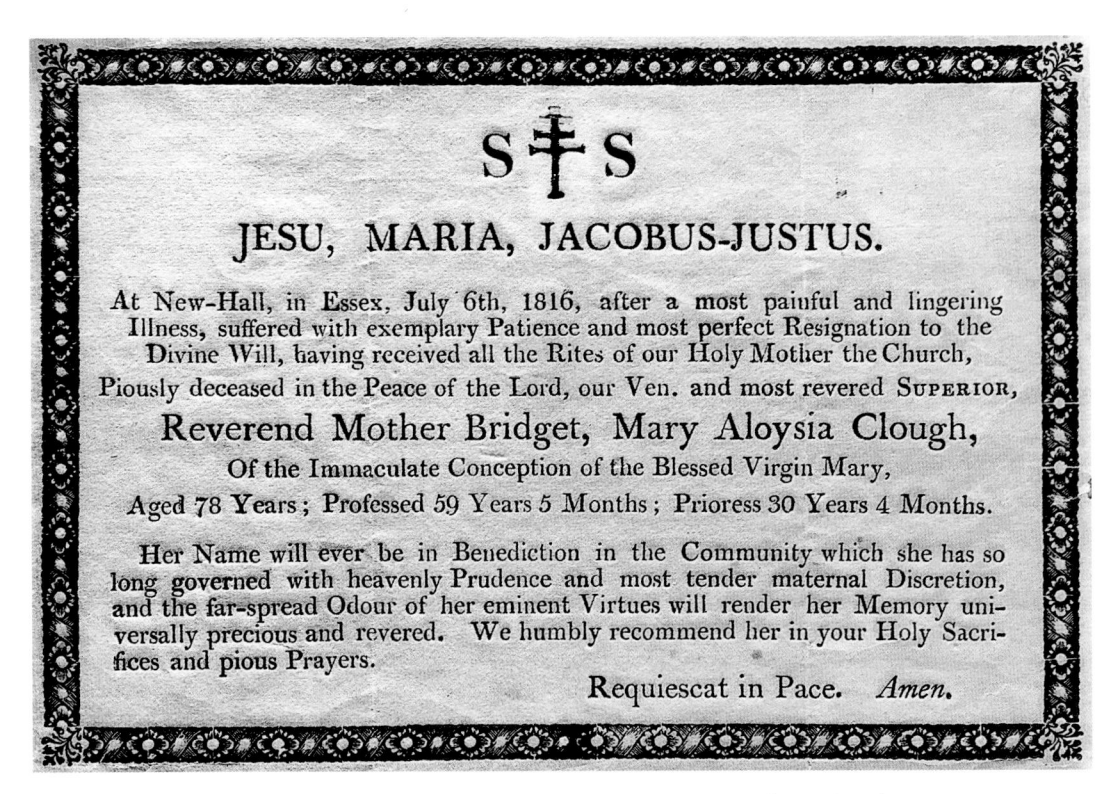

> S ☩ S
>
> ## JESU, MARIA, JACOBUS-JUSTUS.
>
> At New-Hall, in Essex, July 6th, 1816, after a most painful and lingering Illness, suffered with exemplary Patience and most perfect Resignation to the Divine Will, having received all the Rites of our Holy Mother the Church, Piously deceased in the Peace of the Lord, our Ven. and most revered Superior,
>
> ### Reverend Mother Bridget, Mary Aloysia Clough,
>
> Of the Immaculate Conception of the Blessed Virgin Mary,
>
> Aged 78 Years; Professed 59 Years 5 Months; Prioress 30 Years 4 Months.
>
> Her Name will ever be in Benediction in the Community which she has so long governed with heavenly Prudence and most tender maternal Discretion, and the far-spread Odour of her eminent Virtues will render her Memory universally precious and revered. We humbly recommend her in your Holy Sacrifices and pious Prayers.
>
> Requiescat in Pace. *Amen*.

Printed death notice announcing the death of Prioress Bridget Clough in 1816.
Image courtesy of the Canonesses of the Holy Sepulchre.

also comment on the lasting effect of the loss of their matriarch, noting that, 'every one seemed to try in every smallest point to do honour to Reverend Mother's memory, by adhering to the least thing they thought would be her pleasure, so that notwithstanding our grief, she really seemed in a striking manner to be still among us.'[33]

Soon after their arrival at New Hall, nine members of the Community were summoned to appear before the Quarter Sessions on 2 April 1799, and publicly take the oath of obedience on behalf of the Community. Those who had previously taken the same oath at Salisbury in 1797 and 1798 were not required to take it again, and this time, the group was led by the Rt Hon Charlotte Clifford, S. Ann Teresa (1773–1800), eldest daughter of Hugh, fourth baron Clifford of Chudleigh (1726–83). Charlotte had been proposed for profession in December 1793, five months before the migration from Liège, and as a result of the upheaval, was not actually professed until March 1795, when the Community were in Yorkshire. She died only a few months later, in July 1800, aged 28.[34]

A number of her relatives were also among the group of nine. This small group, representing a Community of approximately forty-nine who had travelled from Liège, included several from the same family groups, and also some future leaders of the Community.[35]

Two other Clifford relatives were amongst those who swore the oath on behalf of the Community in 1799, including Charlotte's paternal cousin, Anne Clifford, S. Aloysia Austin (1770–1844), and a cousin by marriage, Ann Hales, S. Christina Juliana (1753–1811).[36] Hales had joined the Community in 1783, about ten years before the migration from Liège, whereas Anne Clifford, like Charlotte, had taken her profession vows in July 1793, a matter of months before the journey to England.

---

[33] ACHS/TB 165/106/Chantress Book 2, 1816–26, p. 4. The Chantress was in charge of the music and choir arrangements for each Mass, and had to ensure that the correct liturgical pieces were sung at the right times and for the right services each day.
[34] O/RB/18.
[35] See Appendix 2. The Liège Community in 1794.
[36] O/RC/21.

Elizabeth Gerard, S. Mary Regis (1771–1843), 9th prioress of the Community from 1816 until her death in 1843. Image courtesy of the Canonesses of the Holy Sepulchre.

PRIORESSES

The cemetery affords a unique opportunity to study the ways in which the Community chose to commemorate these deaths, especially as original headstones have remained in place and are in remarkably good condition. This is particularly useful in the case of the headstones of the various prioresses who have served the Community since 1799, as these headstones tend to include a description of the career and personal attributes of the prioress in question, in contrast with the sparse information recorded on the headstones of the ordinary Community members.

Elizabeth Gerard, S. Mary Regis (1771–1843), was elected the ninth prioress of the Community in July 1816, following the death of Bridget Clough, S. Mary Aloysia. Following such a beloved leader was an unenviable task but Gerard was certainly well suited to the role. Community records describe her with great love and respect, noting that

> it may be doubted if any Superior ever more completely won the love and confidence of her subjects, or the satisfaction and esteem of all who came in contact with her. She had great gifts of mind and heart. She had such courage as to be afraid of nothing, and yet great tenderness for the weaknesses of others.[37]

---

[37] ACHS/D4 'Mss notes on the traditions of our Community, given to me by Reverend Mother' (December 1889); see also *History of the Community*, pp. 154–5.

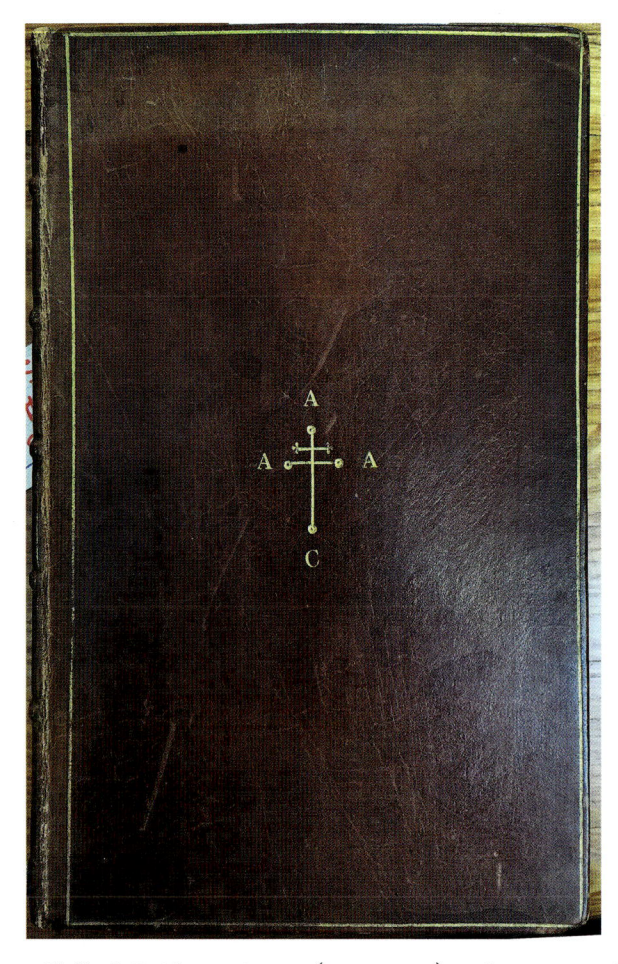

Monogram of Ann Clifford, S. Aloysia Austin (1770–1844), 10th prioress of the Community from 1843 until 1844. The book was a gift from her sister Constantia in 1817.
Image courtesy of the Canonesses of the Holy Sepulchre.

Gerard served as prioress for over twenty-seven years, until her death on 13 June 1843, aged 72. Her headstone conveys the deep affection with which she was regarded, commenting that 'renouncing worldly advantages, she chose for her portion the cross of Christ … we piously now hope [she] rests with it in glory'.[38]

Anne Clifford was elected the tenth prioress of the Community in June 1843. She led the Community for only six months, until her sudden and unexpected death in January 1844, aged 72. Her headstone notes something of her humility and reluctance in accepting the role, commenting that she was 'raised to the painful dignity of Prioress after a humble life of fifty years'.[39] Both Gerard and Clifford were amongst the group who had travelled from Liège, and both were among the nine members of the Community that publicly swore the Oath of Obedience.

The Community was devastated to have lost two prioresses in such a short space of time. A letter sent to a friend by a member of the Community records the deep grief felt by everyone:

> My dear Sister in Christ, I need not tell you that we are indeed afflicted—the loss of two superiors in one year is of itself a calamity, had they not both been as worthy of our regrets as their exalted virtues rendered them, but we have only to say *fiat voluntas tua* [thy will be done] & place ourselves in the hand of the Father of Orphans who in his mercy will no doubt replace them with a worthy successor. Pray with us dear Sister in Christ & obtain the suffrage of your holy community for the intention.[40]

[38] O/LE/20.
[39] O/LE/19.
[40] ACHS/Personnel Files/Prioresses: Gerard. Copy letter, anonymous, sent 1844.

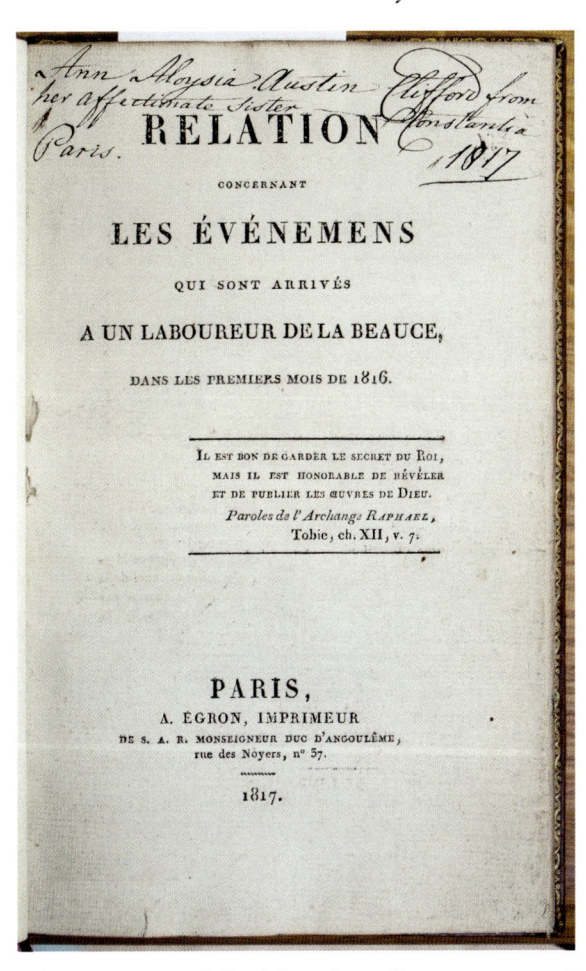

Gift inscription 'Ann Aloysia Austin Clifford from her affectionate sister Constantia, Paris 1817.'
Image courtesy of the Canonesses of the Holy Sepulchre.

Anna Maria Blount, S. Teresa Joseph (1791–1879), was chosen to lead the Community in these difficult circumstances, and was elected to be the eleventh prioress in January 1844. She served as prioress for over 25 years, until ill health forced her to resign in 1869. Despite this, she was able to continue full participation in Community life for a further ten years, until her death in February 1879, aged 88. Blount had joined the school at New Hall in April 1804, alongside her sister Emma. Community records describe her as a very pious and humble person, particularly devoted to all aspects of religious life. Having entered the Community straight after finishing school in 1807, by the time of her death, she had spent seventy-five consecutive years of her life at New Hall, having been professed for nearly seventy years. During that time, she had only left the convent once.[41] Her headstone merely hints at this remarkable career, describing her as 'the Venerable Mother Anna Maria Teresa Joseph Blount' who 'during a religious career extending over more than 70 years, edified and benefited the community by her singular zeal humility and fervour'.

Blount was succeeded by Caroline Corney, S. Mary Alphonsa (1825–73), elected as the twelfth prioress of the Community in April 1869. Corney had also attended school at New Hall from 1837 to 1841, under her maiden name of Dolan, and in the autumn of 1849, married Mr Francis Alexander Corney, a gold and silver refiner, in London. After the death of her husband, and possibly a child, by 1852, and after much prayer and reflection, Corney felt called to join the Community.[42] She was eventually professed as S. Mary Alphonsa in January 1856, and had a productive and fruitful career as procuratrix and then prioress, overseeing extensive building projects including the construction of the ambulacrum. The Community

---

[41] O/LE/9. See also *History of the Community*, pp. 177–89.
[42] Alexander Corney is listed as a gold and silver refiner on the 1851 census, at their family home in the Paddington area of London. He died in February 1852. It is quite likely that Mary Ann Corney, whose birth in the June quarter of 1851 and death in the September quarter of 1852 are registered in the same district, was their daughter.

Anna Maria Blount, S. Teresa Joseph (1791–1879), 11th prioress of the Community from 1844 until 1869. Image courtesy of the Canonesses of the Holy Sepulchre.

Left. Julia Mary Butler, S. Aloysia Austin (1825–1912), 13th prioress of the Community from 1873 until her death in 1912.   *Right.* Mary Agnes Dolan, S. Aloysia Magdalen (1858–1936), 15th prioress of the Community from 1918 until 1936. Images courtesy of the Canonesses of the Holy Sepulchre.

A group photograph of the Community, taken in the 1930s.
Image courtesy of the Canonesses of the Holy Sepulchre.

Left. Community members at work in the garden.
Right. Margaret Ellen Mason, S. Aloysia Stanislaus (1819–75), and Rosina Frances Mason,
S. Ignatia Francis (1825–1909). Images courtesy of the Canonesses of the Holy Sepulchre.

history describes her time as prioress as 'one of bricks and mortar', a period which lasted from 1869 until her death in 1873, aged 48. Her headstone notes that 'her memory will ever be held in benediction by the community which she governed during her short career with maternal charity, prudence and zeal'.[43]

Six other prioresses are also buried in the cemetery: Julia Butler, S. Aloysia Austin (1825–1909), elected thirteenth prioress in 1873 until her retirement in 1912; Cecilia Kendal, S. Joseph Sales (1844–1918), fourteenth prioress from 1912 until her death in 1918; Agnes Dolan, S. Aloysia Magdalen (1858–1936), fifteenth prioress 1918 to 1936; Edith O'Connell, S. Mary Christina (1879–1970), sixteenth prioress 1936 to 1954; Margaret Boland, S. Mary Veronica (1893–1983), seventeenth prioress 1954 to 1966; and Bridget O'Connor, S. Mary Christopher (1921–2003), eighteenth prioress from 1966 until 1978.[44]

[43] O/LE/13.
[44] Butler: O/LE/35; Kendal: O/LE/16; Dolan: O/RD/14; O'Connell: E/L1/13; Boland: E/L1/25 and O'Connor.

THE LIÈGE COMMUNITY

The cemetery also allows the opportunity to closely examine the forty-nine Community members who left Liège in 1794, the youngest of which was aged 17, and the eldest 71.[45] Except for the four who had died during the journey, every member of this Liège Community is buried in the cemetery at New Hall. Analysis of this distinct group allows new patterns to emerge, and a better understanding of the group to be developed. Something that is particularly noticeable about those who migrated from Liège is that many of these Community members were also from the same family groups, including several groups of siblings.

For example, there were three members of the Dennett family, all closely related to Mary Dennett, S. Christina, who had so transformed the Community's school and convent at Liège. Her elder sister, Helen Dennett, S. Mary Teresa (1725–94) had travelled with the Community to England, but died soon after their arrival in London, and was buried in St Pancras in London.[46] Two other members of the Dennett family were also among the Liège community—Elizabeth Dennett, S. Mary Ignatia (1761–1825) and her younger sister Margaret Dennett, S. Mary Stanislaus (1765–1816). Both were nieces of Mary and Helen, and had travelled to Liège to join the Community by 1779.[47]

Two members of the Laurenson family were members of the Community that migrated from Liège in 1794, but there are five members of the family buried in the cemetery, and several others who attended school at New Hall in subsequent generations. The two who migrated from Liège were half-sisters—Catherine Laurenson, S. Mary Agatha (1754–1834), and Mary Laurenson, S. Mary Sales (1777–1812). Similarly to others who were amongst the Liège party, Mary Laurenson had only joined the Community in November 1793, and was not able to profess her final vows until November 1798, during the last few months at Dean House.[48] Her sister Catherine had joined the Community some years earlier, in 1772, and had professed her vows under the Revd Mother Christina Dennett, in September 1774.[49] Their mother Martha is also buried in the cemetery, having outlived both of her children by the time of her own death in 1835.[50] Interestingly, their brother John (1760–1834) was a Jesuit at the English College in Liège from 1773 until their own migration to England in 1794, and was responsible for compiling the chronicle of the journey to Stonyhurst.[51]

Margaret Cross, S. Frances Borgia (1772–1820) and her younger sister Mary, S. Mary Xaveria (1773–1804) were also amongst the group from Liège.[52] As with so many others amongst the group, both Margaret and Mary had only recently joined the Community prior to the evacuation from Liège. Both had entered in 1791, and were professed in July and November 1793 respectively. Their elder brother Joseph (1766–1843) entered the Society of Jesus under the alias Tristram in 1781, and would have been known to the Community during their time in Liège.[53]

Elizabeth Archdeacon, S. Mary Augustine (1765–1849) was the last surviving of the choir sisters from Liège. She joined the Community in 1790, along with her older sister Barbara, S. Mary Aloysia (1764–1833), and the sisters professed their vows together in Liège on 16 June 1792. Barbara Archdeacon had died some years earlier, on 12 June 1833, aged 69.[54] The Archdeacons entered the Community as

---

[45] See Appendix 2. The Liège Community in 1794.
[46] See p. 15 above.
[47] O/RD/21-2.
[48] O/RC/11.
[49] O/RD/28.
[50] O/RD/29.
[51] Stonyhurst College Archives SCA, Lancashire/Ms A.III.22 'A short account of the chief events that took place before, and during, the migration, of the English College, or Academy, from Liège to Stonyhurst in the year 1794'.
[52] O/RA/28 and RB/15 respectively.
[53] Holt, *Jesuits*, p. 249; Henry Foley, SJ, *Records of the English Province of the Society of Jesus: Historic Facts illustrative of the Labours and Sufferings of its Members in the Sixteenth and Seventeenth Centuries*, 7 vols in 8 (London: Burns and Oates, 1877–80), vol. 7, p. 183. Joseph Tristram is also buried in the cemetery—see p. 68 below.
[54] O/LD/20 and O/RC/29 respectively.

choir sisters, and would have been closely involved with the daily running of convent life. Their tasks included singing the daily Office for morning, afternoon and evening prayer, as well as singing any masses or requiems that were taking place each day. These were essential features of the daily spiritual life of the convent, and would have also required proficiency in Latin.

Mary Brown, S. Mary Agnes (1772–1862) was the last of the Liège Community to die, almost seventy years after they had settled at New Hall. She arrived in Liège on 19 June 1791, and entered the noviciate as a lay sister soon after. Although the process of her entering the Community was almost completed by the time the Community left in 1794, it was much delayed by the migration and she was not fully professed until 29 July 1799, at New Hall. She died on 8 February 1862, aged 90, and was buried in the cemetery.[55] Lay sisters were responsible for the bulk of manual labour within the convent, and had a hard and physically demanding role. The lay sisters could not be council members, and were not able to vote in the chapter.

NEW HALL COMMUNITY

As the Community settled in to their new life in England, new members were professed who had no experience of the Liège period in the Community's history. Although it is not possible to examine these in detail within the parameters of this text, analysis of a key example casts light on the nature of religious life in England in the nineteenth century, and within this Community in particular. Lelia Haly (1788–1873), who attended the school between 1805 and 1809, felt drawn to join the Community, and was professed as S. Mary Joseph in 1813.[56] She remained in the Community until her death in 1873, aged 83 years.[57] She is described with great affection in the records, perhaps most notably as 'one of the pillars of the Community all through her life'.[58] As well as the usual documents relating to her time spent at New Hall, the archive also contains a significant number of letters, sent from her family to Prioress Clough in the years between Haly leaving the school and her profession in 1813.[59] The letters provide an unusually detailed description of the process of joining the Community, in both a pragmatic and an emotional sense.

On 13 December 1811, Mr James Haly (1764–1850), Lelia's father, wrote to the Revd Mother Clough to arrange the practicalities of her admission to the noviciate, and to express his support for her decision to join the Community:

> It is no small consolation to me to be able to inform you that my dear daughter Lelia is enabled thro' the bounty of her late uncle William to proceed [with] her design of becoming a Religious, and that she has made choice of your Community, where she first received these happy impressions, is to me an additional source of joy.[60]

Soon afterwards, on 26 December, Lelia's mother Elizabeth (née Flynn, 1764–1834) sent a similar letter to Clough, expressing her feelings about the situation. In contrast with the letter sent by her husband, Elizabeth's letter is a heartfelt exposure of her true feelings, and gives a clear sense of the emotional impact this decision could have upon the families of Community members:

> This letter, most revered Madam, will be handed you by your late pupil, who under your fostering care has imbibed such principles [and] such a distaste for the world that nothing less than returning to your patronage will satisfy her. May that God, who I confidently hope she will humbly and faithfully serve, enable me to resign her as I ought, [and]

---

[55] O/LB/17.
[56] ACHS/School Register 2, 1807–1837. Volume is not paginated, entries are recorded chronologically.
[57] O/LC/12.
[58] *History of the Community*, p. 192.
[59] ACHS/Haly correspondence (bundle of uncatalogued letters). All subsequent quotes from these papers.
[60] An abridged copy of William Haly's will can be found at ACHS/Personnel files/Lelia Haly, S. Mary Joseph. I am very grateful to Mr Richard Haly for his help with the family history, and willingness to share his many years of painstaking research.

A

Christian Directory,

GUIDING MEN TO THEIR

ETERNAL SALVATION.

IN TWO PARTS.

THE FIRST PART WHEREOF APPERTAINS TO RESOLUTION; THE SECOND TREATS OF THE OBSTACLES AND IMPEDIMENTS WHICH HINDER IT, AND HOW THEY MAY BE REMOVED.

NOW SET FORTH

WITH MANY CORRECTIONS AND ADDITIONS.

TO THIS EDITION ARE PREFIXED

THE LIFE OF THE AUTHOR,

AND A

METHOD FOR THE USE OF ALL,

WITH TWO TABLES.

―――

BY THE REV. ROBERT PARSONS,

PRIEST OF THE SOCIETY OF JESUS.

―――

What doth it profit a Man, if he gain the whole World, and lose his own Soul? Or what shall a Man give in exchange for his Soul?   Mat. xvi. ver. 26.
O ye Sons of Men, &c. why do ye love Vanity?   Psalm iv. ver. 3.
But one thing is necessary.   Luke x. ver. 42.

―――

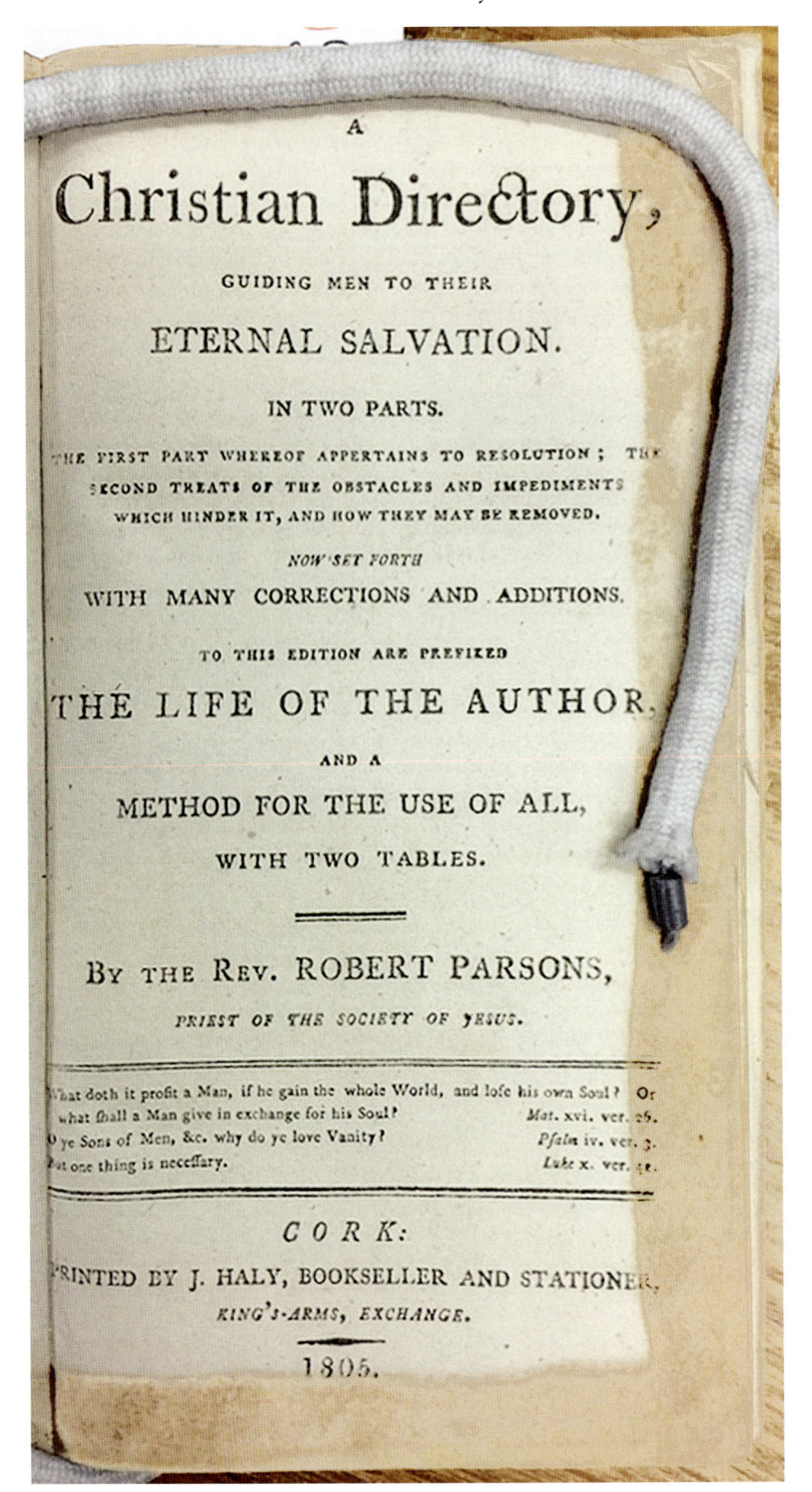

C O R K:

PRINTED BY J. HALY, BOOKSELLER AND STATIONER,
KING'S-ARMS, EXCHANGE.
―――
1805.

A book printed by James Haly (1764–1850), father of Lelia Haly, S. Mary Joseph (1788–1873).
Image courtesy of the Canonesses of the Holy Sepulchre.

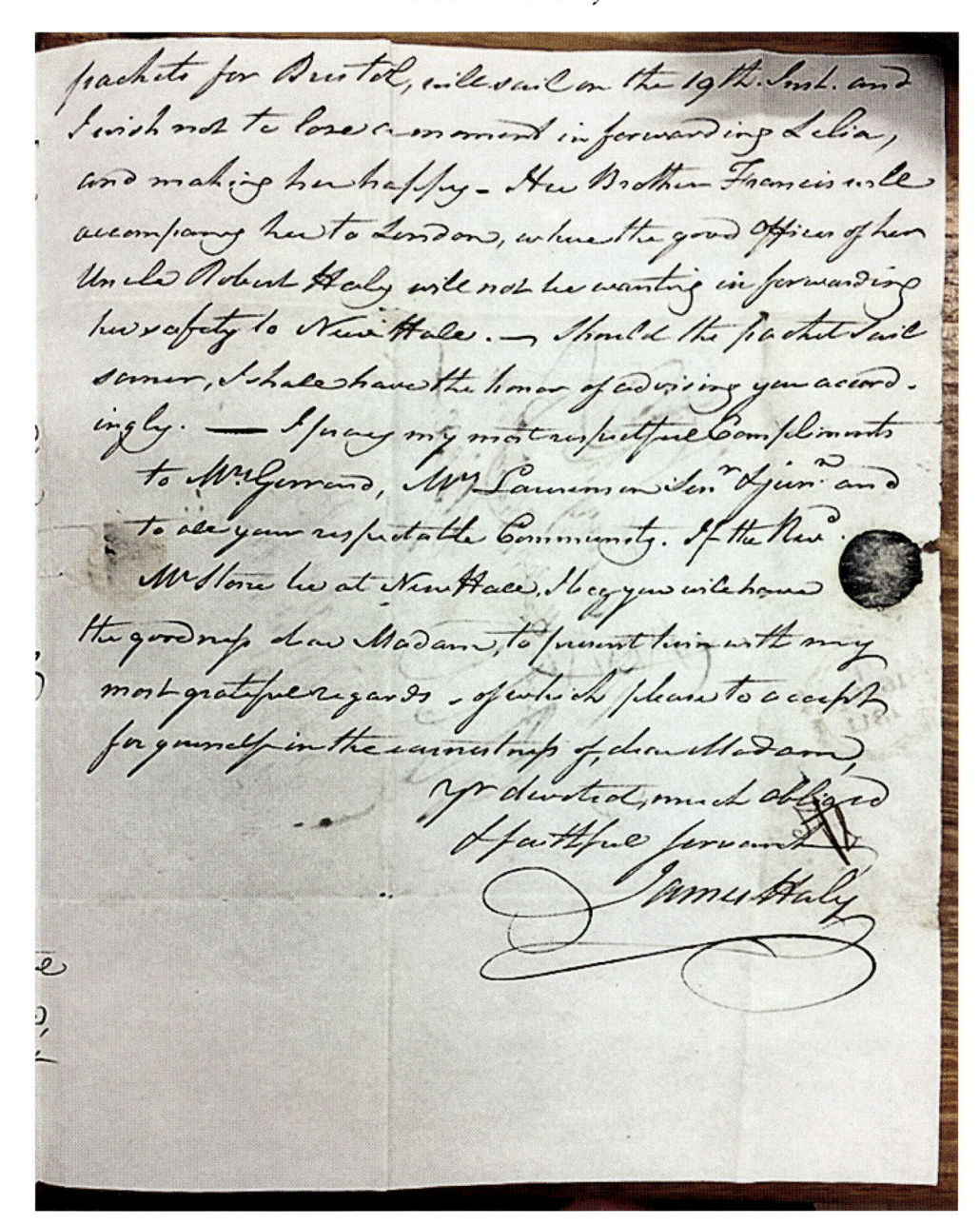

A letter sent by James Haly to Reverend Mother Clough in 1811, regarding his daughter, Lelia, becoming a member of the Community. Image courtesy of the Canonesses of the Holy Sepulchre.

> make the offering of my eldest child at the shrine of the Almighty Being who blessed me with her. Your goodness will, I trust, pardon the incoherency of this scratch & make allowance for my feelings, which in spite of my better judgement, run away with me. May I hope honoured Madam to be sometimes considered in your prayers, from the reflection that none require them more.

Lelia herself notes the role of her parents in enabling her to fulfil her vocation. On 8 January 1812, writing to Clough to confirm her arrival at New Hall a few days later, Haly notes 'I did not expect to join you before late spring—it was a sudden thought suggested by my father and I rejoice in its success'. Later letters include reports from various relatives and friends who visited periodically. A later letter sent by Elizabeth to Lelia on 22 October 1816 even noted 'Mr Dowman is in love with N[ew]. H[all]. Rev[eren]d Mother has made a conquest of him!'

Community members in procession out of the cemetery.
Image courtesy of the Canonesses of the Holy Sepulchre.

Burials: Clergy

There are fourteen members of the clergy buried in the cemetery, most of whom are Jesuits. As with previous groups, a deeper exploration of a representative sample of these men and their links with the Community has much to reveal about the Community themselves, and their role within the wider history of the English Catholic community.

The link between the Canonesses and the Society of Jesus was of profound importance to the development of the Community. Susan Hawley had deliberately located her Community of English Canonesses in Liège so as to allow regular contact with the English College of Jesuits in the same city, and this close working relationship was a continuous part of Community life from 1642 for nearly three hundred years, until the late nineteenth century.

The English Jesuit College in Liège was the largest of four English Jesuit institutions on the continent. These four institutions worked together to prepare future Jesuits for work as missioners to England and Wales. Candidates would typically enter the noviciate at Watten in northern France, spend three years studying philosophy at Liège, followed by some teaching experience at St Omer College, located a few miles away from Watten. A further four years at Liège studying theology was usually followed by ordination and an intensive final year of spiritual preparation at Ghent, before being sent on whichever missionary endeavour that best suited their talents.[61] The English Colleges continued in this fashion until the international suppression of the Society of Jesus in 1773, and the colleges at Watten, St Omer

---

[61] Geoffrey Holt, SJ, *English Jesuits in the Age of Reason* (London: Burns & Oates, 1993), pp. 6–7.

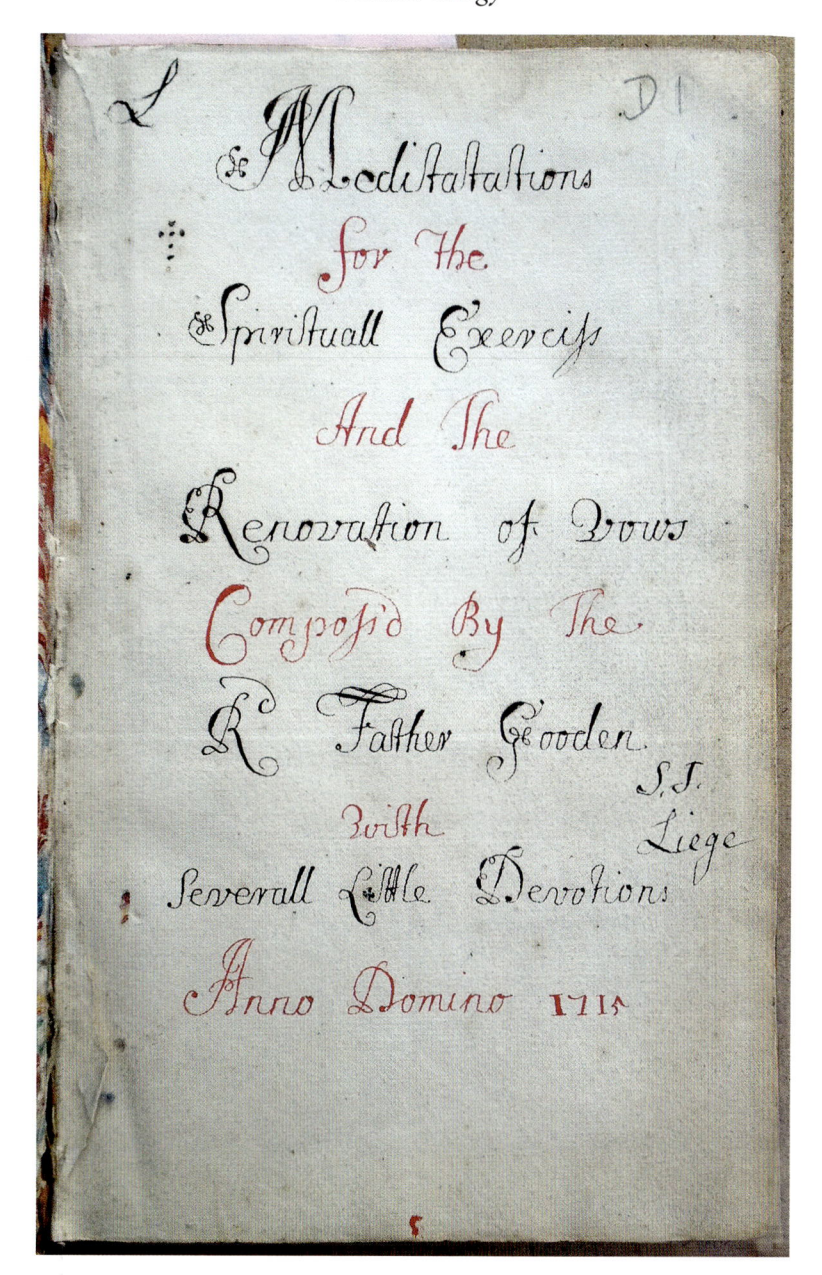

Meditations for the Spiritual Exercises and Renovation of Vows, composed for the Community by Fr James Gooden in 1715. Image courtesy of the Canonesses of the Holy Sepulchre.

and Ghent were closed with immediate effect. The Community's relationship with the English Jesuit College in Liège was so important to the spiritual life of the convent that Prioress Christina Dennett wrote an impassioned plea to the Prince Bishop in 1773, a request for continued access to the 'spiritual and temporal succour' given by the Jesuits, that also illuminates the close relationship between to the two communities:

> My Lord
> The [Community] … having heard of the melancholy situation of the Fathers of the Society of Jesus are in the greatest affliction. We humbly address ourselves to your Highness imploring your paternal protection begging you will permit them to continue to hear our Confessions with the privilege granted us by your Highness & Predecessors. We have always received the Sacraments from the hands of these Fathers without regard to the title of Ordinary or Extraordinary. We settled in this town from no other motive than to be under their direction: It is on this account our House has been constantly furnished with Members. The English Families who send us their children for education do it on no other account but to place them under their direction. Our Peace of Union depend

on their being continued: forty-one of our Religious confess constantly to Fr Howard, as also our Pensioners. It would be hard my Lord to refuse this liberty so necessary for the our spiritual & temporal succour, since it is by these Fathers our House subsists & is conserved. We earnestly entreat your Highness to confirm the above mentioned privileges since our only Confidence is in those Fathers. We more securely confide in your Highnesses granting our request having so often heard the Rector of the English College speak of your goodness.[62]

Unlike the other three English Jesuit institutions, the Liège college was found to be so popular within the locality that it was allowed to stay open, under the authority of the Prince Bishop, and 'rebranded' as the *Academie Anglaise*, as long as the men wore the secular dress of the Liegoise diocesan clergy.[63]

This close working relationship is also visible in the decision of both communities to leave Liège and return to England in 1794. Initially the English Jesuits were sceptical of the need to flee Liège at all, despite being given the same warnings and advice as the Sepulchrines. By July 1794, by when it had become apparent that evacuation was necessary, the Jesuits were able to benefit from the careful plans put in place by the Sepulchrines several months earlier. The Jesuits followed the same route, and also used the house in Maastricht that had been leased by the Sepulchrine Community for six months in January 1794, and which was still available under the terms of that lease, as a safe place to stop and make further arrangements.

GERVAIS GENIN (d. 1800) AND FRANCIS CLIFTON (1742–1812)

Two ex-Jesuits travelled with the Community from Liège, Gervais Genin (d. 1800) and Francis Clifton (1742–1812).[64] Only Genin is buried in the cemetery at New Hall, having died suddenly whilst preparing to say Mass at New Hall in March 1800. He was a French Jesuit who had travelled with the Community in order to escape to the safety of England, and served as the Community's chaplain during the journey in recompense. Clifton referred to Genin in a letter to a friend, sent only a few weeks before Genin's death, in which he noted that, during their travels from Liège, the Community had been 'accompanied by a French clergyman who has resided here during two years and intends to return to France'.[65] Genin died on 19 March 1800, and was buried in the cemetery soon afterwards. His headstone includes the initials 'S.J.' after his name.[66] Although this is the standard abbreviation for members of the Society of Jesus, at the time of Genin's death in 1800, the Society was still prohibited worldwide. It would not be restored in England until 1803, and 1814 internationally.[67] Therefore the use of these initials at this time, and in a public setting such as a cemetery, is extremely unusual. Other contemporary Jesuit burials, such as that of Thomas Ellerker (1738–95), who died in May 1795 and is buried at Stonyhurst College in Lancashire, simply give the name and dates of the deceased, with no indication of religious profession whatsoever.[68]

Francis Clifton, *alias* Dominic Fanning, was particularly important to the Community, and was closely involved in assisting them with their migration from Liège. Prior to that, he had served as their spiritual director and confessor since his ordination in 1773, and was instrumental in arranging many of the practicalities of the migration on behalf of the Community. He stayed with them throughout their search for a permanent home, serving as chaplain and spiritual director. He also

---

[62] ACHS/K/Letter, sent to Prince-Bishop of Liège, September 1773.
[63] Whitehead, *English Jesuit Education*, pp. 111–16.
[64] The term 'ex-Jesuits' is used to describe those who had been members of the Society at the time of the suppression, 1773–1814.
[65] ACHS/Riley-Clifton correspondence/F. Clifton to J. Riley Esq, 18 June 1800.
[66] O/RB/22. see also Tuckwell, *New Hall and its School*, pp. 89 and 96; and *History of the Community*, p. 162.
[67] For a general history of the Jesuits in England in this period, see Hannah Thomas, 'Historiography of the Jesuits in England in the Early Modern Period', *Jesuit Historiography Online*, online edition.
[68] Headstone in Stonyhurst College cemetery, Lancashire; see also SCA/Ms C.II.20 Burial Register 1795–1842; and Holt, *Jesuits*, p. 86.

Above. Headstone of Fr Gervais Genin, a French Jesuit who had travelled with the Community from Liège. He was the first clergyman to be buried in the cemetery. The headstone is inscribed 'The Revd Gervais Genin SJ, deceased 19 March 1800, R.I.P.'

Right. Headstone of Thomas Ellerker, the first English Jesuit to be buried at Stonyhurst College, Lancashire. (Photographs: Hannah Thomas)

assisted with the examination of faith for new novices, and wrote a large number of meditations, prayers and spiritual exercises for use by the Community. Clifton died whilst away on business in London, and was buried at St Pancras church in London, the same church where S. Mary Teresa Dennett had been buried in 1794. Although now removed from the churchyard itself, a sketch of his headstone was made in the late nineteenth century. His will, proved on 6 June 1812, bequeaths 'all his books to the college of Stonyhurst'.[69]

PETER O'BRIEN (1735–1807) AND STEPHEN CHAPON (1751–1826)

Peter O'Brien (1735–1807), was hired by the Community to be their chaplain soon after the death of Genin in 1800. He was probably already known to the Community before this date, having studied theology at the Liège Academy for three years prior to his ordination in 1759. O'Brien was a well-travelled man, and undertook missionary work in Ghent, Liverpool, London and Bristol, as well as three separate missions in Antigua, before moving to New Hall in 1800. He died at New Hall on 28 February 1807, and was laid to rest in the cemetery by his successor, Stephen Chapon, a few days later.[70]

---

[69] TNA/PROB/11/1534, Will of the Revd Francis Clifton, otherwise Fanning, 22 May 1812 (proved 6 June 1812). See also Holt, *Jesuits*, p. 91. It is not clear if Fanning was his true name or an alias. For headstone, see Frederick Teague Cansick, *A Collection of Curious and Interesting Epitaphs: Copied from the Monuments of Distinguished and Noted Characters in the Ancient Church and Burial Grounds of Saint Pancras, Middlesex* (London: J Russell Smith, 1869), p. 130.

[70] O/RC/20; see also Holt, *Jesuits*, pp. 181–2.

Above left. The Revd Fr Edward Heery, later Canon (1843–1928).   *Above right.* Fr James Brownbill (1798–1880).   *Below.* Fr Reuben Butler (1892–1959) and Fr James Nicholson (1855–1934). Images courtesy of the Canonesses of the Holy Sepulchre.

O'Brien's successor, Stephen Chapon (1751–1826), a member of the French secular clergy, was also given refuge by the Community. He arrived at New Hall in 1803 after a brief imprisonment and a narrow escape from the guillotine in France in 1792. His services had been deliberately sought by the Revd Mother Clough after the death of Genin, and the declining health of Clifton and O'Brien, in order to give the 'very numerous' High Masses.[71] He served the Community until his death in June 1826. Unlike many of the others, his headstone is quite detailed, recording that he had been born in Normandy and had been driven from his native country by the persecution of the French Revolution in 1792. It also hints at the dangers he had faced France, noting that 'after having braved danger by land, and the peril of the ocean, was kindly received in this hospitable country, where till the close of life he was protected, supported and cherished'.[72] The notebooks of the then-Chantress, which functioned as a Community diary during this period, record an extraordinarily detailed account of his funeral, both the practical and the ritual elements:

> June 27th 1826. Revd Stephen Chapon died about 11 o'clock at night. Friday 30th we did … the Vespers of the dead in choir: Rev[eren]d McDonnell came that evening from Witham. … Mr McDonnell sung Mass & performed the whole of Mr Chapon's funeral service. Mr C[hapon] was brought to the church during the hours, the corpse was met by the priest outside the chapel door, where the usual ceremony was performed. The corpse was then brought into the chapel & the vestments [etc] laid on it with six yellow candles. three on each side, which were left burning untill [half] past 8. After High Mass, while the choir sang the Miserere, the priest fumed & sprinkled the coffin, Mr R[eeve] carried the cross, Joseph & George who both served the High Mass assisted. At [half] past 8, after night prayers, the corpse was taken to the grave in the following order: George carried the cross (because it was too heavy for Mr Reeve) at the head of the procession, then followed 20 of the pensioners in their hoods, next the nuns (for all had leave but none was obliged to go) in their great cloaks, next the priest in a cope, Mr Reeve on one side & Joseph on the other, then Joseph Emery carried a lantern with three candles in it which were to represent the three virtues, faith, hope and charity.[73]

HERMAN KEMPER (1745–1811)

Herman Kemper (1745–1811), a German Jesuit who served the English province, was also brought to New Hall to alleviate the losses of Genin, Clifton and O'Brien. He arrived in 1808, having undertaken missionary work at Wigan since 1799, and remained at New Hall until his death in April 1811. Kemper had been known to the Community since their time in Liège, where he had undertaken much of his noviciate and, following his ordination in 1774, had spent a successive period of nearly twenty years ministering to the Community there, until the evacuations in 1794.[74] He had also played an important role at an earlier point in the Community's history, urging Elizabeth Smith, S. Mary Joseph (1748–1811), to write her manuscript life of Christina Dennett in 1792, about eleven years after Dennett's death. Smith's manuscript account, although hagiographic in tone, is now one of the only surviving sources for Dennett's work, as Dennett destroyed many of her own writings.[75] Kemper's instruction may have also inadvertently inspired Smith to continue in her role as chronicler, in which capacity she compiled the Community's first manuscript account of their experiences of the revolution in Liège, and the subsequent journey to England.[76]

[71] *History of the Community*, p.162–3.
[72] O/RD/23.
[73] ACHS/TB 165/106/Chantress book 2, 1816–26, pp. 26–7. The Chantress was in charge of the music and choir arrangements for each Mass, and had to ensure that the correct liturgical pieces were sung at the right times and for the right services each day.
[74] O/RD/17; see also Holt, *Jesuits*, p. 136; and *History of the Community*, p. 164.
[75] See pp. 6 and 17 above. See also *History of the Community*, p. 66.
[76] Smith, 'A Short Account'. Elizabeth Smith and her sister Mary, S. Mary Berchmans (1751–1827), were amongst those who migrated from Liège. Both are buried in the cemetery O/RD/15 and RC/26 respectively.

Kemper's death was much felt by everyone. As well as providing spiritual direction and guidance for the Community, he also made a deep impact on those who provided domestic services for the Community and on the wider local population. A manuscript in the Community archives notes that

> Revd Fr Herman Kemper was esteemed as a most holy learned man with a rare talent for direction. He was zealous & loved by all around in the neighbourhood. When he was dying the men entreated to be allowed to see him. Among the number a man in whom Fr Kemper had taken great interest but who had long been a source of great anxiety to him. Henry was under instruction he was a good fellow but there was an inseparable obstacle—he used to come to mass & go to the Protestant Church in the afternoon. The men were kneeling round his bed & the venerable Father fixed his eyes on Henry lifting up his hand he said emphatically 'Ah Henry! You have been master here but as soon as I get to Heaven I will be your Master.' No sooner had the holy man expired than Henry's heart & feelings were entirely changed, he exclaimed 'Never again will I enter a Protestant church!' He kept his word—he became a good practical fervent Catholic.[77]

The 'Henry' mentioned here is identified later on in the manuscript as Henry Lacey (1761–1841), who served the Community for many years as domestic servant and gardener. His conversion to Catholicism was sufficient to allow him burial in the cemetery after his own death in September 1841.[78] Other documents demonstrate the impact of Kemper's death within the wider English Catholic community, a necessarily small and tight-knit group in these pre-Emancipation years. A letter sent to Dorothy Gandolfi, S. Mary Clare (1775–1834), by her father, John Vincent Gandolfi (d. 1815), in 1811, comments 'I received from you the melancholy newse of the exit from this world of my most reverend & worthy friend Mr Kemper with the deepest regret and concern[.] I have, with your Community, in the fullest manner, sustained [this] great loss, [as] have all who knew his greatness.'[79]

Kemper had also been known to the Clifford family, and wrote the epitaph of his close friend Henry Edward Clifford, fifth baron Clifford of Chudleigh (1756–93), at the request of Henry's wife, Apollonia Langdale (1755–1815).[80] Henry was the eldest brother of both Charlotte Clifford, S. Ann Teresa, and Lord Charles Clifford, subsequently sixth baron Clifford of Chudleigh.[81] Through his marriage, he was also related to Catherine Stourton, S. Mary Agatha, and Charlotte Stourton, S. Mary Anne, further illustrating the close family networks within the English Catholic community in this period.[82]

LIÈGE CONNECTIONS CONTINUED

Kemper was replaced with two Jesuits, both of whom served the spiritual needs of the Community and the growing school for over a decade. Thomas Reeve (1752–1826), arrived at New Hall in April 1812, and Charles Forrester (1739–1825), arrived shortly afterwards by November 1813. Reeve had also been known to the Community since their time in Liège, where he had undertaken missionary work for approximately twenty years, from 1773 until the evacuations in 1794. Similarly to Clifton, he died suddenly whilst in London on business, and was also buried at St Pancras church in London, although

---

[77] ACHS/D4 'Mss notes on the traditions of our Community, given to me by Reverend Mother' (December 1889).
[78] O/LA/5.
[79] ACHS/Gandolfi correspondence/John Gandolfi to Dorothy Gandolfi, 11 April 1811. Both Dorothy and her sister Mary, S. Mechtilda Aloysia (1773–1850), attended school at New Hall and later joined the Community. They are buried in the cemetery O/R1/9 and L2/16 respectively, along with several of their relatives. See p. 74 below.
[80] Hugh Clifford, *The House of Clifford from Before the Conquest* (Chichester: Phillimore & Co. Ltd, 1987), pp. 165–6; see also Langdale family tree, *WWTN*. Henry Clifford was buried at the Jesuit church in Munich, having died suddenly whilst visiting the city with his wife as part of their Grand Tour.
[81] See pp. 26, 50 and 52 above.
[82] Charles Stourton, who married Apollonia's sister Mary Landgale, was the brother of Charlotte and Catherine Stourton. See Stourton family tree, *WWTN*, and pp. 26–7 above.

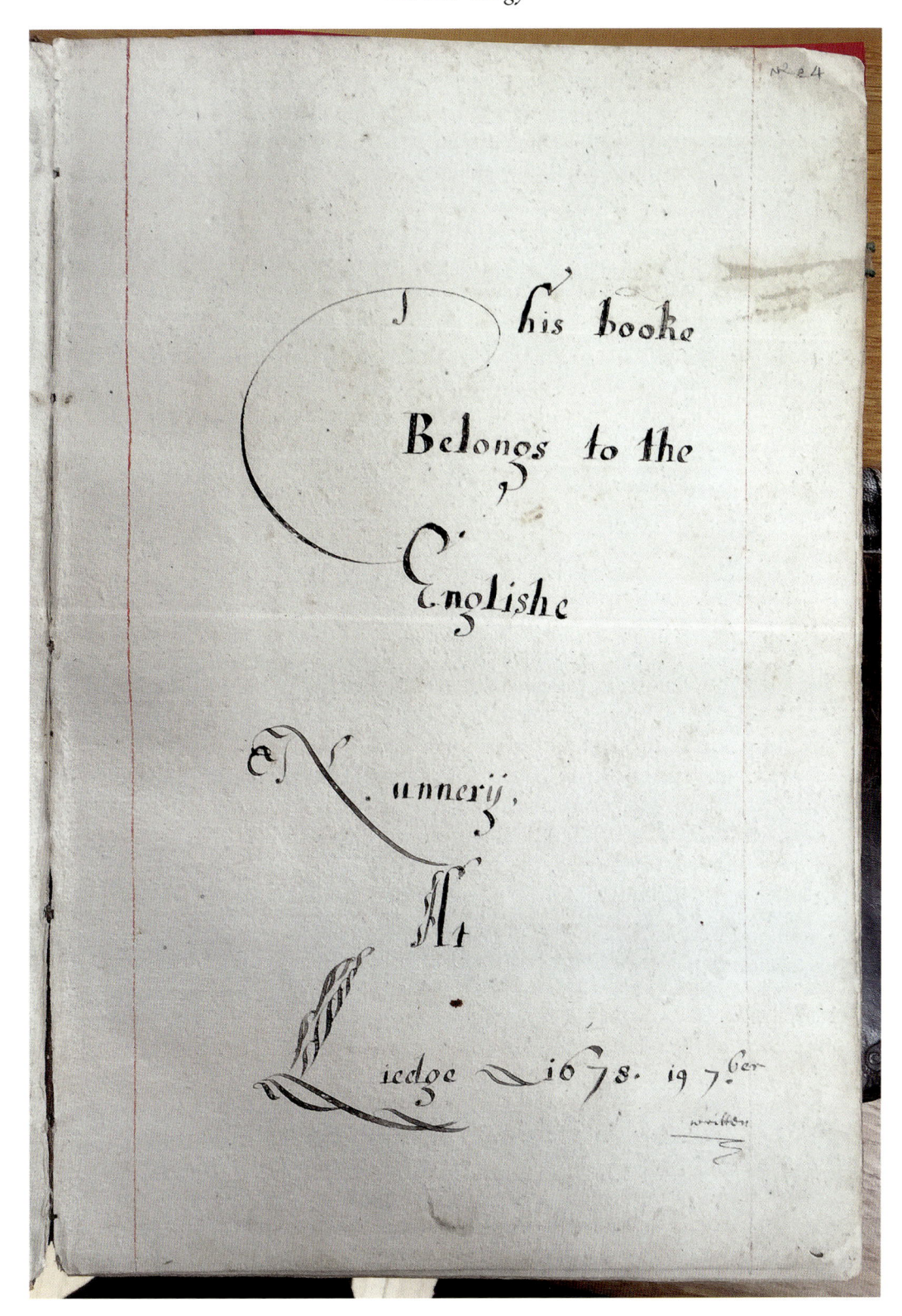

Title page of a service book used by the Community during Mass at Liège.
Image courtesy of the Canonesses of the Holy Sepulchre.

his headstone was not recorded and is no longer visible within the churchyard.[83] Reeve's work at New Hall focused on the chaplaincy of the school, partly due to Forrester's age and infirmity.[84]

[83] Holt, *Jesuits*, p. 208.
[84] See *History of the Community*, pp. 164–5.

Charles Forrester, *vere* Fleury, was a French Jesuit who had entered the Society in France, but had joined the English province soon after the Jesuits had been expelled from France in 1764. He had arrived in England by 1767, and quite likely changed his name at this time to the more English-sounding Forrester, so as to avoid attracting attention. He served the Community as spiritual director and confessor until his death in May 1825, despite severe illness that greatly limited his physical mobility for several years.[85]

Several of the confessors and chaplains at New Hall were known, both to the Community and to each other, through a shared time in Liège, particularly those ex-Jesuits who were trained between 1773 and 1794 at the *Academie Anglaise*. Thomas Angier (1754–1837), and Joseph Tristram, for example, had both spent approximately twenty years in Liège, at the same time as Clifton, Kemper and Reeve, before travelling to England, and working for the Community at New Hall in 1826 and 1837 respectively.[86] It seems that both the Jesuits and the Sepulchrines were able to continue to benefit from their close working relationship, even in the face of the tremendous upheaval, displacement and migration that had brought both groups to England in 1794.

Burials: Lay People

Further to the burials of Community members and clergy, the cemetery is also the final resting place of a significant number of lay people, all of whom have specific connections to the Community.[87] When taken together, an examination of their relationships with the Community adds a further dimension to a better understanding of the history of the Community itself. Equally, analysis of the various means of memorial can reveal different approaches to the funeral as a manifestation of that person's relationship with the Community, where sufficient evidence survives. The lay people in the original half of the cemetery can be loosely divided into three main groups—firstly, school pupils; secondly, family members of the Community; and thirdly, servants and staff members.

SCHOOL PUPILS

Deceased school pupils account for the biggest group amongst the lay people in the original half of the cemetery, twenty of the thirty-six burials. As well as pupils who died during their time at the school, a number of ex-pupils returned to New Hall to be buried in the cemetery, a phenomenon that is quite unusual amongst other similar communities.

In 1805, two young pupils died whilst they were at the school. Firstly, Catherine Nangle (1790–1805), who had joined the school only a year earlier in 1804 with her sister Mary. Catherine died on 30 May 1805, aged 15.[88] Secondly the Rt Hon Miss Anna Maria Clifford (1787–1805), who had joined the school with her sisters Eliza, Charlotte and Christina in August 1797, during their time at Dean House. She and her sisters moved with the Community to New Hall in 1799. Anna died on 14 July 1805, aged 17.[89] Another two pupils died a few years later, in 1813. Catherine Ryan (1796–1813), who died on 13 September, aged 17, and Elizabeth Standish (1798–1813), who died on 19 September, aged 15.[90] Ryan had

---

[85] O/RD/19.
[86] O/RD/30 and O/LE/22 respectively. Tristram was the brother of S. Frances Borgia and S. Mary Xaveria—see p. 56 above.
[87] See Appendix 3. Lay People in the Original Cemetery.
[88] O/RB/11.
[89] O/RB/13. Anna Maria Clifford was the daughter of Charles Clifford, sixth baronet, and therefore the niece of Charlotte Clifford, S. Ann Theresa.
[90] O/RC/9 and RD/9 respectively.

arrived at the school a few years earlier in April 1810, travelling from Copenhagen with her sisters Ellen and Harriett. Standish arrived at a similar time, starting school at New Hall in May 1811.[91]

Members of the Community were deeply saddened by these deaths. S. Aloysia Austin wrote to an ex-pupil, Mary Lucy Weld (1799–1931), in September 1813. Weld had been a classmate of both Ryan and Standish, having arrived at the school in May 1812, where she remained until July 1813:

> I knew, my dear Mary Lucy, you would be much hurt when you heard of poor Ryan's death. I was myself, more so than I should have thought. I pray for her everyday—her Death was very unlike poor little Standish who had all the sacraments & was sensible & very pious to the last moment, whereas the other dear girl never showed the least sense from the time she was taken out of the school. I would certainly keep something belonging to her if I could but every thing is collected & sent to her friends.[92]

Only two years later in 1815, another two pupils died within a few weeks of each other. Sarah Jordan (1799–1815) died on 3 February, aged 16, followed by Anna Maria Lynch (1801–15), who died on 1 April, aged 14. Both Sarah and Anna had travelled overseas to attend school at New Hall. Sarah had travelled from Santa Cruz in the West Indies only six months earlier, arriving at the school in July 1814. A few months later, Anna arrived from Galway in Ireland, joining the school in October of the same year.[93] No causes of death are known for any of these young ladies, and the archive has no further information on these tragedies, but it is likely that the Community were devastated by these losses. The school throughout this early period consisted of no more than fifty pupils, all of whom would have been well known to most members of the Community.

The cemetery also reveals the stories of several deaths as a result of medical conditions and diseases, treatments of which have changed beyond recognition in modern times. In the autumn of 1893, the Community suffered a devastating outbreak of diphtheria, in which three young ladies died within a couple of days of each other: Mary Josephine Kendal, aged 17; her younger sister Ursula Mary Kendal, aged 14; and Antonia Mary Britten, aged 14.[94] Two more were dangerously ill, but recovered, including Antonia's sister, Helen. Two of the maids who served the Community were also ill, but recovered. The Chantress notebooks provide further detail to the names and dates recorded in the cemetery, giving a sense of the rapid development of a contagious disease within such a small community:

> **13th [October 1893]. Friday**. F[athe]r Heery anointed & gave H[oly] Viaticum to little Ursula Kendal & Antonia Britten who were suffering fr[om] diphtheria a relapse after scarletina they are up in the High Nursery. Ursula Kendal died on Saturday morning the bell was not tolled in order that Mary K[endal] her sister should not know it. Mary K is also very ill. The remaining children have dispersed today. Antonia Britten died at 10 0 clock Sat: evening—F[ather] H[eery] with her to the end.

> **15th. Sun. Purity BVM**. Father Heery anointed & gave communion to Mary Kendal… Two maids are now ill, also with diphtheria [*added later:*] not bad now. K Hague is not as ill as MK. A trained nurse for diphtheria came on Friday night.

> **16th. Mon**. Dirge for M M Antonia Britten & Ursula Kendal. Rang to Dead Office 7 minutes to 8. Low Requiem Mass. The funerall put off from 1[.30 pm] to 3.[30 pm] on account of the rain. We wore cloaks at the Office. The sisters served.

> **20th. Friday**. Mary Kendal died at 7 this morning. We had only one Mass at 6[.30pm] as Father Heery was obliged to take some rest.

> **21st. Sat**. Dirge for Mary Kendal. Low Requiem Mass 8[.30pm] after the Dead Office. We wore cloaks. The funeral was at 3[.30pm]. We went.

[91] ACHS/School Register 2, 1807–1837. Volume is not paginated, entries are recorded chronologically.
[92] ACHS/Weld correspondence/Letter from S. Aloysia Austin Clifford to Mary Lucy Weld, 18 October 1813. Weld married Hugh Charles Clifford, seventh baron (1790–1858), younger brother of Anna Maria Clifford (1787–1805).
[93] O/LE/29 and 27 respectively. See ACHS/School Register 2, 1807–37. The volume is not paginated, entries are recorded chronologically.
[94] O/LB/35; O/LA/34; O/LA/35 respectively.

Agnes Kendal, later S. Mary Margaret (1880–1935), and her elder sister Ursula (1879–93).
Ursula and another sister, Mary Josephine, died during a diphtheria outbreak at the school in 1893.
Image courtesy of the Canonesses of the Holy Sepulchre.

29th. Sun. Susan Wye has been taken to the school ill with diphtheria.

10th [November 1893]. Friday. Susan Wye received the Last Sacraments late in the evening. After evening prayers some time.[95]

Mary and Ursula Kendal were two of four sisters who joined the school: Mildred, who arrived in September 1879; Mary, in September 1885; and Agnes and Ursula, who arrived at the school in May 1889. The other two sisters became members of the Community after finishing school: Mildred, also known as Etheldreda (1865–1940), professed her vows as S. Mary Phillip in 1887; and several years later, her youngest sister Agnes returned to New Hall and professed her vows as S. Mary Margaret (1880–1935) in 1913.[96] Similarly, Antonia Britten had joined the school with her siblings only a few months before the outbreak. Antonia and Helen arrived at New Hall in November 1892, joined a few months later by their younger sister Blanche in April 1893.[97]

The notebooks also give some idea of the impact this type of tragedy could have, both practically and emotionally. In a practical sense, the losses had an impact on the spiritual lives of the Community, reducing the number of opportunities available for communal prayer, as a result of an exhausted chaplain. In an emotional sense, in less than a month, the Community had to deal with three deaths, two serious illnesses, two funerals and a school full of grieving children, not to mention their own grief at these losses.

[95] ACHS/ TB 165/112/ Chantress Book 9, 1886–1904, not paginated.
[96] ACHS/School Register 4, 1872–1947, pp. 67 and 133. S. Mary Phillip and S. Mary Margaret are buried in the cemetery, O/RC/27 and O/LA/6 respectively.
[97] ACHS/School Register 4, 1872–1947, pp. 148 and 153.

Antonia Britten (1879–93) and her younger sister Lily. Antonia died during a diphtheria outbreak at the school in 1893; her headstone is shown below. Images courtesy of the Canonesses of the Holy Sepulchre.

Nora Riddell and her sister, Mary Josephine (1879–95), who attended New Hall in the 1880s,
following their elder sister Laura. Mary died of peritonitis at the school in 1895, after a long illness.
Image courtesy of the Canonesses of the Holy Sepulchre.

So soon after these losses, another two pupils died as a result of medical conditions. In March 1895, Mary Josephine Riddell (1879–95) died, aged 16. She had joined the school only a year earlier, along with her younger sister Nora, following their elder sister Laura, who was at the school from 1884 to 1887. The school records show that both Mary and Nora were quite sickly: having survived measles, whooping cough, scarletina and diphtheria, Mary died of peritonitis after a long and painful decline.[98] A few years later, in November 1898, another pupil, Agnes Russell (1885–98), died of appendicitis, aged 14. Her school record provides some detail about the medical procedures employed in her treatment:

> [Agnes] fell ill about 11 November [18]98, underwent a most serious operation on the
> night of the 14th, a London specialist and two Chelmsford doctors leaving this at 1am
> on the 15th. She died on the 22nd at 9.55pm, her mother and Fr Heery by her bedside.
> A most holy death full of faith and resignation. Illness: grave internal inflammation.[99]

Some information is given for both funerals. The Chantress books record the arrival of Mrs Riddell the day after Mary's death, concluding that 'The child to be buried here'. A brief description is provided of the funeral Mass, which was attended by Riddell's parents and two brothers:

> A few children & nuns went & the parents walked last. A beautiful cross of flowers was
> on the white coffin & the bier was covered with the white pall used at M Fitzpatrick
> funeral. A fine day.[100]

---

[98] O/LB/34; see ACHS/School Register 4, 1872–1947, p. 98.
[99] ACHS/School Register 4, 1872–1947, p. 163.
[100] ACHS/TB 165/112/ Chantress Book 9, 1886–1904, not paginated.

Agnes Russell (1885–98) on her Communion day. She died of appendicitis at the school in 1898; her headstone is shown above. Image courtesy of the Canonesses of the Holy Sepulchre.

In contrast, Russell's memorial is described in the barest of terms: 'Low Requiem. Cloaks. Funeral 1[.30pm]. Nuns & children did not go to it, weather being bad. The child's parents followed the corpse.'[101]

Despite these experiences of illness, loss and grief, records of the lay people in the cemetery also bear witness to the strong feeling of family felt by those who attended the school. This is perhaps particularly visible in the number of elderly ex-pupils who have been laid to rest in the cemetery. Some have family members amongst the Community; others had stayed on at the school as fee-paying boarders, and chose to be buried in the Community cemetery.[102] Some left posthumous requests for their mortal remains to be returned to the school for burial, an indication of the depth of love and affection felt for their time with the Community.

Louisa Fermor (1778–1820) had been with the Community since joining the school in Liège in 1792, aged 14. She was one of the small number of pupils who had travelled with the Community in 1794, and remained at New Hall until her death in June 1820, aged 42.[103] Her will, dated shortly before her death, left a sizeable bequest of £5,500 to the Community, the annual interest of which was 'to be paid unto my servant Elizabeth Pratt'. No information about her funeral has survived, but in thanks for her generous donation, the Community offered several annual masses for both Louisa and her family.[104]

---

[101] ACHS/TB 165/112/ Chantress Book 9, 1886–1904, not paginated.
[102] A boarder was usually an elderly spinster who paid for bed and board within the convent.
[103] O/RA/26.
[104] TNA PROB 11/1632: Will of Louisa Fermor, 3 June 1820 (proved 6 July 1820); see also ACHS/Benefactors Book, 1820. £5,500 in 1820 had the spending equivalent of £250,000 in today's money. Her servant Elizabeth Pratt is also buried in the cemetery, see p. 77 below.

Louisa's sister Henrietta (1771–1806) had also been at the Community's school in Liège since 1788, and was professed as S. Teresa Joseph soon afterwards in November 1792.[105]

Headstone of Louisa Gandolfi (1785–1866). Image courtesy of the Canonesses of the Holy Sepulchre.

Several members of the Gandolfi family are buried in the cemetery. Louisa Gandolfi (1785–1866) and her sister Anna (1783–1842) had joined the school whilst they were at Dean House in 1797, and were joined by another unnamed sister in May 1799, at New Hall. Their elder sisters Mary (1773–1850) and Dorothy (1775–1834), had professed their vows and joined the Community as S. Mary Mechtilda and S. Mary Clare in 1799 and 1800 respectively.[106] It is likely this was a factor in Louisa's return to New Hall as a boarder by 1841. She is described on both the 1851 and 1861 census returns as 'infirm', and died at New Hall in June 1866, aged 81.[107] Her sister Anna also returned to New Hall at the same time, but died a few months later in July 1842.[108]

Some lay people buried in the cemetery were not always well known to the whole Community, but instead, families were given the comfort of laying their loved ones to rest in the special atmosphere of the Community cemetery. For example, in May 1859, Bernard Hammond died suddenly while visiting his aunts at New Hall, following an epileptic seizure. At the request of his parents, and with the permission of the Prioress, he was buried in the cemetery on 7 May 1859. No physical memorial or headstone survives, but the circumstances of his death have been preserved in the Community archive.[109]

---

[105] O/RC/18.
[106] O/LD/19 and O/RD/26.
[107] O/LD/4.
[108] O/LE/24.
[109] For example, a detailed account of his death was recorded in the burial register by the Revd Brownbill, the priest who conducted the service: see ACHS/J1.11/Burial Register 1803–1979, p. 83.

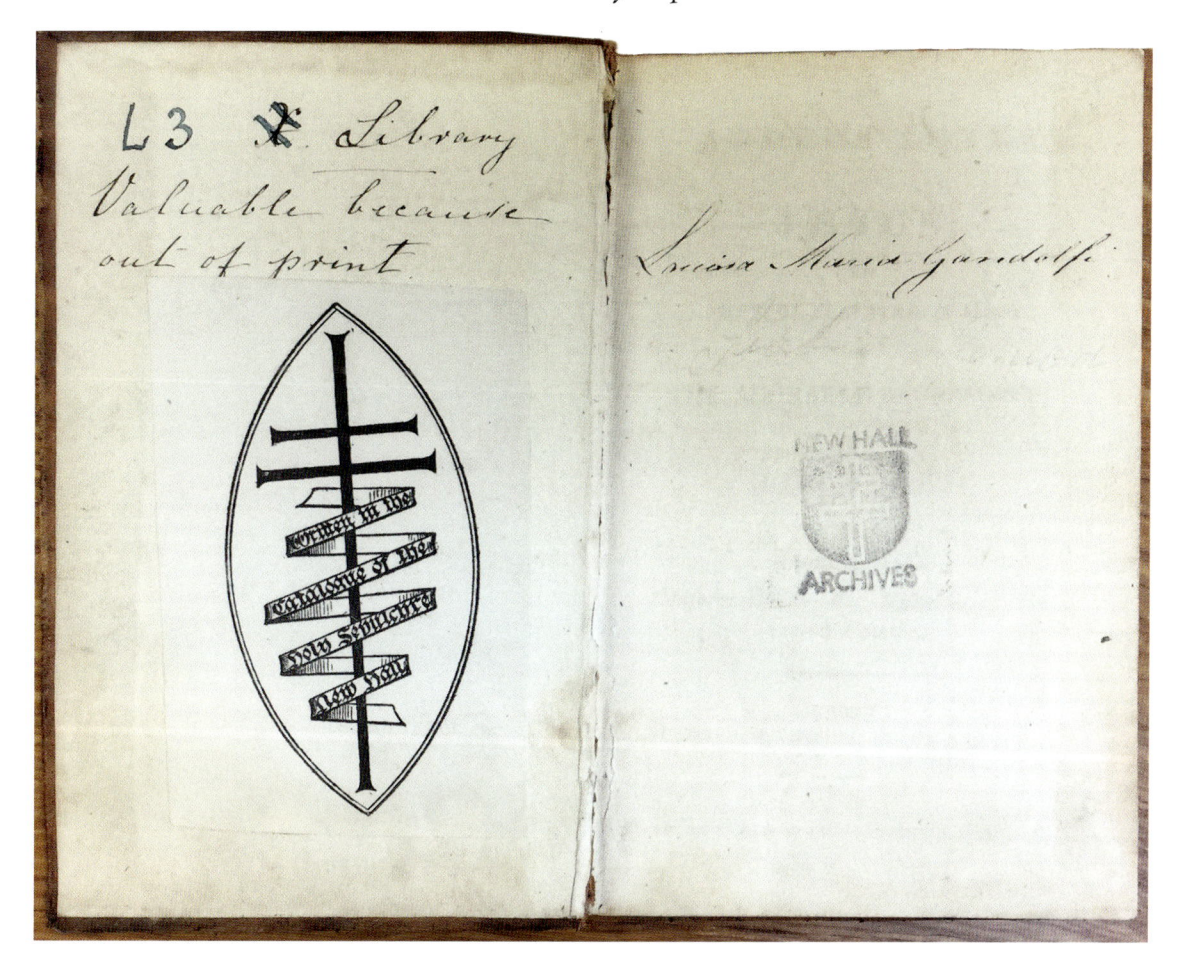

An 1819 edition of The Ardent Lover of Jesus ... with a devout method of hearing Mass, *owned by Louisa Maria Gandolfi (1785–1866). Image courtesy of the Canonesses of the Holy Sepulchre.*

Others made arrangements for burial in the cemetery as a result of previous associations with the Community, confirming the strong feeling of family and togetherness fostered at the school. On 7 April 1899, Mrs Minnie Plowden was laid to rest in the cemetery, having died in Edinburgh, in Scotland, a few days earlier. The headstone does not provide much information on these intriguing circumstances, simply noting that Minnie Plowden, wife of Roger Plowden of Strachur Farm in Argyleshire, had died on 4 April 1899, with no indication of how or why her body had been transported nearly four hundred miles for burial.[110] The Chantress notebooks help to cast some light on this mystery, noting that Mrs Plowden, who had been a pupil at the school in the 1870s under her maiden name of Tump, had sought special permission from Cardinal Vaughan, Archbishop of Westminster, before her death, requesting that, in the event of her decease, she be buried at her old home in Essex:

> 7th [April]. First Fri. Had the half hours prayer but no Exposition. The cause was this. Mrs Roger Plowden (Minnie Tump) died on the 4th & left a written paper, asking to be buried here. The Cardinal having given leave, the body was brought from Edinburgh. It arrived about [quarter] to 11 Friday morning, when a low Requiem Mass was said by Fr Heery ... the funeral followed the Requiem. The Community went up privately to the cemetery & there waited for the funeral procession. We chanted a few verses of the Miserere when it came in sight. Minnie's husband & little son, her brother & his wife, her cousin Mr Broadbent & Miss Maggie Maguire were present. It poured rain. The Community left the cemetery as soon as the burial was over. We had dinner when we returned, a little after 12.[111]

[110] O/LB/8. Because she died in Scotland, she did not appear on the national index of births, marriages and deaths, which covers England and Wales only.
[111] ACHS/ TB 165/112/ Chantress Book 9, 1886–1904, not paginated.

Mary 'Minnie' Plowden (1861–99), an ex-pupil who requested to be buried at New Hall. Her body was transported from Edinburgh in April 1899. Image courtesy of the Canonesses of the Holy Sepulchre.

SERVANTS AND STAFF MEMBERS

As well as school pupils and family members, the cemetery is also the final resting place of several members of staff who worked with and for the Community. The first lay person to be buried in the cemetery was one Mary Delraye (d. 1804), who died in June 1804. She was one of only two servants who travelled with and looked after the Community, clergy and school children during the migration. The second servant, Mary Jane Moers (1776–1848), died in 1848, and she is also buried in the cemetery.[112]

Some were given a full burial service as if they were one of the Community, such as Euphrasina Nadit (d. 1827), a governess at the school, who had died on 1 April 1826.[113] The Chantress notes:

> April 3rd 1827. We did a service for Miss Euphrasina Nadit who had been with us as a governess in the little class from July 1826. She died on the 1st April. We wore our great cloaks as also at the burial which was at 10 o clock on the 4th. All the young ladies Community and sisters followed the corps as for one of the Religious. She was brought to the chapel during the hours on her service day where she remained untill she was carried to the grave.[114]

[112] O/RA/13 and O/LC/27 respectively.
[113] O/RA/30.
[114] ACHS/ TB 165/106/Chantress Book 3, 1826–9, p. 3.

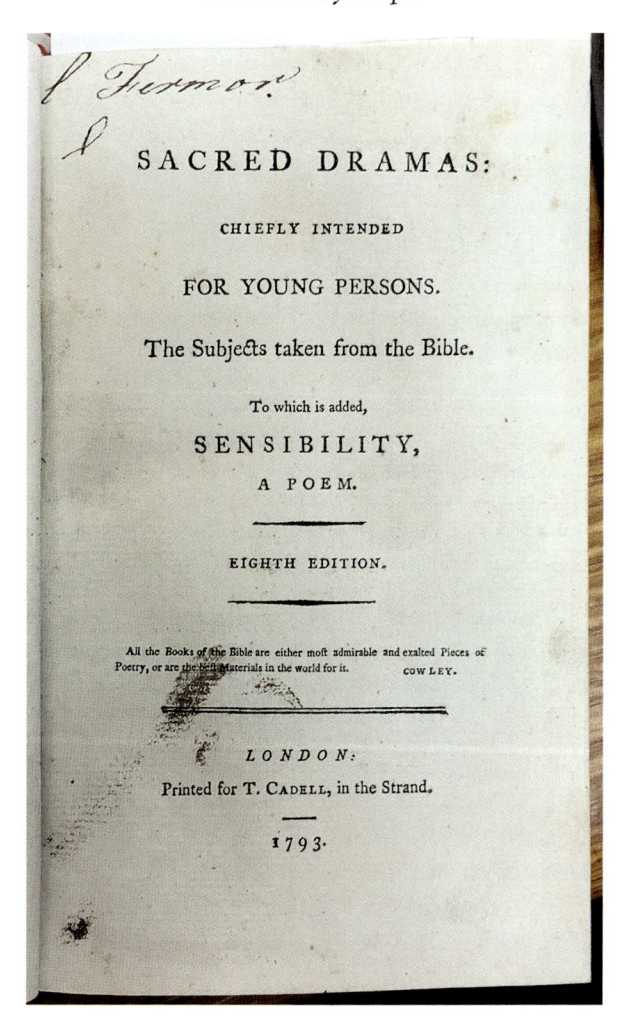

A 1793 edition of *Sacred Dramas chiefly intended for Young Persons*, owned by Louisa Fermor (1778–1820). Image courtesy of the Canonesses of the Holy Sepulchre.

A quite different service is described for the funeral of Elizabeth Pratt, also known as Patty, who had died unexpectedly on 14 February 1832.[115] She was the maid servant of Louisa Gandolfi, and Louisa Fermor, both of whom were benefactors of the Community.[116] The Chantress simply notes '[Patty] was buried on Friday morning. As it was very wet & cold there were but two Community went to the grave'.[117] It is likely that the generous bequest left to Patty in Louisa Fermor's will also had an impact on the decision to bury Patty in the cemetery, as it allowed Patty to become a benefactor to the Community in her own right. Letters in the archives record that the bequest was approximately £30 per annum, a sizeable amount that had the spending equivalent of approximately £1300 in modern currency.

The funeral of Angelique Molliet (c. 1760–1833) is described in similarly sparse terms by the then-Chantress, and with considerably less ceremony than previous funerals. Molliett died on 30 January 1833, aged 71.[118] She had been with the Community as a boarder since they had been in Liège, and was among those who made the journey in 1794. The account of her funeral service simply notes that 'she was put under the great stairs & taken solemnly into the chapel during Vespers. No one of the religious went to the grave as it was very wet weather.'[119]

Research into some individuals has also highlighted a 'policy' of sorts, particularly when it came to allowing lay people to be buried in the cemetery. One example is Mr Simon Van Ham (1761–1824),

[115] O/RB/32.
[116] See p. 73 above.
[117] ACHS/TB 165/107/Chantress Book 4, 1830–44, p. 58.
[118] O/RB/31.
[119] ACHS/TB 165/107/Chantress Book 4, 1830–44, p. 79.

who had been the music master at Liège. Although he did not migrate with the Community in 1794, he and his wife had joined them at New Hall by 1801 where he remained until his death in 1824. He served the Community and the school as music master, composing several mass settings and other liturgical pieces that were in frequent use by the Community from 1801 until at least the 1850s. However, he is not buried in the cemetery, despite his widow, Martha (1785–1864), professing her vows as S. Mary Ursula and becoming a member of the Community by 1830.[120] Van Ham's will reveals that he was not Catholic, suggesting that this was a necessary condition for burial in the Community cemetery in this period.[121] A requiem Mass was celebrated at New Hall for the repose of his soul, and he was buried in the large parish cemetery of the Anglican church of All Saints in Springfield with the following inscription:

> To the memory of SIMON GUILLAUIME VAN HAM Esq of this parish, who departed this life Sep[tembe]r 26th 1824 / in his 63d year. Formerly a distinguished member of the University of Louvain. He was a man of most upright character str[ict] morality, integrity and justice. Joined to great literary and musical acquirements … This tomb was erected by his [–] / widow as a tribute of gratitude, affection and love to the … most ind[ulg]ent of husbands. R.I.P.[122]

Only one member of the Phillipson family is buried at the cemetery, but the family are a key part of the Community's history, having served the Community continuously for over a century as groundsmen and maintenance staff. William Abraham Phillipson (1787–1839) died on 23 November 1839, aged 52, and was buried at the cemetery a few days later.[123] Several successive generations of his family were buried in the All Saints cemetery in Springfield.[124] Very little information has been preserved about their roles at New Hall, simply an effusive note of thanks 'recording our appreciation of the devoted service of many members of the Phillipson family … earning our best thanks and acknowledgement for their most loyal and intelligent zeal for our interests'.[125]

When members of staff passed away unexpectedly, celebrating a funeral Mass and arranging burial in the cemetery could be a means for the Community to offer comfort and an appropriate tribute. This is particularly visible in the death of Lydia Hilliard (1899–1937), a member of teaching staff who died suddenly in November 1937, aged 38.[126] The then-Chantress describes the circumstances of her death, noting that

> Miss Hilliard, a member of the school staff was found dead upstairs just after 9 o'clock. She had been to Mass & communion that morning & breakfasted as usual. She was anointed conditionally and the Doctor arrived almost immediately. On Friday 26th the body was taken to Chelmsford for a 'post mortem' examination. She was found to have died from cerebral haemorrhage and is to be buried in our cemetery as she has no home or near relations living. She has taught in the school for 5 years.[127]

It seems from this account that offering burial in their cemetery was one of the few means available to the Community for expressing their grief at this sudden loss. An obituary printed in the chronicle of St Hugh's College in Oxford, which Hilliard had attended, also draws attention to the difficulties still experienced by the Catholic community at this time, even more than a century after emancipation had been granted. The obituary notes that

> Her courage and more particularly her faith never seemed to desert her, and they inspired and supported her in taking a few years ago what she admitted to be the risk of

---

[120] O/LB/14.
[121] TNA/PROB 11/1691/202: Will of Simon Guillauime Van Ham, 19 February 1824 (proved 26 October 1824).
[122] Essex Society for Family History ESFH, *Monumental Inscriptions at All Saints, Springfield and Cemetery at Trinity Road, Springfield, 1421–1989* (Chelmsford: Essex Society for Family History, 2001), entry 162.
[123] O/LA/4.
[124] See ESFH, *Monumental Inscriptions at All Saints*, entries 179–83.
[125] *History of the Community*, p. 205.
[126] O/LB/33.
[127] ACHS/D2/Chantress Book 14, 1937– 51. Entries are not paginated, but are arranged chronologically.

diminishing her chances in the field of history teaching, by joining the Roman Catholic Church, in which she found great happiness and fulfilment.[128]

These accounts demonstrate the wide range of lay people that have been laid to rest in the Community cemetery, and the rich depth of their relationships and connections with the Community themselves. Taken together, they confirm the strong feeling of family felt by those who were part of daily life within the school, whether as pupil, family member or staff member.

John Phillipson (1834–1907) standing outside his workshops, *c.* 1900. He was one of several generations of the Phillipson family who served the Community as groundsmen and maintenance staff. Image courtesy of the Canonesses of the Holy Sepulchre.

---

[128] 'Lydia Maud Hilliard', *St Hughes College, Oxford, Chronicle 1937-8* (Oxford: privately printed, 1938), p. 32.

CONCLUSION

In 1794, political conditions forced the English Canonesses of the Holy Sepulchre, and seventeen other English religious communities in exile, to leave their homes on the continent and seek shelter in England. Catholicism was still illegal in England, and although conditions were generally more tolerant than they had been a century earlier, those who practised the faith were still viewed with suspicion and hostility. For the Canonesses, the search for a permanent home in England took five years, prompting necessary changes in the practicalities of daily conventual life. These changes are brought into sharp relief when examined through the lens of death and burial. In the context of anti-Catholic suspicion and hostility, traditional Community practices had to be set aside in order to allow any burial to take place at all, and often only with the consent of the local Anglican vicar. After arrival at New Hall in March 1799, the Community were at last able to recreate the conventual environment they had left behind at Liège, constructing a chapel, a convent and cemetery within the enclosure walls for the first time since 1794.

The aim of this book has been to examine in detail the history and importance of the Community cemetery at New Hall, and to present a lasting record of this unique example of its place and period. The cemetery is, and always has been, an important part of Community spiritual and liturgical life, representing a place of commemoration and remembrance for deceased members of the Community family. The cemetery is deeply rooted within Community life, representing a closely linked group of people with a shared religious outlook. As such, it offers an opportunity to examine the wider context of the individuals buried within its walls, in this case the wider history of English Catholicism in the eighteenth, nineteenth and early twentieth centuries, as well as the context of the development of the cemetery in England and Wales. The Community cemetery's role in these two national contexts is perhaps best encapsulated by the physical boundary that divides the burial space from the rest of the estate. In the case of the history of Catholicism, the wall represents the creation of a sanctuary, a necessarily secretive commemorative space, that allowed conventual funerary rituals to continue in a manner more suited to their new environment. As England grew more tolerant of Catholicism, the wall took on a new significance, demarcating a physical separation of ground consecrated for Catholic burials from that which was not consecrated. Later versions of the wall were stylistically similar to those found at local municipal cemeteries, perhaps reflecting the further relaxation of attitudes towards Catholicism, and a more inclusive society.

The move towards inclusivity begins within the cemetery itself, and is particularly visible in the combination of priests, servants, school children and Community laid to rest within its walls. This sense of family and togetherness continues in the extension to the cemetery, used for all burials since 1956, which now includes those of other denominations, and persists in the spirit of the Community to the present day.

Conclusion

Above. The left-hand side of the extension to the cemetery, where members of the Community have been buried since 1956.   *Below*. The right-hand side of the extension to the cemetery, where lay people with a special connection to the Community have been buried since 1956.

Above. Memorial plaques in the new half of the cemetery.

Below. Older-style wooden markers have largely been replaced with stone—
these are the first burials in the extension.

APPENDIX 1. MEMORIAL INSCRIPTIONS

Recorded by the Essex Society for Family History [ESFH], November 2003.[1] ESFH team: Yvonne Tunstill (Leader), Fred Eaton, Doug Harris, Christine Jemmeson, Linda Lee, Rosemary Mountjoy, Bob Newman, Jean Spence, Adrian Stockton, Keith Tunstill and Ann Church. Additional notes and some corrections made by Hannah Thomas, September 2016.

Entries are colour coded and divided into three main groups: Community (black), Lay People (red) and Clergy (green). Each entry includes a location reference, which takes the format of Side-Row/Grave Number. Burials in the original half are preceded by 'O', and those in the extension by 'E'. See fold-out map/plan for the detailed locations within the cemetery. Information in italics beneath each entry has been added from existing cemetery plans, Community lists and archive research.

NOTES ON TRANSCRIPTION

The inscriptions in the typescript have been 'run on', with an oblique stroke indicating the end of a line on the memorial. Doubtful letters or figures have been enclosed in square brackets, along with additional information added from other sources. Contracted or incomplete words have been expanded or completed inside square brackets. Parentheses indicate that brackets actually appear on the inscription. With the fading of lettering and figures and the use of elaborate fonts by the stonemasons, the recorder had to use his or her best judgment and experience to determine the original inscription. Common difficulties with figures include deciding between the numbers 1 and 4, 2 and 8, 3 and 5, 6 and 9 and 0, and 7 and 3.

Cautionary note: whilst we endeavour to ensure total accuracy, we cannot guarantee it.

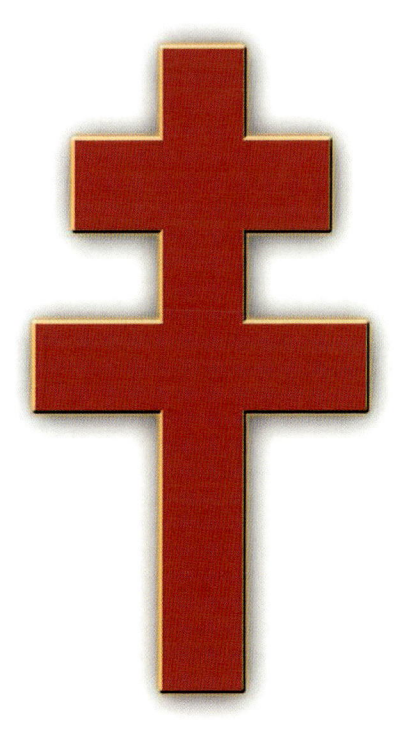

---

[1] Reg. Charity No. 290552.

Monumental Inscriptions

1: O/RA/35 Headstone, round top with raised round shoulders and etched Patriarchal cross of Jerusalem top centre with S S either side.
Mother MARY ELIZA / Magdalen Joseph KELLY /
deceased 14th July 1898 / aged 50 years / R.I.P. /
Sister Magdalen Joseph

2: O/RA/34 Headstone, round top with raised round shoulders and etched Patriarchal cross of Jerusalem top centre with S S either side.
Sister ANNE Magdalen / Stanislaus FITZPATRICK /
deceased 11th November 1897 / aged 2[8] years / R.I.P. /
Sister Magdalen Stanislaus

3: O/RA/33 Headstone, round top with raised round shoulders and etched Patriarchal cross of Jerusalem top centre with S S either side.
Sister MARGARET Mary / Agatha MADDEN /
deceased 29th April 1897 / aged 73 years / R.I.P. /
Sister Agatha

4: O/RA32 Headstone, round top with raised round shoulders and etched Patriarchal cross of Jerusalem top centre.
Mrs / ELIZABETH NORRIS / deceased May 2[4]th 1831 /
aged 74 years / R.I.P. /
Sister Catherine

5: O/RA/31 Headstone, round top with raised round shoulders.
Mrs / JANE PORTER / deceased March 26th 1831 /
aged 5[8] years / R.I.P. /
Sister Winifred

6: O/RA/30 Headstone, round top with raised round shoulders, badly eroded.
[*line illegible*] / **EUPH[RASINE] [NA]D[IT]/**
dece[ased April] 27[th 1827] / [——]rs /
Governess

7: O/RA/29 Headstone, round top with raised round shoulders and etched Patriarchal cross of Jerusalem top centre.
Miss / ANNE WICKWAR / deceased / Feb[ruar]y the 13th 1823 /
aged 22 years / R.I.P. /
Sister Teresa Stanislaus

8: O/RA/28 Headstone, round top with raised round shoulders and etched Patriarchal cross of Jerusalem top centre.
Mrs / MARGARET CROSS / deceased / June the 23d 1820 /
aged 48 years / R.I.P. /
Sister Francis Borgia [TRISTRAM]

Memorial Inscriptions

9: O/RA/26 Headstone, round top with raised round shoulders.
Miss / LOUISA FERMOR / deceased / June the 8th 1820 / aged 42 years / R.I.P. /
Ex-pupil; benefactor

10: O/RA/25 Headstone, round top with raised round shoulders and etched Patriarchal cross of Jerusalem top centre.
ELIZABETH / WINNARD / deceased Oct[obe]r 28th / 1818 / aged 41 years / R.I.P. /
Sister Baptist

11: O/RA/23 Headstone, round top with raised round shoulders and etched Patriarchal cross of Jerusalem top centre.
Mrs. MARY SEYMORE / died 3rd May 1803 / aged 56 / R.I.P. /
Sister Loyola

12: O/RA/22 Headstone, round top with raised round shoulders and etched Patriarchal cross of Jerusalem top centre.
Mrs / MARY MARSHALL / died the 14th of March / 1799 / aged [7]5 yrs. / R.I.P. /
Sister Cleophae

13: O/RA/21 Headstone, round top with raised round shoulders and etched Patriarchal cross of Jerusalem top centre.
Mrs EMELIA / Barbara FREEMAN / died the 13th of June / 1799 / aged 24 yrs / R.I.P. /
Sister Barbara [DUFRENE]

14: O/RA/20 Headstone, round top with raised round shoulders and etched Patriarchal cross of Jerusalem top centre.
Mrs. / ELIZABETH EVENS / died the 25th of June / 1799 / aged 57 yrs / R.I.P. /
Sister Mary Clare

15: O/RA/19 Headstone, gothic top with Patriarchal cross of Jerusalem top centre with S S either side.
Sister Mary Francis / ELIZABETH McCONVILLE / 20 July 1939 / aged 78 / R.I.P. /
Sister Francis

16: O/RA/18 Headstone, round top with raised round shoulders and etched Patriarchal cross of Jerusalem top centre, badly eroded.
Mrs JANE [Joan] REYNOLDS / de[ceas]ed / [11] Aug[ust] 1842 / aged 7[3] years / R.I.P. /
Sister Teresa Chantal

17: O/RA/17 Headstone, flat top with carved Patriarchal cross of Jerusalem top centre.
Mrs. / ELIZABETH POOLE / died the 3rd of July / 1800 / R.I.P. /
Sister Mary Gonzaga [STEVENSON]

18: O/RA/16   Headstone, gothic top with Patriarchal cross of Jerusalem with S S either side.
Sister Mary FRANCES / Cecily BUDD / deceased 27 July 1937 / aged 67 years / R.I.P. /
Sister Cecily

19: O/RA/15   Headstone, round top with raised round shoulders and etched Patriarchal cross of Jerusalem top centre with S S either side.
Mrs. ELIZABETH POISMAN / died 15th of Oct[obe]r 1803 / aged [5]8 / R.I.P. /
Sister Alexia

20: O/RA/14   Headstone, gothic top with Patriarchal cross of Jerusalem top centre with S S either side.
Venerable Mother / Aloysia Berchmans / ROSE ELLISON / deceased [20] May 1935 / aged [77 ye]ars / R.I.P. /
Sister Aloysia Berchmans

21: O/RA/13   Headstone, flat top.
MARY DELRAYE / died 21st June / 1804 / R.I.P. /
Servant

22: O/RA/11   Headstone, flat top.
Mrs DIANA STRICKLAND / died on the 2d August / 1804 / R.I.P. /
Boarder

23: O/RA/9   Headstone, round top with raised round shoulders and etched Patriarchal cross of Jerusalem top centre.
ELIZABETH MARY PRICE / deceased / July the 17th 1838 / aged 86 years / R.I.P. /
Sister Cicely Price

24: O/RA/7   Headstone, round top with raised round shoulders and etched Patriarchal cross of Jerusalem top centre with S S either side.
Mother ANNA MARIA / Francis Regis STOURTON / deceased 18 Nov[ember] 1877 / aged 68 years / R.I.P. /
Sister Francis Regis

25: O/RA/5   Headstone, round top with raised round shoulders and etched Patriarchal cross of Jerusalem top centre with S S either side.
Venerable Mother / TERESA Mary Anne / Joseph GILLOW / deceased 17th Feb[ruary] 1878 / aged 78 years / R.I.P. /
Sister Ann Joseph

26: O/RA/3   Headstone, round top with raised round shoulders and etched Patriarchal cross of Jerusalem top centre with S S either side.
Mother MARY / Teresa Stanislaus / BUTLER / deceased 1[0] April 1880 / aged [70] years / R.I.P. /
Sister Teresa Stanislaus

Memorial Inscriptions

27: O/RA/1 — Headstone, round top with raised round shoulders and etched Patriarchal cross of Jerusalem top centre with S S either side.
Sister JANE / Paul COUPE / deceased May 5th 1882 / aged 93 years / R.I.P. /
Sister Paul

28: O/RC/20 — Broken headstone leaning against wall, curved top with flat and scooped shoulders with cross carved in relief in roundel top centre.
Revd. PETER [O'B]RIEN / [line illegible] / on the [28 February] 1807 / [line illegible] /
Jesuit, chaplain to Community 1800–7

29: O/RB/1 — Headstone, round top with raised round shoulders and etched Patriarchal cross of Jerusalem top centre with S S either side.
Mother HELEN Mary / Bernard BURKE / deceased / 22nd July 1884 / aged 45 years / R.I.P. /
Sister Mary Bernard

30: O/RB/3 — Headstone, round top with raised round shoulders and etched Patriarchal cross of Jerusalem top centre with S S either side.
Mother GEORGIANA / Mary Magdalen LOUGH[N]AN / deceased / December [1] 1882 / aged [82] years /
Sister Mary Magdalen

31: O/RB/5 — Headstone, round top with raised round shoulders and etched Patriarchal cross of Jerusalem top centre with S S either side.
Mother Angelique / MARY Angela MITCHEL / deceased 18th of Dec[embe]r 1878 / aged 66 years / R.I.P. /
Sister Mary Angela

32: O/RB/7 — Headstone, gothic top with Patriarchal cross of Jerusalem at top with S S either side.
Mother Mary Stanislaus / Ju[b]ilarian / BLANCHE O'BYRNE / 5 March 1939 / aged 82 / R.I.P. /
Sister Mary Stanislaus

33: O/RB/9 — Headstone, round top with raised round shoulders and etched Patriarchal cross of Jerusalem top centre.
Mrs FRANCES HILL / deceased April 12 / 1842 / aged 75 years / R.I.P. /
Sister Mary Angela

34: O/RB/11 — Headstone, flat top.
Miss CATHARINE NANGLE / died the 30th of May / 1805 / R.I.P. /
Pupil, died at school aged 15

35: O/RB/13 — Headstone, flat top.
The Honorable / Miss ANNA MARIA CLIFFORD / died the 14th July 1805 / aged 17 / R.I.P. /
Pupil, died at school

36: O/RB/14   Headstone, gothic top with Patriarchal cross of Jerusalem at top with S S either side.
Sister / Mary Monica / MARY ANN WEAVER / deceased / 25th November 1954 / aged 73 years / R.I.P. /
Sister Monica

37: O/RB/15   Headstone, flat top with Patriarchal cross of Jerusalem at top.
Mrs. MARY CROSS / died the 23d Dec[embe]r / 1804 / aged 31 yrs / R.I.P. /
Sister Mary Xaveria [TRISTRAM]

38: O/RB/17   Headstone, flat top with Patriarchal cross of Jerusalem at top.
Mrs BRIDGET / WEBBE / deceased the 3rd / of March 1801 / aged [70] years / R.I.P. /
Sister Anne Xaveria

39: O/RB/18   Headstone, flat top with Patriarchal cross of Jerusalem at top.
Mrs / CHARLOTTE CLIFFORD / died the 13th of July / 1800 / aged [28] yrs / R.I.P. /
Sister Ann Teresa

40: O/RB/19   Headstone, gothic top with Patriarchal cross of Jerusalem at top with S S either side.
Sister / Mary Winifred / MARGARET BOARDMAN / deceased / 13th June 1956 / aged 75 years / R.I.P. /
Sister Winefride

41: O/RB/20   Headstone, flat top with Patriarchal cross of Jerusalem at top.
Mrs / MARY HARGITT / died the 5th of April / 1800 / aged 29 yrs / R.I.P. /
Sister Magdalen

42: O/RB/21   Headstone, round on flat with scooped shoulders.
Mrs / ELIZABETH STRAFFEN / deceased / the 23d of Jan[uary] 1837 / aged 85 years / R.I.P. /
Sister Anne Xaveria

43: O/RB/22   Headstone, round on flat with scooped shoulders and IHS with Latin cross above in relief in roundel at top.
The Revd GERVAIS GENIN S J / deceased the 19th of March / 1800 / R.I.P. /
French ex-Jesuit, chaplain to Community 1794–1800

44: O/RB/23   Headstone, flat top with Patriarchal cross of Jerusalem at top.
Mrs. ELIZABETH REEKS / died the 1st Oct[obe]r 1805 / aged 63 / R.I.P. /
Sister Martha

45: O/RB/24   Slate headstone, gothic top with Patriarchal cross of Jerusalem at top with S S either side.
Sister Mary Ursula / GERTRUDE SMITHERS / 17 February 1940 / aged 78 / R.I.P. /
Sister Ursula

Memorial Inscriptions

46: O/RB/25   Headstone, gothic top with raised gothic shoulders and Patriarchal cross of Jerusalem at top.
Mrs CLARE SEMMES / deceased May 7th 1820 / aged 75 years / R.I.P. /
Sister Mary Ursula

47: O/RB/26   Headstone, round on flat with raised round shoulders and Patriarchal cross of Jerusalem at top.
Mrs / ANNA WRIGHT / deceased / the 7[th] of Dec[embe]r 1819 / aged 76 years / R.I.P. /
Sister Aloysia Joseph

48: O/RB/28   Headstone, round on flat with raised round shoulders.
Mrs / MARY B[U]RCHAL / deceased Jan[uary] 31 1832 / aged 61 years / R.I.P. /
Sister Magdalen

49: O/RB/29   Headstone, round on flat with raised round shoulders.
Mrs / ANN PARKINSON / deceased / March the 30th 1832 / aged 72 years / R.I.P. /
Sister Salome

50: O/RB/30   Headstone, round on flat with raised round shoulders.
Mrs / CHRISTINA CLEMENT / deceased / on the 13th of Nov[ember] 1833 / aged [35] years / R.I.P. /
Sister Mary Euphrasia

51: O/RB/31   Headstone, round on flat with raised round shoulders.
Mad[e]ll(e) / ANGELI[Q]U[E] MOLLIET / deceased Jan[uary] 30th 1833 / aged 7[1 or 4] years / R.I.P. /
Boarder

52: O/RB/32   Headstone, round on flat with raised round shoulders.
Mrs / ELIZABETH PRATT / deceased / Feb the 1[4th] 1832 / aged [?]6 years[2] / R.I.P. /
Servant, known as 'Patty'

53: O/RB/33   Headstone, round on flat with raised round shoulders and Patriarchal cross of Jerusalem at top with S S each side.
Sister MARY Winefride / BLAKE / deceased September 27th 1899 / aged 44 years / R.I.P. /
Sister Winefride

54: O/RB/34   Headstone round on flat with raised round shoulders and Patriarchal cross of Jerusalem at top with S S each side.
Sister SARAH ANN Mary / Salome EMERY / deceased April 2nd 1900 / aged 79 years / R.I.P. /
Sister Salome

---

[2] Originally transcribed as 'aged 16 years'; Pratt is noted as the servant of Louisa Fermor in the latter's will of 1820, making it very unlikely Pratt was born in 1816. No record of Pratt's age at death has been found.

55: O/RB/35   Headstone, round on flat with raised round shoulders and Patriarchal cross of Jerusalem at top with S S each side.
Sister JULIA Mary / Monica DALY / deceased 9th November 1900 / aged 56 years / R.I.P. /
Sister Monica

56: O/RC/35   Headstone, round top with raised round shoulders and etched Patriarchal cross of Jerusalem top centre with S S either side.
Sister CATHARINE Mary / Flaviana MARSH / deceased 24th July 1909 / aged 74 years / R.I.P. /
Sister Flaviana

57: O/RC/34   Headstone, round top with raised round shoulders and etched Patriarchal cross of Jerusalem top centre with S S either side.
Sister ANNE Mary / Aloysia Joseph COSTELLO / deceased 16th August 1907 / aged 26 years / R.I.P. /
Sister Aloysia Joseph

58: O/RC/33   Headstone, round top with raised round shoulders and etched Patriarchal cross of Jerusalem top centre with S S either side.
Mother WINEFRIDE MARY / Francis Xavier SCOLES / deceased 31st January 1900 / aged 47 years / R.I.P. /
Sister Francis Xavier

59: O/RC/32   Headstone, round on flat with scooped shoulders.
Mr(s) / HARRIET WHATTOLLEY / deceased / the 26th of Jan[uary] 1837 / aged 53 years / R.I.P. /
Sister Mary Clementina

60: O/RC/31   Headstone, round top with raised round shoulders and etched Patriarchal cross of Jerusalem top centre.
Mrs MARY ANN HEAD / deceased / the 13th of May 1837 / aged 77 years / R.I.P. /
Sister Mary Ann

61: O/RC/30   Headstone, round top with raised round shoulders and etched Patriarchal cross of Jerusalem top centre with S S either side.
Mrs / ANN Mary McEVOY / deceased / the 3rd of Feb[ruary] 1836 / aged 68 years / R.I.P. /
Sister Aloysia Stanislaus

62: O/RC/29   Headstone, round top with raised round shoulders and etched Patriarchal cross of Jerusalem top centre with S S either side.
Mrs / BARBARA ARCHDEACON / deceased / the 12th of June 1833 / aged 69 years / R.I.P. /
Sister Mary Aloysia

63: O/RC/28   Headstone, round on flat with scooped shoulders.
Mrs / CATHERINE PERRIN / deceased Nov[embe]r 9th 1832 / aged 81 years / R.I.P. /
Sister Mary Rose

64: O/RC/27		Headstone, gothic top with Patriarchal cross of Jerusalem at top with S S either side. **Mother Mary Philip / Jubilarian / ETHELDREDA KENDAL / 14 May 1940 / aged 76 / R.I.P. /** *Sister Mary Philip*
65: O/RC/26		Headstone, round top with raised round shoulders and etched Patriarchal cross of Jerusalem top centre. **Mrs MARY [LOUISE] SMITH / deceased June 24th / 1827 / aged 76 years / R.I.P. /** *Sister Mary Berchmans*
66: O/RC/25		Headstone, round on flat with scooped shoulders. **Mrs / MARY SUSANNA / HOWARD / deceased / the 22d of December 1813 / aged 67 years / R.I.P. /** *Sister Frances*
67: O/RC/24		Headstone, gothic top with Patriarchal cross of Jerusalem at top with S S each side. **Mother / Mary Magdalene / Jubilarian / MILDRED FALLS / 7 September 1947 / aged 84 / R.I.P. /** *Sister Mary Magdalene*
68: O/RC/23		Headstone, round top with raised round shoulders and etched Patriarchal cross of Jerusalem top centre. **Mrs / ELIZABETH FULLWOOD / deceased / the 23d of May 181[3] / aged 73 years / R.I.P. /** *Sister Paul*
69: O/RC/22		Headstone, round on flat with scooped shoulders and Patriarchal cross of Jerusalem at top. **Mrs BRIDGET CHAMPNEY / deceased / April the 5th 1812 / aged 81 years / R.I.P. /** *Sister Mary Magdalen*
70: O/RC/21		Headstone, round top with ogee shoulders and Patriarchal cross of Jerusalem at top. **[Mrs] ANN HALES / deceased / the 21st of May 1811 / aged 58 years / R.I.P. /** *Sister Christina Juliana*
71: O/RC/18		Headstone, round on flat. **Mrs / HENRIETTA FERMOR / deceased / Dec[ember] the 30th 1806 / aged [35] years / R.I.P. /** *Sister Teresa Joseph*
72: O/RC/17		Headstone, flat top with Patriarchal cross of Jerusalem at top. **Mrs SARAH TRANT / deceased on the / 7th of Feb[ruar]y 1807 / aged 43 / R.I.P. /** *Sister Francis Xaveria*

73: O/RC/15   Headstone, flat top with Patriarchal cross of Jerusalem at top.
Mrs ELIZABETH STUTTER / deceased / the 10th of June 1807 / R.I.P. /
Sister Mary Baptist

74: O/RC/14   Headstone, gothic top with Patriarchal cross of Jerusalem at top with S S either side.
Venerable Mother / Mary Teresa / GERTRUDE PETRE /
deceased 7th June 1934 / aged 78 years / R.I.P. /
Sister Mary Teresa

75: O/RC/13   Headstone, round on flat with scooped shoulders and Patriarchal cross of Jerusalem at top.,
Mrs ELIZABETH TALBOT / died / the 20th of April 1808 /
aged [70] / R.I.P.
Sister Mary Helen Aloysia

76: O/RC/11   Headstone, round on flat with scooped shoulders and Patriarchal cross of Jerusalem at top.
Mrs MARY LAWRENSON (*sic*) **/ deceased / the 12th of July 1812 /**
aged 35 years / R.I.P. /
Sister Mary Sales [LAURENSON]

77: O/RC/9   Headstone, round on flat with scooped shoulders.
Miss / CATHARINE RYAN / died the 13th of Sept[ember] 1813 / aged [17] years /
Pupil, died at school

78: n/a   Headstone, round top with raised round shoulders and etched Patriarchal cross of Jerusalem top centre, in front of number 79. Completely worn.
Perhaps S. Mary Philip [MARY JOSEPHINE BURKE] 14 August 1878. Grave not located

79: O/RC/7   Headstone, round top with raised round shoulders and etched Patriarchal cross of Jerusalem top centre with S S either side.
Mother DELPHINE / Mary Aloysia Francis / PEREIRA /
deceased Feb[ruary] 3rd 1880 / aged 31 years / R.I.P. /
Sister Aloysia Francis

80: O/RC/5   Headstone, round top with raised round shoulders and etched Patriarchal cross of Jerusalem top centre with S S either side.
Mother ISABELLA / Mary Francis Helen / STEUART /
deceased Feb[ruary] 23[d] 1880 / aged 66 years / R.I.P. /
Sister Francis Helen

81: O/RC/3   Headstone, round top with raised round shoulders and etched Patriarchal cross of Jerusalem top centre with S S either side.
Sister SARAH ANN / Mary Scholastica / TAYLOR /
deceased August 23rd 1885 / aged 47 years / R.I.P. /
Sister Scholastica

82: O/RC/1   Headstone, round top with raised round shoulders and etched Patriarchal cross of Jerusalem top centre with S S either side.
Sister Marie CAMILLE / Teresa Stanislaus / HENRY / deceased 30th Oct[ober] 1886 / aged 29 years / R.I.P. /
Sister Teresa Stanislaus

83: O/RD/1   Headstone, round top with raised round shoulders and etched Patriarchal cross of Jerusalem top centre with S S either side.
Sister BRIDGET / Paul WADDEN / deceased 14th May 1891 / aged 39 years / R.I.P. /
Sister Paul

84: O/RD/3   Headstone, round on flat with raised round shoulders with Patriarchal cross of Jerusalem at top with S S either side.
Mother GEORGINA / Mary Aloysia / Joseph PEREIRA / deceased 3rd August 1891 / aged 60 years / R.I.P. /
Sister Aloysia Joseph

85: O/RD/5   Headstone, round on flat with raised round shoulders with Patriarchal cross of Jerusalem at top with S S either side.
Sister ANNE Mary / Martha MATHEWS / deceased 3rd May 1889 / aged 37 years / R.I.P. /
Sister Martha

86: O/RD/7   Headstone, round on flat with raised round shoulders with Patriarchal cross of Jerusalem at top with S S either side.
Mother Mary / ELIZABETH Christina / Joseph NANGLE / deceased 24th May 1887 / aged 63 years / R.I.P. /
Sister Christina Joseph

87: O/RD/9   Headstone, round on flat with scooped shoulders.
Miss / ELIZABETH STANDISH / died the 19 of Sep[tembe]r 1813 / aged 15 years / R.I.P. /
Pupil, died at school

88: O/RD/11   Headstone, round on flat with scooped shoulders and Patriarchal cross of Jerusalem at top.
Mrs / TERESA JONES / deceased / the 19th of August 181[3] / aged 25 years / R.I.P. /
Sister Mary Christina

89: O/RD/13   Headstone, round on flat with scooped shoulders and Patriarchal cross of Jerusalem at top.
M[rs] SARAH TRANT / deceased / the 18th of May 1811 / aged 76 years / R.I.P. /
Sister Mary Christina

90: O/RD/14   Headstone, gothic top with Patriarchal cross of Jerusalem at top with S S either side.
Venerable Mother / Aloysia Magdalene / of the Sacred Heart / AGNES DOLAN / 15th Superior of this community / who died on 8th August 1936 / aged 78 years / Professed 52 years Prioress 18 years / R.I.P. / O Lord my God in Thee have I put my trust / Ps. VII.l /
Sister Aloysia Magdalene

91: O/RD/15   Headstone, round on flat with scooped shoulders with Patriarchal cross of Jerusalem at top.
M[rs] / ELIZABETH SMITH / deceased / the [5] of May 1811 / aged 63 years / R.I.P. /
Sister Mary Joseph

92: O/RD/17   Headstone, curved top on flat with scooped shoulders and slightly slanting Latin cross on base in relief in roundel at top.
The Revd / HERMAN KEMPER / S · J / deceased the 8th of April / 1811 / aged 65 years / R.I.P. /
German Jesuit, chaplain to Community 1776–94 and 1808–11

93: O/RD/18   Slate headstone, curved top on flat with round and flat shoulders and Patriarchal cross of Jerusalem in oval at top.
D.O.M / Here lie the remains of / the Reverend Prioress / B.M.A. CLOUGH / who after having for more / than 30 years governed / those committed to her charge / with uncommon indications / of heavenly wisdom, fortitude / and sweetness / departed this life / in the 79th year of her age / July 6th 1816 / R I P /
Sister Mary Aloysia, 8th Prioress

94: O/RD/19   Headstone, curved top on flat with scooped shoulders with Latin cross and IHS at top.
The Revd. / CHARLES HENRY [FLEURY] FORRESTER / S. J. / deceased the 2nd of May / 1825 / aged 86 years / R I P /
French Jesuit, chaplain to Community 1813–25

95: O/RD/20   Headstone, gothic top with Latin cross and IHS in roundel at top.
Reverend / JAMES NICHOLSON S. J. / deceased November 7 1934 / aged 79 years / 10 years Chaplain to this / community / R.I.P. / "Mane autem facto, stetit Jesus / in litore." Joan XXI. IV /
Jesuit, chaplain to Community 1924–34

96: O/RD/21   Headstone with chipped top, round top on flat with scooped shoulders and Patriarchal cross of Jerusalem at top.
[Mrs] / MARGARET DENNETT / deceased the 6th of April / 1816 / aged [5]1 years / R I P /
Sister Mary Stanislaus

Memorial Inscriptions

97: O/RD/22 — Headstone, round top on flat with scooped shoulders and Patriarchal cross of Jerusalem at top.
Mrs / ELIZABETH DENNETT / deceased July 19th / 1825 / aged 64 years / R.I.P. /
Sister M Ignatia Joseph

98: O/RD/23 — Headstone, round top with raised shoulders and Latin cross in roundel at top.
The Revd STEPHEN CHAPON / deceased June 27th 182[6] / He was born on the sixth of March 17[5]1 / in the parish of Percy / Diocese of Coutances Normandy / In the year 1792 he was driven from his / native country by the persecution of / the French Revolution / and after having braved danger by land / and the peril of the ocean / wa[s] kindly received in this hospitable / country[3]: / where till the close of life he was / protected, supported, and cherished / R I P /
French secular priest, chaplain to Community 1803–26

99: O/RD/25 — Headstone, curved top with flat shoulders and Patriarchal cross of Jerusalem at top.
Miss / MARGARET Mary RORK[E] / deceased / August the 2d 1826 / aged 21 years / R.I.P. /
Sister Teresa Austin, died during noviciate

100: O/RD/26 — Headstone, round top with raised round shoulders.
Mrs / DOROTHY Mary / GANDOLFI / deceased the 26th of March / 1834 / aged 61 years / R.I.P. /
Sister Mary Clare

101: O/RD/28 — Headstone, round top with raised round shoulders.
Mrs / CATHERINE LAURENSON / deceased / the 4th of August 1831 / aged 76 years / R.I.P. /
Sister Mary Agatha

102: O/RD/29 — Headstone, round top on flat with scooped shoulders.
Mrs / MARTHA LAURENSON / deceased / Oct[ober] the 24th 1835 / aged 88 years / R.I.P. /
Mother of S. Mary Agatha and S. Mary Sales

103: O/RD/30 — Headstone, round top with shaped shoulders and Latin cross with IHS in roundel at top.
The Revd THOMAS ANGIER, S. J. / deceased the 18th of Jan[uary] / 1837 aged 81 years / R.I.P. /
Jesuit, chaplain to Community 1826–37

---

[3] Inscription written by Chapon himself some years before his death; Community records note that 'this was found to be so flattering to the Community that part of it was left out, and even in the inscription actually on the stone, instead of hospitable 'Community', the word has been changed to 'country'. See *History of the Community*, p. 163.

104: O/RD/31   Headstone, round top with raised round shoulders and Patriarchal cross of Jerusalem at top.
Mrs ALICE PARKINSON / deceased / February 8 1843 / aged 78 years / R.I.P. /
Sister Lucy

105: O/RD/32   Headstone, round top with raised round shoulders and Patriarchal cross of Jerusalem at top with S S either side.
Mrs BARBARA O CONNOR / deceased / the 22nd of May 1837 / aged 44 years / R.I.P. /
Sister Mary Gonzaga

106: O/RD/33   Headstone, gothic top with Patriarchal cross of Jerusalem at top.
Mother Mary / Josephine / ANNA WILLIAMS / deceased at / Newnham Paddox Rugby[4] / 5th March 1941 / aged 92 years / R.I.P. /
Sister Mary Josephine

107: O/RD/34   Headstone, round top with raised round shoulders and Patriarchal cross of Jerusalem at top with S S either side.
Venerable Mother MARIA / Mary Margaret WATTS / deceased 17th October 1906 / aged 77 years / R.I.P. /
Sister Mary Margaret

108: O/RD/35   Headstone, round top with raised round shoulders with Patriarchal cross of Jerusalem at top with S S either side.
Venerable Mother ROSINA / Mary Ignatia Francis MASON / deceased 21st February 1909 / aged 84 years / R.I.P. /
Sister Ignatia Francis

109: O/LE/1   Headstone, gothic top with Patriarchal cross of Jerusalem at top with S S either side.
Mother Mary Catherine / PAULINE CAPECE GALEOTA / DELLA REGINA / deceased 26th October 1926 / aged 69 years / R.I.P. /
Sister Mary Catherine

110: O/LE/2   Headstone, gothic top with Patriarchal cross of Jerusalem at top with S S either side.
Venerable Mother / ROSE / Mary Francis ROSKELL / deceased 30th April 1926 / aged 79 years / R.I.P. /
Sister Mary Francis

111: O/LE/3   Headstone, gothic top with Patriarchal cross of Jerusalem at top with S S either side.
Venerable Mother / Mary Agnes / MARY ELLEN KEOGH / deceased 22nd February 1927 / aged 83 years / R.I.P. /
Sister Mary Agnes

---

[4] The Community and School were evacuated to Newnham Paddox during World War II. Two members of the Community died during that period, and were discretely brought back to the cemetery for burial, using a green tradesman's van in order to avoid attracting attention.

Memorial Inscriptions

112: O/LE/4   Headstone, gothic top with central IHS.
The Very Reverend / Canon EDWARD HEERY / Chaplain during 36 years / to our Community / died October 6th 1928 / aged 85 years / R.I.P. / I have loved O Lord the beauty of Thy house and / the place where Thy glory dwelleth / Ps 25 /
Chaplain to Community 1892–1928

113: O/LE/5   Headstone, gothic top with Patriarchal cross of Jerusalem at top with S S either side.
Venerable Mother / AGNES Mary / Aloysia James KENDAL / deceased 17th November 1925 / aged 83 years / R.I.P. /
Sister Aloysia James

114: O/LE/7   Headstone, round top with raised shoulders and Patriarchal cross of Jerusalem at top with S S either side.
Venerable Mother PAULINA (*sic*) **/ Mary Anne CADDELL / deceased 13th May 1911 / aged 94 years / R.I.P. /**
Sister Mary Anne

115: O/LE/8   Headstone, round top with raised shoulders and Patriarchal cross of Jerusalem at top with S S either side.
The Venerable Mother MARIA / Mary Anne Xavier (*sic*) **WHEBLE / deceased / August 12th 1882 / aged 79 years / R.I.P. /**
Sister Ann Xaveria

116: O/LE/9   Headstone, gothic top with central IHS.
The Revd JAMES BATEMAN S. J. / deceased 17th June 1879 / aged 73 years / R.I.P. /
Jesuit, chaplain to Community 1877–9

117: O/LE/11   Headstone, gothic top with heavily embossed Patriarchal cross of Jerusalem at top with S S either side.
The Venerable Mother / ANNA MARIA Teresa / Joseph BLOUNT / of the Blessed Sacrament / deceased February 7th 1879 / aged 88 years / Professed 69 years and Prioress 25 years / During a religious career extending over more / than 70 years she edified and benefited the / community by her singular zeal humility / and fervour / Beati immaculati in via qui ambulant / in lege domini / R.I.P. /
Sister Teresa Joseph, 11th Prioress

118: O/LE/13   Headstone, gothic top with heavily embossed Patriarchal cross of Jerusalem at top with S S either side.
The Reverend Mother / CAROLINE Mary Alphonsa / CORNEY / XIIth Superior of this community / who died on the 6th Feb[ruary] 1873 / aged 48 years / R.I.P. / Her memory will ever be held in benediction / by the community which she governed during / her short career with maternal charity, prudence / and zeal for the greater glory of God /
Sister Mary Alphonsa, 12th Prioress

119: O/LE/14   Headstone, gothic top with raised gothic shoulders and central IHS.
Revd. GEORGE BAMPTON S. J. / died Nov[ember] 10th 1865 / aged 49 years / R.I.P. /
Jesuit, chaplain to Community 1864–5

120: O/LE/15   Headstone, round top with Patriarchal cross of Jerusalem at top with S S either side.
Mrs JANE Anne / Teresa GREHAN / deceased 17th April 1863 / aged 70 years / R.I.P. /
Sister Ann Teresa

121: O/LE/16   Headstone, gothic top with heavily embossed Patriarchal cross of Jerusalem at top with S S either side.
The Venerable Mother / CECILIA Mary / Joseph Sales KENDAL / of the Holy Ghost / 14th Superior of this community / who died on the 3rd February 1918 / aged 74 years / Professed 50 years Prioress 6 years / R.I.P. / Ecce ancilla domini / fiat mihi secundum verbum (tuum) /
Sister Joseph Sales, 14th Prioress

122: O/LE/17   Headstone, round top with raised shoulders and Patriarchal cross of Jerusalem at top.
Mrs / MARY Benedict STOWRTON (*sic*) **/ deceased 27th December / 1850 / aged 70 / R I P /**
Sister Mary Benedict [STOURTON]

123: O/LE/19   Headstone, round top with scooped shoulders and heavily embossed DOM over Patriarchal cross of Jerusalem at top with S S either side.
The Reverend Mother Prioress / ANNE Mary Aloysia Austin CLIFFORD / of the Sacred Heart / deceased January 14th 1844 / aged 71 years / Professed 50 years Prioress 6 months / Raised to the painful dignity of Prioress / after an humble life of fifty years / she soon (*possible mason's errors:* **enchaseddiitt is we) piously hope / for the (wenly) crown the reward of / virtues / by which she had long edified the / community / Requiescat in pace /**
Sister Aloysia Austin, 10th Prioress

124: O/LE/20   Headstone, round top with scooped shoulders and heavily embossed DOM over Patriarchal cross of Jerusalem at top with S S either side.
The Reverend Mother Prioress / ELIZABETH Mary Regis GERARD / of the Infant Jesus / deceased June 13th 1843 / aged 72 years Professed 35 years / Prioress 27 years / Renouncing great wordly advantages / she chose for her portion the cross of Christ / at a period when earth and hell / were leagued against it / Faithfully and meekly she bore it / through life / and as we piously hope now rests / with it in glory / Requiescat in pace /
Sister Mary Regis, 9th Prioress

125: O/LE/22   Headstone, round top with scooped shoulders and embossed cross.
The Reverend JOSEPH TRISTRAM / S J / deceased April 14 1843 / aged 77 years / Requiescat in pace /
Jesuit, chaplain to Community 1837–43 [CROSS]

126: O/LE/24   Headstone, round top with raised shoulders and embossed cross at top.
Mrs ANNA MARIA GANDOLFI / deceas[ed 23] July 184[2] / aged 59 years / R.I.P.
Ex-pupil; Boarder

127: O/LE/25   Headstone, round top with raised shoulders and small cross.
Miss MATILDA KING / deceased Jan[uary] 14 1841 / aged 18 years / R.I.P. /
Ex-pupil; Boarder

128: O/LE/27   Headstone, gothic top.
Miss / ANNA MARIA LYNCH / deceased / 1st April 1815 / aged 14 / R.I.P. /
Pupil, died at school

129: O/LE/29   Headstone, round top with scooped shoulders.
Miss / SARAH JORDAN / deceased / Feb[ruar]y 3rd 1815 / aged 16 years / R.I.P. /
Pupil, died at school

130: O/LE/30   Cross with central IHS and ribboned 'Crux ave spes unica', on triple plinth and kerb.
North side, top plinth: **I.H.S / In grateful memory /**
Middle plinth: **of my dear father and friend / the Rev. JAMES BROWNBILL. S. J. / who died at New Hall Jan[uar]y 14th 1880 / aged 82 years /**
Bottom plinth: **Anima serena memento mei / in valle lacrymarum / cum animam meam videris / in divina Christi facie / R.I.P. /**
Jesuit, chaplain to Community 1863–80

131: O/LE/32   Headstone, round top with raised shoulders and Patriarchal cross of Jerusalem at top with S S either side.
Ven Mother ELEONORA / Mary Aloysia WELD / deceased March 20th 1893 / aged 79 years / R.I.P. /
Sister Mary Aloysia

132: O/LE/34   Headstone, round top with raised shoulders and Patriarchal cross of Jerusalem at top with S S either side.
Venerable Mother MARIA / Aloysia Sales LOUGHNAN / deceased 30th May 1904 / aged 88 years / R.I.P. /
Sister Aloysia Sales

133: O/LE/35	Headstone, gothic top with heavily embossed Patriarchal cross of Jerusalem at top. **The Venerable Mother / JULIA Mary / Aloysia Austin BUTLER / of the Sacred Hearts of Jesus & Mary / 13th Superior of this community / who died on the 29th May 1915 / aged 91 years / Professed 63 years Prioress during 39 years / R.I.P. / In te domino sperat / non confundia in (eteri)um /** *Sister Aloysia Austin, 13th Prioress*
134: O/LD/36	Headstone, curved top with raised round shoulders with Patriarchal cross of Jerusalem at top with S S either side. **Sister GRACE Mary / Rose HARWOOD / deceased April 19th 1895 / aged 38 years / R.I.P. /** *Sister Rose*
135: O/LD/35	Headstone, curved top with raised round shoulders with Patriarchal cross of Jerusalem at top with S S either side. **Sister LOUISA Mary / Aloysia Stanislaus / ERRINGTON / deceased April 26th 1895 / aged 26 years / R.I.P. /** *Sister Aloysia Stanislaus*
136: O/LD/34	Headstone, curved top with raised round shoulders with Patriarchal cross of Jerusalem at top with S S either side. **Mother ADELAIDE Mary / Loyola CABALLERO / deceased 24th February 189[5] / aged 64 years / R.I.P. /** *Sister Mary Loyola*
137: O/LD/32	Headstone, curved top with raised round shoulders with Patriarchal cross of Jerusalem at top with S S either side. **Mother HARRIET Mary / Gertrude BARRAUD / deceased 14 December 1894 / aged 7[5] years / R.I.P. /** *Sister Mary Gertrude*
138: O/LD/30	Headstone, curved top with raised round shoulders with Patriarchal cross of Jerusalem at top with S S either side. **Mother MARIA Mary / Berchmans CRONIN / deceased 7th May 1890 / aged 37 years / R.I.P. /** *Sister Mary Berchmans*
139: O/LD/29	Headstone, curved top with raised round shoulders. **Miss / LUCY GALLWEY / deceased / on the 10th of Jan[uar]y 18[34] / aged 1[4] years / R.I.P. /** *Pupil, died at school*
140: O/LD/27	Headstone, curved top with raised round shoulders. **Miss / JANE WHITESIDE / deceased / on the 14th of Jan[uary] 1837 / aged 16 years / R.I.P. /** *Pupil, died at school*

Memorial Inscriptions

141: O/LD/25   Headstone, curved top with scalloped shoulders and leaning Latin cross in roundel top centre.
Miss [THERESA] THOMAS / deceased March 28 1844 /
aged 58 years / R.I.P. /
The angel of the Lord shall encamp / around about them that fear him: /
and shall deliver them(:) taste and / see that the Lord is sweet /
Infirmarian and Organist

142: O/LD/24   Headstone, gothic top with Patriarchal cross of Jerusalem top centre.
Mrs MARGARET BARRY / deceased Nov[ember] 1(5) 1846 /
aged 45 years / R.I.P.
Sister Mary Christina

143: O/LD/23   Headstone, gothic top with Patriarchal cross of Jerusalem at top with S S either side.
Mother Mary Cecilia / HERMIONE de FONTENAY / deceased at /
Newnham Paddox Rugby[5] / 24th April 1945 / aged 53 years / R.I.P. /
Sister Mary Cecilia

144: O/LD/22   Headstone, curved top with raised round shoulders with slanting Patriarchal cross of Jerusalem at top.
Mrs MARY Sales / LAURENSON / deceased 24th August / 1848 /
aged 44 years / R.I.P. /
Sister Mary Sales [the younger]

145: O/LD/21   Headstone, gothic top with Patriarchal cross of Jerusalem at top with S S either side.
Sister Teresa Ignatius / MARY FITZGERALD /
deceased 18 September 1937 / aged 51 years / R.I.P. /
Sister Teresa Ignatius

146: O/LD/20   Headstone, curved top with raised round shoulders with Patriarchal cross of Jerusalem at top with S S either side.
Mrs / ELIZABETH ARCHDEACON / deceased 25th April 1849 /
aged 84 years / R.I.P. /
Sister Mary Augustine

147: O/LD/19   Headstone, curved top with raised round shoulders with Patriarchal cross of Jerusalem at top with S S either side.
Mrs / MARY Mechtilda GANDOLFI / deceased 22nd October 1850 /
aged 79 years / R.I.P. /
Sister Mary Mechtilda

148: O/LD/18   Headstone, gothic top with Patriarchal cross of Jerusalem at top with S S either side.
Mother Mary Angela / ISABELLA COVENTRY /
deceased 2nd March 1936 / aged 81 years / R.I.P. /
Sister Mary Angela

---

[5]   See note 3 above.

149: O/LD/17 Headstone, curved top with raised round shoulders with slanting Patriarchal cross of Jerusalem at top.
Mrs LAURA Mary Josephine / LAWRENSON /
deceased 16th May 1853 / aged 41 years / R.I.P. /
Sister Mary Josephine

150: O/LD/16 Headstone, gothic top with Patriarchal cross of Jerusalem at top with S S either side.
Mother Mary Dismas / ANGELA WELD /
deceased 7th December 1933 / aged 58 years / R.I.P. /
Burial ground plan shows Sister Mary Dismas

151: O/LD/15 Headstone, curved top with raised round shoulders with slanting Patriarchal cross of Jerusalem at top with S S either side.
Mrs. EMMA Mary / Rose FREEMAN / deceased 26th July 1863 /
aged 63 years / R.I.P. /
Sister Rose

152: O/LD/14 Headstone, curved top with raised round shoulders with Patriarchal cross of Jerusalem at top with S S either side.
Sister ROS[ALINDA] / Bridget OSMOND /
deceased Sept[ember] 13 1866 / aged 85 years / R.I.P. /
Sister Bridget

153: O/LD/13 Headstone, curved top with raised round shoulders with Patriarchal cross of Jerusalem at top with S S either side.
Mother / Mary Francis Xavier / CATHERINE RORKE /
deceased 27 Feb[ruary] 1869 / aged 68 years / R.I.P. /
Sister Francis Xavier

154: O/LD/12 Headstone, curved top with raised round shoulders with Patriarchal cross of Jerusalem at top with S S either side.
Mother Lucretia / FRANCES Mary / Stanislas (*sic*) **HUBBARD /**
deceased 19 of May 1873 / aged 68 years / R.I.P. /
Sister Mary Stanislaus

155: O/LD/11 Headstone, curved top with raised round shoulders with Patriarchal cross of Jerusalem at top with S S either side.
Mother MARY / Catherine KENDAL / deceased 2nd April 187[5] /
aged 76 years / R.I.P. /
Sister Mary Catherine

156: O/LD/9 Headstone, curved top with raised round shoulders with Patriarchal cross of Jerusalem at top with S S either side.
Mother WILLIAMINA / Mary Xavier / RUTHERFORD /
deceased 19 Jan[uary] 1877 / aged 55 years / R.I.P. /
Sister Mary Xavier

157: O/LD/7 Headstone, curved top with raised round shoulders with Patriarchal cross of Jerusalem at top with S S either side. Face badly eroded.
Je[sus] Ma[ry] / Mother [ISABEL]LA) /

Memorial Inscriptions

[M]ary A[LOYSIA] [P]ORTER /
deceased [12th Nove]mber 19[11] / aged 74 years / R.I.P. /
Sister Mary Aloysia, Religious of the Réunion an Sacre Coeur

158: O/LD/5   Headstone, curved top with raised round shoulders with Patriarchal cross of Jerusalem at top with S S either side.
Venerable Mother / ELIZABETH / Mary Sales PORTER /
deceased 23rd January 1913 / aged 78 years / R.I.P. /
Sister Mary Sales

159: O/LD/4   Slate headstone, gothic top with raised gothic shoulders and cross in oval top centre.
Miss LOUISA / MARIA GANDOLFI / deceased June 27th 1866 /
aged 81 years / R.I.P. /
Ex-pupil; Boarder

160: O/LD/3   Headstone, gothic top with Patriarchal cross of Jerusalem at top with S S either side.
Venerable Mother / ANDALUSIA Mary Anne / Teresa PURCELL /
deceased 18th February 1921 / aged 79 years / R.I.P. /
Sister Anne Teresa

161: O/LD/2   Headstone, gothic top with Patriarchal cross of Jerusalem at top with S S either side.
Mother ELIZABETH / Mary Joseph FALLS / deceased 3rd June 1922 /
aged 63 years / R.I.P. /
Sister Mary Joseph

162: O/LD/1   Headstone, gothic top with Patriarchal cross of Jerusalem at top with S S either side.
Sister MARY ANNE / Elizabeth MESCHER / deceased 18th April 1925 /
aged 86 years / R.I.P. /
Sister Elizabeth

163: O/LC/1   Headstone, gothic top with Patriarchal cross of Jerusalem at top with S S either side.
Sister MARY / Philomena LUCAS / deceased 28th April 1923 /
aged 78 years / R.I.P. /
Sister Philomena

164: O/LC/2   Headstone, gothic top with Patriarchal cross of Jerusalem at top with S S either side.
Sister CHARLOTTE Mary / Magdalen Sales THUNDER /
deceased 28th November 1921 / aged 39 years / R.I.P. /
Sister Magdalen Sales

165: O/LC/3   Headstone, round top with raised round shoulders and Patriarchal cross of Jerusalem top centre with S S either side.
Mother CATHERINE Mary / Ann Joseph HIGGINS /
deceased 16th December 1918 / aged 76 years / R.I.P. /
Sister Anne Joseph

The Secret Cemetery

166: O/LC/4 Headstone, round top with raised round shoulders and Latin cross at angle at top.
Mrs MARY HE[N]SON / deceased 29th Sept[ember] 1864 / aged 66 years / R.I.P. /
Servant

167: O/LC/5 Headstone, round top with raised round shoulders and Patriarchal cross of Jerusalem at top with S S either side.
Sister MARY ANN FINN / deceased 2nd November 1913 / aged 78 years /R.I. P. /
Sister Anne

168: O/LC/6 Headstone, gothic top with Patriarchal cross of Jerusalem at top with S S either side.
Mother Angela Joseph / VICTORIA RUSHBROOKE / deceased 21st February 19[3]2 / aged [72] years / R.I.P. /
Sister Angela Joseph

169: O/LC/7 Headstone, round top with raised round shoulders and Patriarchal cross of Jerusalem at top with S S either side.
Venerable Mother / ANNE Mary Austin / McSWINEY / deceased 25th November 1915 / aged 85 years / R.I.P. /
Sister Mary Austin

170: O/LC/8 Fleury cross with 'M' surmounted by a crown at intersection, on pedestal and plinth.
Pedestal, north side: **Sacred to the memory of / AGNES MARY daughter / of MICHAEL RUSSELL / of Glanmore Charleville / Ireland / born 14th January 1885 / died 22nd November 1898 /**
Pupil, died at school

171: O/LC/9 Headstone, round top with raised round shoulders and Patriarchal cross of Jerusalem at top with S S either side.
Sister FRANCES CLARE / Mary Joseph ELLISON / Novice / deceased 13th October 1876 / aged 21 years / R.I.P. /
Sister Mary Joseph

172: O/LC/11 Headstone, round top with raised round shoulders and Patriarchal cross of Jerusalem at top with S S either side.
Ven[era]ble Mother MARY / Anne Teresa BUNNEY / deceased [31] Jan[uary] 1875 / aged [87] years / R.I.P. /
Sister Anne Teresa

173: O/LC/12 Headstone, round top with raised round shoulders and Patriarchal cross of Jerusalem at top with S S either side.
Venerable Mother / LELIA Mary / Joseph HALY / deceased 1 of April 1873 / aged 8[3] years / R.I.P. /
Sister Mary Joseph

174: O/LC/13 Headstone, round top with raised round shoulders and Patriarchal cross of Jerusalem at top with S S either side.

Memorial Inscriptions

**Mother Mary Josephine / PAULINA JERNINGHAM /
deceased 4 Feb[ruary] 1868 / aged 31 years / R.I.P. /**
Sister Mary Josephine

175: O/LC/14   Headstone, round top with raised round shoulders and Patriarchal cross of Jerusalem at top with S S either side.
**Mrs ANNE / Juliana BLEASDALE / deceased 28 April 1865 /
aged 80 years / R.I.P. /**
Sister Juliana

176: O/LC/15   Headstone, round top with raised round shoulders and slanting Patriarchal cross of Jerusalem at top with S S either side.
**Mrs MARY Martha LILLY / deceased 16 of Nov[ember] 1863 /
aged 79 years / R.I.P. /**
Sister Martha

177: O/LC/17   Headstone, round top with raised round shoulders and slanting Patriarchal cross of Jerusalem at top with S S either side.
**Mrs ANN Mary / Anselm BLEASDALE / deceased 31st Jan[uar]y 1863 /
aged 48 years / R.I.P. /**
Sister Anselm

178: O/LC/19   Headstone, round top with raised round shoulders and slanting Patriarchal cross of Jerusalem at top.
**Mrs / MARY Helen CRAVEN / deceased 22nd May / 1852 /
aged 56 years / R.I.P. /**
Sister Helen

179: O/LC/20   Headstone, round top with raised round shoulders and slanting Patriarchal cross of Jerusalem at top.
Mrs / MARGARET Elisabeth (*sic*) **BEAUMONT /
deceased 20th March / 1852 / aged 70 / R.I.P. /**
Sister Elizabeth

180: O/LC/22   Headstone, round top with raised round shoulders and slanting Patriarchal cross of Jerusalem at top.
**Mrs / ELIZABETH Mary STEEL / deceased 27th May 1851 /
aged 70 years / R.I.P. /**
Sister Mary

181: O/LC/24   Headstone, round top with raised round shoulders, shaled at top.
[Mrs ELIZABETH COLES] (*remainder illegible*) **/
[died 18 December 1848] aged [34 year]s / R.I.P. /**
Sister Aloysia Joseph

182: O/LC/25   Headstone, round top with raised round shoulders and slanting Patriarchal cross of Jerusalem at top.
**Mrs CATHERINE [JEMIMA] HAL[L] / deceased 18th October / 1848 /
aged 57 years / R.I.P. /**
Sister Felicitas

183: O/LC/27	Headstone, round top with raised round shoulders and slanting Latin cross at top. **Mrs MARY JANE / MOERS / deceased 27th August / 1848 / aged 72 years / R.I.P. /** *Servant*	
184: O/LC/29	Headstone, round top with raised round shoulders and slanting Latin cross at top, shaled at top. **[Elizabeth Barwell, died 1 September] 1847 / aged 73 years / R.I.P. /** *Servant*	
185: O/LC/30	Headstone, round top with Patriarchal cross of Jerusalem at top with S S either side. **Sister ELIZABETH / Mary Cleophœ / MUTTER / deceased 15th July 1892 / aged 79 years / R.I.P. /** *Sister Cleophae*	
186: O/LC/32	Headstone, round top with Patriarchal cross of Jerusalem at top with S S either side. **Sister SARAH Mary / Veronica KING / deceased 12th Feb[ruar]y 1894 / aged 72 years / R.I.P. /** *Sister Veronica*	
187: O/LC/34	Headstone, round top with Patriarchal cross of Jerusalem at top with S S either side. **Sister LOUISA Mary / Felicitas MORTLOCK / deceased 12th February 1895 / aged 53 years / R.I.P. /** *Sister Felicitas*	
188: n/a	List of lay people shows BERNARD L. HAMMOND died 3rd May 1859, of Greenwich. No memorial found. *Died whilst visiting his aunts at New Hall*	
189: O/LB/35	Fleury cross with 'M' surmounted by a crown at intersection, on pedestal, within kerb. *North side:* **MARY JOSEPHINE KENDAL / died October 20 1893 / He that is mighty hath / done great things to me: / and Holy is His name /** *Pupil, died at school*	
190: O/LB/34	Cross on pedestal within kerb. *North side:* **Of your charity pray for / MARY / daughter of J.G. RIDDELL / of Felton Park / died March 4th 1895 / aged 15 years 11 months / R.I.P. /** *Pupil, died at school*	
191: O/LB/33	Cross now broken from pedestal and base. *North side:* **Pray for the soul / of / LYDIA M. HILLIARD / deceased at New Hall / 25 Nov[ember] 1937 / aged 38 years / R.I.P. /**	

Memorial Inscriptions

192: O/LB/30   Headstone, curved top with raised round shoulders with Patriarchal cross of Jerusalem at top with S S either side.
**Mother ALICE Mary / Anthony Joseph / CLEVERLY /
deceased 20th October 1889 / aged 39 years / R.I.P. /**
Sister Antony Joseph

193: O/LB/29   Headstone, curved top with raised round shoulders with Patriarchal cross of Jerusalem at top.
**Mrs ANN Scholastica HACKING / deceased 25th Feb[ruar]y 1854 /
aged 57 years / R.I.P. /**
Sister Scholastica

194: O/LB/27   Headstone, curved top with raised round shoulders with Patriarchal cross of Jerusalem at top with S S either side.
**Mrs ELIZABETH Mary / Gertrude NEWSHAM /
deceased 15th November / 1854 / aged 70 years / R.I.P. /**
Sister Mary Gertrude

195: O/LB/25   Headstone, curved top with raised round shoulders with the letter M surmounted by a Latin cross at top.
**Miss / CATHERINE CRISPIN / deceased 21st Feb[ruar]y / 1856 /
[aged] 16 / R.I.P. /**
Pupil, died at school

196: O/LB/24   Headstone, curved top with raised round shoulders with Patriarchal cross of Jerusalem at top with S S either side.
**Mrs BARBARA POOLE / deceased 11th December / 1856 /
aged 54 / R.I.P. /**
Sister Magdalen Sales

197: O/LB/22   Headstone, curved top with raised round shoulders with Patriarchal cross of Jerusalem at top with S S either side.
**Mrs CLARE Mary Joseph / Sales DIGNAN / deceased / March 23 1857 /
aged 70 / R.I.P. /**
Sister Joseph Sales

198: O/LB/20   Headstone, curved top with raised round shoulders with Patriarchal cross of Jerusalem at top with S S either side.
**Mrs Mary TERESA / Bernard CARPUE /
deceased 9th Oct[ober] / 1857 / aged 75 / R.I.P. /**
Sister Mary Bernard

199: O/LB/19   Headstone, curved top with raised round shoulders with slanting Patriarchal cross of Jerusalem at top with S S either side.
**Mrs. / LOUISA Mary / Constantia COLEMAN /
deceased 22nd July 1861 / aged 80 / R.I.P. /**
Sister Mary Constantia

200: O/LB/17	Headstone, curved top with raised round shoulders with Patriarchal cross of Jerusalem at top with S S either side.
Mrs MARY Agnes BROWN / deceased / 8th of February 1862 / aged 89 years / R.I.P. /
Sister Agnes

201: O/LB/15	Headstone, curved top with raised round shoulders with slanting Patriarchal cross of Jerusalem at top with S S either side.
Mrs Mary / BARBARA SIMMONS / deceased 16 Feb[ruary] 1864 / aged 84 years / R.I.P. /
Sister Barbara

202: O/LB/14	Headstone, curved top with raised round shoulders with Patriarchal cross of Jerusalem at top with S S either side.
Mrs MARTHA Mary / Ursula VAN HAM / deceased 28 of Nov[ember] 1864 / aged 79 years / R.I.P. /
Sister Mary Ursula

203: O/LB/13	Headstone, curved top with raised round shoulders with Patriarchal cross of Jerusalem at top with S S either side.
Mrs MARY ANN Aloysia / Gertrude WRIGHT / deceased 21 Feb[ruary] 1865 / aged 47 years / R.I.P. /
Sister Aloysia Gertrude

204: O/LB/12	Headstone, curved top with raised round shoulders with Patriarchal cross of Jerusalem at top with S S either side.
Mother Mary Francis / MATILDA CARTER / deceased 2nd Nov[ember] 1866 / aged 78 years / R.I.P. /
Sister Francis Xavier

205: O/LB/11	Headstone, curved top with raised round shoulders with Patriarchal cross of Jerusalem at top with S S either side.
Sister MARY / Winefrid RICHARDS / deceased Nov[ember] 24 1874 / aged 52 years / R.I.P. /
Sister Winifred

206: O/LB/9	Headstone, curved top with raised round shoulders with Patriarchal cross of Jerusalem at top with S S either side.
Mother MARGARET / Mary Aloysia / Stanislass MASON / deceased 22nd May 1875 / aged 56 years / R.I.P. /
Sister Aloysia Stanislaus

207: O/LB/8	Cross on double plinth and base within kerb. North side of cross decorated with carved flowers wrapped with ribbon with 'My Jesus mercy Mary help'. *North side, top plinth:* **Pray for the repose / of the soul of / MINNIE / beloved wife of /** *Bottom plinth:* **ROGER HERBERT PLOWDEN / of Strachur Farm, Argylleshire / died April 4th 1899, aged 38 / R.I.P. /**
Ex-pupil; née Tump

Memorial Inscriptions

208: O/LA/1   Headstone, gothic top with Patriarchal cross of Jerusalem at top.
**Sister CATHERINE / Mary [O']DONOHUE /
deceased 21st April 1921 / aged 89 years / R.I.P. /**
Sister Mary

209: O/LA/2   Headstone, round top with raised round shoulders and Patriarchal cross of Jerusalem at top with S S either side.
**Sister MADELINE Mary / Agnes Philip DICKINSON /
deceased 5th February 1919 / aged [37] years / R.I.P. /**
Sister Agnes Philip

210: O/LA/3   Headstone, round top with raised round shoulders and Patriarchal cross of Jerusalem at top with S S either side.
**Venerable Mother AGNES / Mary Clare SCOLES /
deceased 13th November 1918 / aged 84 years / R.I.P. /**
Sister Mary Clare

211: O/LA/4   Headstone, curved top with raised round shoulders.
**WILLIAM / ABRAHAM PHILLIPSON /
deceased / November 23 1839 / aged [5]2 years / R.I.P. /**
Groundsman

212: O/LA/5   Headstone, curved top with raised round shoulders.
**HENRY LACEY / deceased / September 20 1841 / aged 80 years /
R.I.P. /**
Servant

213: O/LA/6   Headstone, gothic top with Patriarchal cross of Jerusalem at top with S S either side.
**Sister Mary Margaret / AGNES KENDAL /
deceased 29th November 1935 / aged 56 years / R.I.P. /**
Sister Mary Margaret

214: O/LA/7   Headstone, round top with raised round shoulders.
**Mrs / ELIZABETH KNIGHT / deceased 22nd Feb[ruar]y 1860 /
aged 59 / R.I.P. /**
Servant

215: O/LA/8   Headstone, round top with raised round shoulders and slanting Latin cross at top.
**Mrs CATHERINE JARRETT / deceased 6th April 186[4] /
aged 89 years /R.I.P. /**
Governess

216: O/LA/10   Headstone, gothic top with Patriarchal cross of Jerusalem at top with S S either side.
**Sister MARY HELEN / Helen TRAVERS / 4th September 1949 /
aged 73 / R.I.P. /**
Sister Helen

217: O/LA/13   Headstone, gothic top with Patriarchal cross of Jerusalem at top with S S either side.
Sister / Mary Winefride / EMILY HUGHES / deceased 24th April / 1954 / aged 71 / R.I.P. /
Sister Mary Winefride

218: O/LA/15   Headstone, gothic top with Patriarchal cross of Jerusalem at top with S S either side.
Sister Mary / Christina Magdelene / MURIEL LLOYD-THOMAS / deceased / 18th December 1953 / aged 73 years / R.I.P. /
Sister Christina Magdalene

219: O/LA/16   Headstone, gothic top with Patriarchal cross of Jerusalem at top with S S either side.
Sister / Mary Ann Frances / FRANCES / TRAPPES-LOMAX / deceased 4th January / 1954 / aged 80 /
Sister Ann Frances

220: O/LA/18   Headstone, gothic top with Patriarchal cross of Jerusalem at top with S S either side.
Sister Mary / Margaret Francis / CATHERINE / TRAPPES-LOMAX / deceased / 2nd August 1953 / aged 82 years / R.I.P. /
Sister Margaret Francis

221: O/LA/20   Headstone, gothic top with Patriarchal cross of Jerusalem at top with S S either side.
Sister / Mary Cleophae / ELLEN LANE / deceased 16th November / 1952 / aged 78 years / R.I.P. /
Sister Cleophae

222: O/LA/21   Headstone, gothic top with Patriarchal cross of Jerusalem at top with S S either side.
Sister / Mary Ignatia / Joseph ALOYSIA / BRENNFLECK / deceased 20th May / 1951 / aged 80 years / R.I.P. /
Sister Ignatia Joseph

223: O/LA/23   Headstone, gothic top with Patriarchal cross of Jerusalem at top with S S either side.
Sister / Mary Margaret / Angela CATHERINE / WHELAN / deceased 2nd October / 1952 / aged 90 years / R.I.P. /
Sister Margaret Angela

224: O/LA/32   Large tapered double plinth with part of cross now fallen and within kerb.
Top plinth: **Jesu mercy / Mary help /** *Bottom plinth:* **Of your charity / pray for the repose of the soul of / Rev. JOSEPH DALY / who died July 24th 1892 / aged 29 years / R.I.P. /**

225: O/LA/33   Decorative fleury cross on tapered plinth with cross surmounting the letter M at top, south end of kerb.
In memory of / CLARA MAUD FITZPATRICK / child of Mary / deceased March 28th 1890 / aged 2[1] years / R.I.P. /

**Beati qui habitant in domo tua domine /
in sæcula sæculorum laudabunt te /**
Pupil, died at school

226: O/LA/34 — Fleury cross on plinth, south end of kerb.
**URSULA MARY KENDAL / died October 14 189[3] /
I rejoiced at the things that / were said to me; we shall go /
into the house of the Lord / [aged 14 years]**
Pupil, died at school

227: O/LA/35 — Fleury cross on plinth, south end of kerb.
**MARY ANTONIA / JOSEPHINE BRITTEN / died October 14. 1893 /
In peace in the self same / I will sleep and I will rest / [aged 14 years]**
Pupil, died at school

228: E1/1 — Large wooden cross surmounted by wooden sloping roof.
**ELIZABETH FLORINDA / de BURGH ATKINSON /
25th November / 1956 / aged 14 / R.I.P. /**

229: E1/2 — Large wooden cross surmounted by wooden sloping roof.
TERESA MERRELLS / died 6 July / 195[7] / [aged 46 years]

230: E1/3 — Large wooden cross surmounted by wooden sloping roof.
**WINIFRED MARY DOLAN T.O.S.F. / died June [11] / [1958] /
[aged 90 years]**

231: E1/4 — Large wooden cross surmounted by wooden sloping roof.
**Reverend REUBEN BUTLER S.J / died 5 Dec[ember] / 1959 /
aged / (6)7 /**

232: E1/5 — Large wooden cross surmounted by wooden sloping roof.
**KATHLEEN ISOBEL TERNAN / died 28 Oct[ober] / 1[962] /
aged / 61 /**

233: E1/6 — Large wooden cross surmounted by wooden sloping roof.
**EDITH JOYCE SYGROVE / died 15th December 1970 aged 72 /
PERCY SYGROVE / died 23rd February 1979 aged 78 / R.I.P. /**

234: E1/7 — Large wooden cross surmounted by wooden sloping roof.
**MARGARET EILEEN KIRK [née HARTARD] / born 20th March /
1919 / died / 25th Oct[ober] / 1976 / R.I.P. /**

235: E1/8 — Large wooden cross surmounted by wooden sloping roof, and small bronze plaque, and small red and white and blue rugby ball at base of cross.
**In / loving / memory / IAN McLEOD JONES /
died [2nd] July, 1979 aged 45 /**
Plaque: **SHAUN McLEOD-JONES / 20th May 1963 / 31st May 2003 /
"I won't back down" /**
Sister Mary Magdalen, Archivist, says Shaun was a rugby player

236: E1/9   Headstone, gothic top.
FRANCISCA FUSTER / CORTES / Fallecio / el 23 de Noviembre 1983 / A los 66 anos de edad / Recuerdo de tus hijos / nietos y companeros /

237: E1/10   Headstone, curved top with small flat shoulders, on base with separate flower holder.
In / loving memory of / PENELOPE / darling daughter of / JOAN and DAVID WAITE / 20.10.1954–30.3.1984 / "She will make the face of / heaven so bright" /

238: E1/11   Stone cross.
MIKE [MICHAEL WILLIAM] KING / 1934–1990 / [died 23rd January]

239: E/L1/1   Headstone, gothic top with Patriarchal cross of Jerusalem etched at top centre.
S. Mary Gabriel / MARGARET ANN WAUD WAUD / died 19th December 1956 / aged 89 / R.I.P. /
Sister Mary Gabriel

240: E/L1/2   Headstone, gothic top with Patriarchal cross of Jerusalem etched at top centre.
S. Mary Gertrude / EMILY TURNER / died 8th October 1958 / aged 77 / R.I.P. /
Sister Mary Gertrude

241: E/L1/3   Headstone, gothic top with Patriarchal cross of Jerusalem etched at top centre.
S. Magdalene Joseph / NORA HAGUE / died 16th November 1958 / aged 78 / R.I.P.
Sister Magdalene Joseph

242: E/L1/4   Headstone, gothic top with Patriarchal cross of Jerusalem etched at top centre.
S. Mary Agnes / MAUD COOPER / died 30th January 1959 / aged 63 / R.I.P.
Sister Mary Agnes

243: E/L1/5   Headstone, gothic top with Patriarchal cross of Jerusalem etched at top centre.
S. Magdalene Philip / ALICE MARY CREWSE / died 21st April 1960 / aged 90 / R.I.P. /
Sister Magdalene Philip

244: E/L1/6   Headstone, gothic top with Patriarchal cross of Jerusalem etched at top centre.
S. Mary John / MILDRED DALY / died 5th August 1960 / aged 62 / R.I.P. /
Sister Mary John

245: E/L1/7   Headstone, gothic top with Patriarchal cross of Jerusalem etched at top centre.
S. Mary Alfonsa / GLADYS SWALLOW / died 19th October 1961 / aged 70 / R.I.P. /
Sister Mary Alfonsa

246: E/L1/8   Headstone, gothic top with Patriarchal cross of Jerusalem etched at top centre.
S. Mary Salome / ELLEN CLANCY / died 4th February 1965 / aged 88 / R.I.P. /
Sister Mary Salome

247: E/L1/9   Headstone, gothic top with Patriarchal cross of Jerusalem etched at top centre.
S. Mary Catherine / ELIZABETH ANN CLANCY / died 26th March 1965 / aged 94 / R.I.P. /
Sister Mary Catherine

248: E/L1/10   Headstone, gothic top with Patriarchal cross of Jerusalem etched at top centre.
S. Mary Paul / EVELYN POWER / died 21 Nov[ember] 1965 / aged 69 / R.I.P. /
Sister Mary Paul

249: E/L1/11   Headstone, gothic top with Patriarchal cross of Jerusalem etched at top centre.
S. Mary Veronica / SARAH McCARTNEY / died 25th February 1967 / aged 91 / R.I.P. /
Sister Mary Veronica

250: E/L1/12   Headstone, gothic top with Patriarchal cross of Jerusalem etched at top centre.
S. Magdalene Helen / MONICA MARY WARRINGTON / died 1st May 1968 / aged 85 / R.I.P. /
Sister Magdalene Helen

251: E/L1/13   Headstone, gothic top with Patriarchal cross of Jerusalem etched at top centre.
S. Mary Christina 16th Prioress / EDITH O'CONNELL / died 15th November 1970 / aged 91 / R.I.P. /
Sister Mary Christina, 16th Prioress

252: E/L1/14   Headstone, gothic top with Patriarchal cross of Jerusalem etched at top centre.
S. Antony Magdalene / FRANCES RUSSELL / died 30th December 1972 / aged 92 / R.I.P. /
Sister Antony Magdalene

253: E/L1/15   Headstone, gothic top with Patriarchal cross of Jerusalem etched at top centre.
S. Mary Genevieve / MARY POWER / died 12th January 1973 / aged 86 / R.I.P. /
Sister Mary Genevieve

254: E/L1/16   Headstone, gothic top with Patriarchal cross of Jerusalem etched at top centre.
S. Mary Berchmans / BLANCHE DESOMBRES / died 6th August 1973 / aged 82 / R.I.P. /
Sister Mary Berchmans

255: E/L1/17   Headstone, gothic top with Patriarchal cross of Jerusalem etched at top centre.
S. Mary Bernard ETHELDREDA RUSSELL / died 27 Dec[ember] / 1974 / aged / 87 / R.I.P /
Sister Mary Bernard

256: E/L1/18   Headstone, gothic top with Patriarchal cross of Jerusalem etched at top centre.
S. Antony MARY MYERSCOUGH / died 3 Sept[ember] / 1976 / aged / 99 / R.I.P. /
Sister Antony

257: E/L1/19   Headstone, gothic top with Patriarchal cross of Jerusalem etched at top centre.
S. Magdalen Dolores NORAH WILSON / died 7th Dec[ember] / 1978 / aged / 91 / R.I.P. /
Sister Magdalen Dolores

258: E/L1/20   Headstone, gothic top with Patriarchal cross of Jerusalem etched at top centre.
Sister Mary Gerard ELIZABETH DEVINE / died 4th October / 1980 / aged / 91 / R.I.P. /
Sister Gerard

259: E/L1/21   Headstone, gothic top with Patriarchal cross of Jerusalem etched at top centre.
S. Mary Ignatius / KATHLEEN KERENHAPPUCH BROWN / died 5th Jan[uary] / 1981 / aged / 66 / R.I.P. /
Sister Mary Ignatius

260: E/L1/22   Headstone, gothic top with Patriarchal cross of Jerusalem etched at top centre.
S. JOY Mary CAREY / died 8th July / 1981 / aged / 78 / R.I.P. /
Sister Joy

261: E/L1/23   Headstone, gothic top with Patriarchal cross of Jerusalem etched at top centre.
S. Mary Emmanuel / DOROTHY MINCHIN FLAVIN / died 6th Sept[ember] / 1981 / aged / 84 / R.I.P. /
Sister Mary Emmanuel

262: E/L1/24   Small slate headstone, gothic top with Patriarchal cross of Jerusalem incised at top centre.
Sister Mary / MARGARET MARY HOGG / died 1st Sept[ember] 1983 / aged 88 / R.I.P. /
Sister Mary

263: E/L1/25   Small slate headstone, gothic top with Patriarchal cross of Jerusalem incised at top centre.
S. Mary Veronica / 17th Prioress / MARGARET FRANCES / BOLAND / died 8th Dec[ember] 1983 / aged 90 / R.I.P. /
Sister Mary Veronica

264: E/L1/26   Small slate headstone, gothic top with Patriarchal cross of Jerusalem incised at top centre.
S. Teresa Magdalen / FRANCES NAIRNE ROFFEY / died 11th Dec[ember] 1984 / aged 79 / R.I.P. /
Sister Teresa Magdalen

265: E/L1/27   Small slate headstone, gothic top with Patriarchal cross of Jerusalem incised at top centre.
S. Mary Paul / NAOMI E.M. FALKINER / died 28th Jan[uary] 1986 / aged 80 years / R.I.P. /
Sister Mary Paul

266: E/L1/28   Small slate headstone, gothic top with Patriarchal cross of Jerusalem incised at top centre.
S. Anne / ELSIE YOUNG / died 15th April 1986 / aged 97 years / R.I.P. /
Sister Anne

267: E/L1/29   Small slate headstone, gothic top with Patriarchal cross of Jerusalem incised at top centre.
S. Philomena / JANE M.A. McDERMOTT / died 29th Dec[ember] 1987 / aged 84 years / R.I.P. /
Sister Philomena

268: E/L1/30   Small slate headstone, gothic top with Patriarchal cross of Jerusalem incised at top centre.
S. Mary Benedict / BEATRICE MARY / COVERDALE / died 9th February 1990 / aged 75 years / R.I.P. /
Sister Mary Benedict

269: E/L1/31   Small slate headstone, gothic top with Patriarchal cross of Jerusalem incised at top centre.
S. Teresa / EMMA ANNE / EWERS / died 11th May 1992 / aged 87 years / R.I.P. /
Sister Teresa

270: E/L1/32   Small slate headstone, gothic top with Patriarchal cross of Jerusalem incised at top centre.
Sister Mary Joseph / RHODA CLARE / REYNOLDS / died 10th August 1993 / aged 86 years / R.I.P. /
Sister Mary Joseph

271: E/L1/33   Small slate headstone, gothic top with Patriarchal cross of Jerusalem incised at top centre.
Sister Anne Joseph / JOYCE ELIZABETH ROWLAND / died 29th October 1994 / aged 83 years / R.I.P. /
Sister Anne Joseph

272: E/L1/34   Headstone, gothic top with Patriarchal cross of Jerusalem etched at top centre.
Sister Mary / Andrew AMALIA / HERTHA ENGEL / died 1st July 1998 / aged 80 years / RI.P. / RUTH MARGOT / ENGEL / 27.12.1918–9.10.1999 / aged 80 years / R.I.P.
Sister Mary Andrew

273: E/L1/35   Headstone, gothic top with Patriarchal cross of Jerusalem etched at top centre.
Sister Mary / Martha JOAN / MERRELLS / died 26th November 1998 / aged 82 years / R.I.P. /
Sister Mary Martha

274: E/L1/36   Headstone, gothic top with Patriarchal cross of Jerusalem etched at top centre.
Sister Mary / Peter MIRIAM / DAVIES / died 11th February 1999 / aged 76 years / R.I.P. /
Sister Mary Peter

275: E/L2/2   Headstone, gothic top with Patriarchal cross of Jerusalem etched at top centre.
Sister Mary Christopher / 18th Prioress / MARY DOROTHY BRIDGET O'CONNOR / *died 31st August 2003, aged 82* **/ R.I.P. /**
Sister Mary Christopher, 18th Prioress

276: E/L2/1   Headstone, gothic top with Patriarchal cross of Jerusalem etched at top centre.
Sister / Margaret Helen / MARGARET MAY / TERNEY / died 12th December 2000 / aged 95 years / R.I.P. /
Sister Margaret Helen

277: E/L2/3   Headstone, gothic top with Patriarchal cross of Jerusalem etched at top centre.
Sister / Magdalen John / MADELEINE CONSTANCE / EARLE / died 25th September 2006 / aged 92 years / R.I.P. /
Sister Magdalen John

278: E/L2/4   Headstone, gothic top with Patriarchal cross of Jerusalem etched at top centre.
Sister / PAULINE / MARY / CROWTHER / died 18th April 2014 / aged 64 years / R.I.P. /
Sister Pauline

279: E/L2/5   Headstone, gothic top with Patriarchal cross of Jerusalem etched at top centre.

Memorial Inscriptions

Sister / MARY THÉRÈSE / ANN ELIZABETH / BAMFORD / died 21st November 2015 / aged 87 years / R.I.P. /
Sister Thérèse

280: E/L2/6 — Headstone, gothic top with Patriarchal cross of Jerusalem etched at top centre.
Sister / ALICE BELLORD / died 12th September 2016 / aged 77 years / R.I.P.
Sister Alice

281: E/R1/1 — Cross on double plinth.
Cross: **VIRGINIA SHAKERLEY / MASKELL /**
Top plinth, north side: **27 February 1936 / 25 January 1968 /**
Bottom plinth: **Give beauty back to God / G.M.H. /**
Ex-pupil

282: E/R1/2 — Flat tablet with Celtic cross incised at top.
EMMA / CATHERINE / FRANCES / COOKE /
South side: **daughter of / W. R. & A. J. M. COOKE /**
West side: **born 30th Dec[ember] 1962 / died 10th March 1974 /**
Pupil, died at school

283: E/R1/3 — Wooden cross with roof.
Pray / for / NANCY COOKE / born 5 June / 1929 / died / 5 April / 1976 / R.I.P. /
Emma's mother

284: E/R1/4 — Small stone cross on plinth.
North side: **FRANCES EAGAR / 1940–1978 / Faith, humour, courage /**
Ex-pupil; Née REID

285: E/R1/5 — Headstone, curved top.
ELIZABETH GERTRUDE / WARRINGTON / died 24th July 1980 / aged 97 / R.I.P.
Sister of Monica

286: E/R1/6 — Headstone, curved top, on base with flower holder.
JEAN MARGARET / CAMPBELL HALL / 1929–1987 / Darling wife and mother / so much loved and missed / by her husband WILLIAM / and their daughters / JANE, ANNA and CLARE / WILLIAM ERNEST HALL / 1914–2007 / A GREAT MAN—THE MOST LOVED / HUSBAND, FATHER AND GRANDFATHER / HE LIVED A LIFE OF LOVE AND KINDNESS / 'Loves last gift remembrance' /
School staff

287: E/R1/7 — Headstone, flat top.
ROSAMOND / WHATELEY / nee PETRE / 1928 / 1990 / Requiescat / in pace /
Ex-pupil

288: E/R1/8   Headstone, gothic top with Maltese cross at top. Small wooden cross.
GWYNETH ROSALIND / MORRIS née HILL / 1903–1993 / R.I.P. / JOHN WILLIAM TALWIN / MORRIS MBE TD / 1902–2000 /
Cross: **Major JOHN / TALWIN MORRIS MBE / died 26th April 2000 / aged 97 years /**
Parents of Sister Angela

289: E/R1/9   Headstone, curved top with etched roses, on base with flower holder.
In / loving / memory of / JOHN ARNOLD [Jack] FURZE / a dear husband and father / who died 27th March 1994 / aged 80 / Rest in peace /
Local friend

290: E/R1/10   Headstone, gothic top with Patriarchal cross of Jerusalem.
DIANA IRVING PAULINE / JACKSON / [Margot] / 1898–1997 / R.I.P. /
Ex-pupil

291: E/R1/11   Headstone, curved top with etched scenic view, on base with flower holder.
In loving memory of / a beloved wife, mother / & grandmother / GERTRUDE [Trudi] / KITCHEN / born Switzerland 1902 / died 16 August 1997 / Rest in peace / HAROLD HERBERT KITCHEN / 3.10.1919 to 11.8.2001 / Reunited with / the love of his life / Rest in peace /
Springfield Parish.

292: E/R1/12   Headstone, gothic top with Patriarchal cross of Jerusalem.
MAUREEN SYLVIA / CALLOW / née LANIGAN-O'KEEFFE / 29.2.1919–25.12.1999 / Returned home /
Ex-pupil

293: E/R1/13   Headstone, curved top, on base.
In / loving memory of / MARSHALL / DOMINIC de SOUZA 9.10.1912–17.1.2001 / Sadly missed by his wife / children and grandchildren /
Springfield Parish

294: E/R1/14   Headstone, curved top.
ANNABEL PARSONS / 1961–2002 / aged 41 / Most treasured / daughter, sister, / mother & / friend /
Niece of Sister Angela

295: E/R1/15   Headstone, curved top.
Noah Gabriel Beere / Beautiful first born son of / Mahri-Claire and Greg / Stillborn on 11th June 2005 / Always Loved, / Never Forgotten /
Grandson of Jacque McGlynn

296: E/R1/16   Headstone, curved top, on base.
JAMES MULLARKEY / 1945–2007 / Pray for me, as I will for thee, / that we may merrily meet in heaven / St. Thomas More /
Local friend

Memorial Inscriptions

297: E/R1/17   Headstone, curved top, on base.
BETTE / In Peace and / Happiness / 14 . 10 . 1929 / ~ / 11 . 4 . 2010 /
[*Née Parry*]

298: E/R1/18   New grave.
James "Jim" McGhee / died 4 October 2015 / aged 82
Parishioner and friend of the Community

299: E/R2/1   Square cremation tablet on wall.
In / loving memory of / EDNA MAY WILLIAMS / died / 15th Nov[ember] 1983 / aged 83 years /
Household Staff

300: E/R2/2   Square cremation tablet on wall.
In memory / of / ERNIE PALMER / died 19th May 1988 / aged 76 years /
Groundsman

301: E/R2/3   Square cremation tablet on wall.
To the memory / of / DOROTHY MARY / STOKES / 16.3.1913–25.6.1985 / R.I.P. /
Mother of Elizabeth Scott Townsend

302: E/R2/4   Rectangular cremation tablet on wall.
NICOLA KENNEDY / 8.12.69–2.12.89 / Forever in our hearts /
Ex-pupil

303: E/R2/5   Square cremation tablet on wall.
BARRY JAMES / KENNEDY / Beloved husband / father and grandfather / 20.6.1939–1.5.2009 / Always there for us / God Bless /

304: E/R2/6   Square cremation tablet on wall with stencil design of rose in top left corner. Flower holder at foot of wall.
Cherished / memories of / ROSIE SCHMIDT / 1920–1990 / "You were always there / you always cared / We miss you" /
Flower holder: **Rosie / R.I.P. /**
Household Staff

305: E/R2/7   Square cremation tablet on wall with cross in top left corner.
In memory of / MAURICE JOHN / BIRMINGHAM / 1906–1991 / Loving husband, father / and grandfather / And his wife / ETHEL MAUD / 1912–2001 Loving mother / and grandmother /
Parents of Sister Mary Christina

306: E/R2/8   Square cremation tablet on wall.
In loving memory of / TREVOR JOHN EVANS / much loved husband / cherished father and / devoted grandfather / always in our thoughts / 7.7.32–1.9.97 /
Local friend and taxi driver

307: E/R2/9 — Small black gold edged cremation plaque on wall. Black and gold flower holder at foot of wall.
**In loving memory of / JEAN PEARSON / 7.8.1923–19.2.1999 /
In loving memory of / ERIC PEARSON / 20.11.1922–28.12.2005 /
Rest in peace /**
Flower holder, side 1: **In / loving / memory /**
Side 2: **JEAN / PEARSON / 1923–1999 /**
Side 3: **DORY / PEARSON / 1955–1984 /**
Staff member

308: E/R2/10 — Small metal cremation plaque on wall.
**In loving memory of / DAVID CLARKE / 08.01.1937–21.03.1999 /
Dearest husband / devoted father / and grandfather /
always in our thoughts /**
Groundsman

309: E/R2/11 — Small metal cremation plaque on wall.
**In loving memory of / COLIN [*EDWARD GEOFFREY*] ROBERTS /
died 11 July 2000 / aged 64 years / Rest in peace /**
Springfield Parish

310: E/R2/12 — Small metal cremation plaque on wall.
**In loving memory of / GUILIA ROBERTS / died 1st August 2010 /
age 79 years / Rest in peace together /**
Springfield Parish

311: E/R2/13 — Small metal cremation plaque on wall.
**GEOFFREY WILLIAM / FORD / devoted husband / and father /
20th Nov[ember] 1940 to / 8th July 2000 /**
Local friend

312: E/R2/14 — Small metal cremation plaque on wall.
**HAROLD LESLIE / DUBOIS / In loving memory /
[died 29th April 2005]**
Local friend

313: E/R2/15 — Small metal cremation plaque on wall.
**In loving memory of / REGINALD S. CROWTHER /
28.6.1912–7.9.1987 / AND / KATE CROWTHER / NEÉ NEILAN /
21.9.1916–12.8.2006 /**
Parents of Sister Pauline

314: E/R2/16 — Small metal cremation plaque on wall.
**In loving memory of / MARY CHAPLIN / 19.12.1935–07.06.2012 /
DEARLY LOVED / At peace with the Angels /**
Springfield Parish

315: E/R2/17 — Small metal cremation plaque on wall.
**In loving memory of / DORIS KIRBY / (NEÉ BROYD) /
4.4.1913–7.4.2013**
Known as Margaret; friend of the Community

Memorial Inscriptions

316: E/R2/18		Small metal cremation plaque on wall. **DANIEL MICHAEL / O'CONNOR / BORN 11.03.1930 / DIED 28.09.2008 /** *Brother of Sister Mary Christopher*
317: E/R2/19		Small metal cremation plaque on wall. **JAN NEWTON / 1940–2014** *Senior School Staff, Governor, Friend*
318: E/R2/20		Small metal cremation plaque on wall. **MARGARET HELEN / MURRAY / 27.2.1945–5.8.2015 / BELOVED WIFE / DEVOTED MOTHER / AND GRANDMOTHER / R.I.P /** *Senior School Staff, Friend*
319: E/R2/21		Small metal cremation plaque on wall. **ANTHONY FRANCIS / DOHERTY / (TONY) / 1939–2016 / REST IN PEACE /** *Springfield Parish*

MEMORIAL PLAQUES

320: Metal plaque on pedestal with statue of Virgin Mary.
Pray for / HELEN TRAPPES-LOMAX / of Clayton Hall / June 15th 1924 / R.I.P. /

321: Memorial bench (round)
[Harold] THO[MA]S PARSONS / 1912–2007 / Much loved by his family / a great friend to the Community & School /
Frederick J. French Builders; Benefactor

APPENDIX 2. THE LIÈGE COMMUNITY IN 1794

denotes lay sister; bold denotes leaders of migration.
All burial locations at New Hall, unless otherwise stated

Name	Religious name	Dates	Burial
Archdeacon, Barbara	S. Mary Aloysia	(1764–1833)	O/RC/29
Archdeacon, Elizabeth	S. Mary Au[gu]stin	(1765–1849)	O/LD/20
Brown, Mary	*S. Mary Agnes	(1772–1862)	O/LB/17
Champney, Bridget	S. Mary Magdalen	(1731–1812)	O/RC/22
Clifford, Anne	S. Mary Aloysia Austin	(1771–1844)	O/LE/19
Clifford, Charlotte	S. Ann Theresa	(1773–1800)	O/RB/18
Clough, Bridget	**S. Mary Aloysia**	**(1739–1816)**	**O/RD/18**
Cross/Tristram, Margaret	S. Frances Borgia	(1772–1820)	O/RA/28
Cross/Tristram, Mary	S. Mary Xaveria	(1773–1804)	O/RB/15
Dennett, Elizabeth	S. Mary Ignatia	(1761–1825)	O/RD/22
Dennett, Helen	S. Mary Theresa	(1725–1794)	St Pancras, London
Dennett, Margaret	S. Mary Stanislaus	(1765–1816)	O/RD/21
Evens, Elizabeth	*S. Mary Clare	(1734–1799)	O/RA/20
Fermor, Henrietta	S. Mary Teresa Joseph	(1771–1806)	O/RC/18
Freeman [Dufrene], Emilia	S. Mary Barbara	(1776–1799)	O/RA/21
Fullwood, Elizabeth	*S. Mary Paul	(1740–1813)	O/RC/23
Gerard, Elizabeth	S. Mary Regis	(1771–1843)	O/LE/20
Hales, Ann	S. Christina Juliana	(1753–1811)	O/RC/21
Hargitt, Mary	*S. Mary Magdalen	(1770–1800)	O/RB/20
Head, Mary Ann	S. Mary Anne	(1759–1837)	O/RC/31
Hill, Frances	S. Mary Angela Aloysia	(1767–1842)	O/RB/9
Howard, Mary Susanna	*S. Mary Frances	(1746–1813)	O/RC/25
Laurenson, Catherine	S. Mary Agatha	(1754–1834)	O/RD/28
Laurenson, Mary	S. Mary Sales	(1777–1812)	O/RC/11

The Liège Community in 1794

Lynch, Mary	S. Mary Joseph	(1757–1797)	West Dean, Wilts
McEvoy, Anne	S. Aloysia Stanislaus	(1768–1836)	O/RC/30
Marshall, Mary	*S. Mary Cleophae	(1723–1799)	O/RA/22
Norris, Elizabeth	*S. Mary Catherine	(1757–1831)	O/RA/32
Parkinson, Alice	*S. Mary Lucy	(1765–1843)	O/RD/31
Parkinson, Ann	*S. Mary Salome	(1760–1832)	O/RB/29
Perrin, Catherine	S. Mary Rose	(1751–1832)	O/RC/28
Poisman, Elizabeth	*S. Mary Alexius	(1746–1803)	O/RA/15
Price, Elizabeth Mary	*S. Mary Cicely	(1752–1838)	O/RA/9
Reeks, Elizabeth	*S. Mary Martha	(1744–1805)	O/RB/23
Reynolds, Jane	S. Teresa Chantal	(1769–1842)	O/RA/18
Roper, Winefred	S. Mary Constantia	(1743–1796)	Holme, Yorks
Semmes, Clare	S. Mary Ursula	(1745–1820)	O/RB/25
Seymour, Mary	*S. Mary Loyola	(1747–1803)	O/RA/23
Smith, Elizabeth	S. Mary Joseph	(1748–1811)	O/RD/15
Smith, Mary	S. Mary Berchmans	(1751–1827)	O/RC/26
Stevenson/Poole, Elizabeth	S. Mary Gonzaga	(1754–1800)	O/RA/17
Straffen, Elizabeth	*S. Mary Ann Xaveria	(1754–1837)	O/RB/21
Stutter, Elizabeth	S. Mary Baptist	(1753–1807)	O/RC/15
Talbot, Elizabeth	**S. Mary Helen**	**(1738–1808)**	**O/RC/13**
Trant, Elizabeth	S. Benedict Joseph	(1767–1797)	West Dean, Wilts
Trant, Sarah	**S. Frances Xaveria**	**(1764–1807)**	**O/RC/17**
Trant, Sarah	S. Mary Christina	(1735–1811)	O/RD/14
Webbe, Bridget	S. Ann Xaveria	(1731–1801)	O/RB/17
Wright, Anna	S. Aloysia Joseph	(1743–1819)	O/RB/26

APPENDIX 3. LIST OF CLERGY

All burial locations are at New Hall, unless otherwise stated

Name	Dates	Buried	Notes
Angier, Thomas, SJ	(1754–1837)	O/RD/30	
Bampton, George, SJ	(1816–1865)	O/LE/14	
Bateman, James, SJ	(1805–1879)	O/LE/9	
Brownbill, James, SJ	(1798–1880)	O/LE/30	
Butler, Reuben	(1892–1959)	E1/4	
Chapon, Stephen	(1751–1826)	O/RD/23	French secular clergy, sought refuge at New Hall
Clifton, Francis, SJ	(1742–1812)	St Pancras, London	*alias* Dominic Fanning
Daly, Joseph	(1863–1892)	O/LA/32	
Forrester, Charles, SJ	(1739–1825)	O/RD/19	*alias* Charles Fleury
Genin, Gervais, SJ	(d. 1800)	O/RB/22	French Jesuit, escaped with Community
Heery, Canon Edward	(1843–1928)	O/LE/4	
Kemper, Herman, SJ	(1745–1811)	O/RD/17	German Jesuit
Nicholson, James, SJ	(1855–1934)	O/RD/20	
O'Brien, Peter, SJ	(1735–1807)	O/RC/20	
Reeve, Thomas, SJ	(1752–1826)	St Pancras, London	*alias* Thomas Haskey
Tristram, Joseph, SJ	(1766–1843)	O/LE/22	*alias* Joseph Cross

APPENDIX 4. LAY PEOPLE IN THE ORIGINAL CEMETERY

Name	Dates	Buried	Relationship with Community
Barwell, Elizabeth	1774–1847	O/LC/29	Servant
Britten, Mary Antonia	1879–1893	O/LA/35	Pupil, died at school
Clifford, Anna Maria	1788–1805	O/RB/13	Pupil, died at school
Crispin, Catherine	1840–1856	O/LB/25	Pupil, died at school
Delraye, Mary	d. 1804	O/RA/13	Servant; travelled from Liège
Fermor, Louisa	1778–1820	O/RA/26	Ex-pupil; Benefactor
Fitzpatrick, Clara Maud	1869–1890	O/LA/33	Pupil, died at school
Gallwey, Lucy	1820–1834	O/LD/29	Pupil, died at school
Gandolfi, Anna Maria	1783–1842	O/LE/24	Ex-pupil; Boarder
Gandolfi, Louisa Maria	1785–1866	O/LD/4	Ex-pupil; Boarder
Hammond, Bernard	c.1842–1859	not known	Died whilst visiting his aunts at New Hall
Henson, Mary	1798–1864	O/LC/4	Servant
Hilliard, Lydia	1899–1937	O/LB/33	Teaching staff
Jarrett, Catherine	1775–1864	O/LA/8	Governess
Jordan, Sarah	1799–1815	O/LE/29	Pupil, died at school
Kendal, Mary Josephine	1876–1893	O/LB/35	Pupil, died at school
Kendal, Ursula Mary	1879–1893	O/LA/34	Pupil, died at school
King, Matilda	1823–1841	O/LE/25	Ex-pupil; Boarder
Knight, Elizabeth	1799–1860	O/LA/7	Servant
Lacey, Henry	1761–1841	O/LA/5	Servant
Laurenson, Martha	1747–1835	O/RD/29	Mother of S. Mary Agatha and S. Mary Sales
Lynch, Anna Maria	1801–1815	O/LE/27	Pupil, died at school
Moers, Mary Jane	1776–1848	O/LC/27	Servant; travelled from Liège
Molliet, Angelique	c.1760–1833	O/RB/31	Boarder
Nadit, Euphrasine	d. 1827	O/RA/30	Governess

Nangle, Catherine	1790–1805	O/RB/11	Pupil, died at school
Phillipson, William Abraham	1787–1839	O/LA/4	Groundsman
Plowden, Minnie [Mary]	1861–1899	O/LB/8	Ex-pupil
Pratt, Elizabeth	d. 1833	O/RB/32	Servant; Benefactor
Riddell, Mary	1879–1895	O/LB/34	Pupil, died at school
Russell, Agnes Mary	1885–1898	O/LC/8	Pupil, died at school
Ryan, Catherine	1796–1813	O/RC/9	Pupil, died at school
Standish, Elizabeth	1798–1813	O/RD/9	Pupil, died at school
Strickland, Diana	d. 1804	O/RA/11	Boarder
Thomas, Theresa	1786–1844	O/LD/25	Infirmarian and Organist
Whiteside, Jane	1821–1837	O/LD/27	Pupil, died at school

BIBLIOGRAPHY AND FURTHER READING

COMMUNITY HISTORY

Anon., *History of the New Hall Community of Canonesses Regular of the Holy Sepulchre* (Roehampton: Manresa Press, 1899).

Canonesses of the Holy Sepulchre, *Fishy Tales: Living Memories of New Hall 1930–2012* (privately printed, 2012).

Dumont, Bruno, 'La ferme de La Vache, Rue Pierreuse, nº 115–119: Sur les traces des dames anglaises', *Bulletin de la Société Royale le Vieux-Liège* 339 (2012), pp. 217–52.

Essex Society for Family History, *Monumental Inscriptions at New Hall Burial Ground, Boreham, 1799–2003* (Chelmsford: Essex Society for Family History, 2003).

Goldie, Henrietta, *Days of Yore: An Account of her School Days at Dean House* (privately printed in the New Hall Chronicle, 1926), pp. 25–36.

Tuckwell, Tony, *New Hall and its School: 'A True School of Virtuous Demeanour'* (King's Lynn: Free Range Publishing, 2006).

BACKGROUND READING

Aries, Phillippe, *The Hour of Our Death* (New York: Alfred A. Knopf, 1981).

Bellenger, Dom Aidan, Gerald Brine and Frances Daniels, *St Benedict's, Stratton on the Fosse, Somerset: A History* (Radstock: Downside Abbey Press, 2014).

Bellenger, Dom Aidan, *Fearless Resting Place* (Radstock: Downside Abbey Press, 2015).

Bence-Jones, Mark, *The Catholic Families* (London: Constable & Co. Ltd, 1992).

Bettey, J. H., 'The Suppression of the Benedictine Nunnery at Shaftesbury in 1539', *Hatcher Review* 4 (1992), pp. 3–11.

Bossy, John, *The English Catholic Community 1570–1850* (London: Darton, Longman & Todd, 1979).

Bowden, Caroline, and James E. Kelly, *The English Convents in Exile, 1600–1800: Communities, Culture and Identity* (Farnham: Ashgate, 2013).

Camm, Bede, *Forgotten Shrines: An Account of Some Old Catholic Halls and Families in England and of Relics and Memorials of the English Martyrs* (Burns, Oates & Washbourne: London, 1936).

Chadwick, Hubert, SJ, *St Omers to Stonyhurst: A History of Two Centuries* (London: Burns & Oates, 1962).

Clifford, Hugh, *The House of Clifford from before the Conquest* (Chichester: Phillimore & Co. Ltd, 1987).

Coleridge, Henry James (ed.), *St Mary's Convent Micklegate Bar York, 1686–1887* (London: Burns & Oates, 1887).

Collett, Barry (ed.), *Female Monastic Life in Early Tudor England* (Farnham: Ashgate, 2002).

Davies, Douglas J., *Death, Ritual and Belief: The Rhetoric of Funerary Rites* (London: Continuum, 2002).

Davies, Douglas J., *Mors Britannica: Lifestyle and Death-Style in Britain Today* (Oxford: Oxford University Press, 2015).

Doyle, Peter (ed.), *The Correspondence of Alexander Goss, Bishop of Liverpool, 1856–1872* (Woodbridge: Catholic Record Society, 2014).

Duffy, Eamon, *The Stripping of the Altars: Traditional Religion in England, c. 1400–c. 1580* (London: Yale University Press, 2005).

Essex Society for Family History, *Monumental Inscriptions at All Saints, Springfield and Cemetery at Trinity Road, Springfield, 1421–1989* (Chelmsford: Essex Society for Family History, 2001).

Foley, Henry, SJ, *Records of the English Province of the Society of Jesus: Historic Facts Illustrative of the Labours and Sufferings of its Members in the Sixteenth and Seventeenth Centuries*, 7 vols in 8 (London: Burns and Oates, 1877–80).

Haigh, Christopher, *English Reformations: Religion, Politics and Society under the Tudors* (Oxford: Clarendon Press, 1993).

Harding, Vanessa, *The Dead and the Living in Paris and London, 1500–1670* (Cambridge: Cambridge University Press, 2002).

Holt, Geoffrey, SJ, *The English Jesuits 1650–1829: A Biographical Dictionary* (Southampton: Catholic Record Society, 1984).

Holt, Geoffrey, SJ, *English Jesuits in the Age of Reason* (London: Burns & Oates, 1993).

Houston-Ball, Henry, and Joseph S. Hansom (eds), 'Catholic Registers of Holme-on-Spalding Moor, E. R. Yorks, 1744–1840', as printed in *Miscellanea IV* (London: Catholic Record Society, 1907).

Humphery-Smith, Cecil R., *The Phillimore Atlas and Index of Parish Registers* (Chichester: Phillimore & Co. Ltd, 2003).

Jones, Colin, *The Longman Companion to the French Revolution* (New York: Longman, 1990).

Jones, Edward Alexander, and Alexandra Walsham, *Syon Abbey and its Books: Reading Writing and Religion, c. 1400–1700'* (Woodbridge: Boydell & Brewer, 2010).

Lee, Charles E., *St Pancras Church and Parish* (London: privately printed, 1955).

McCoog, Thomas M., SJ, *English and Welsh Jesuits* (Southampton: Catholic Record Society, 1994 and 1995).

Mangion, Carmen M., 'Avoiding "rash and impudent measures": English Nuns in Revolutionary Paris, 1789–1801', in Caroline Bowden and James E. Kelly (eds), *The English Convents in Exile, 1600–1800: Communities, Culture and Identity* (Farnham: Ashgate, 2013), pp. 247–63.

Mangion, Carmen M., *Contested Identities: Catholic Women Religious in Nineteenth-Century England and Wales* (Manchester: Manchester University Press, 2008).

Marshall, Peter, *The Oxford Illustrated History of the Reformation* (Oxford: Oxford University Press, 2015).

Marshall, Peter, 'Confessionalisation and Community in the Burial of English Catholics, c. 1570–1700', in Nadine Lewycky and Adam Morton (eds), *Getting Along? Religious Identities and Confessional Relations in Early Modern England—Essays in Honour of Professor W. J. Sheils* (Farnham: Ashgate, 2012), pp. 57–75.

Milburn, David, *A History of Ushaw College* (Ushaw: Ushaw College, Durham, 1964).

Palmer, Samuel, *St Pancras, being Antiquarian, Topographical and Biographical Memoranda relating to the Extensive Metropolitan Parish of St Pancras, Middlesex* (London: Field & Tuer, 1870).

Rugg, Julie, *Churchyard and Cemetery: Tradition and Modernity in Rural North Yorkshire* (Manchester: Manchester University Press, 2015).

Rutherford, Sarah, *The Victorian Cemetery* (Oxford: Shire Publications Ltd, 2008).

Scott, Geoffrey, OSB, *Gothic Rage Undone: English Monks in the Age of Enlightenment* (Radstock: Downside Abbey, 1992).

Tingle, Elizabeth C., and Jonathan Willis (eds), *Dying, Death, Burial and Commemoration in Reformation Europe* (Farnham: Ashgate, 2015).

Walsham, Alexandra, *Catholic Reformation in Protestant Britain* (London: Ashgate, 2014).

Whitehead, Maurice, *English Jesuit Education: Expulsion, Suppression, Survival and Restoration, 1762–1803* (Farnham: Ashgate, 2013).

Williams, J. Anthony, *Catholic Recusancy in Wiltshire 1660–1791* (Newport: Catholic Record Society, 1968).

Bibliography and Further Reading

PRIMARY SOURCES

The Laws Against Papists and Popish Recusants, Nonconformists and Nonjurors (London: Printed for W. Bickerton, 1744).

Little, J. Brook, *The Law of Burial: including all the burial acts and official regulations, with notes and cases* (London: Shaw and Sons, 1902).

10 and 11 Victoria cap. 65: Cemeteries Clauses Act 1847

52 Geo 3 cap. 146: Parochial Registers Act 1812

3 Jac 1 cap. 5: An Act to Prevent and avoid Dangers which may grow by Popish Recusants 1606

ARCHIVE MATERIAL

Archives of the Canonesses of the Holy Sepulchre, Colchester [ACHS]

Benefactors Book 1662–1871
Chapter Book 1642–1800
Chapter Book 1800–1976
Clifford correspondence
McEvoy correspondence
Riley-Clifton correspondence
Weld correspondence
School Register 1, 1785–1805
School Register 2, 1805–38
School Register 3, 1838–72
School Register 4, 1872–1947
D1a/Certificate of taking Oath of Allegiance, 17 October 1797.
D2 'A short account of some particulars which happen'd during the Revolutions at Liège and of our journey from thence to England', by Elizabeth Smith
D4 'Mss notes on the traditions of our Community, given to me by Reverend Mother' (December 1889).
J1.11/Burial Register 1803–1979
K/Letter, sent to Prince-Bishop of Liège, September 1773
List of Repairs 1866–86
List of Repairs 1868–73 and 1889–1941
TB 165/106/Chantress Book 2, 1816–26
TB 165/106/Chantress Book 3, 1826–9
TB 165/107/Chantress Book 4, 1830–44
TB 165/112/ Chantress Book 9, 1886–1904

Downside Abbey, Somerset [DAA]

Papers of the English Benedictines at Brussels, later Winchester and Haslemere
Accounts 1794–1853
Annals of the Community of the Glorious Assumption of the Blessed Virgin Mary, 1628–1878
Book of Visitations to the Benedictine Convent, Winchester
Receipts, Disbursements and Debts of our Monastery from the year 1794 to 1806
Fasti Gregoriani 1793–1932.

Douai Abbey, Reading [DAA]

CA Papers of the English Carmelite Community at Antwerp, later Lanherne
CA/1/C/2 Registry of deaths of the community of Lanherne
CA/VII/C Death records, including obituaries, necrologies and anniversaries

CA/1/B Annals of the English Carmelites, 1619–1794
TI Papers of the English Benedictine Community at Dunkirk, later Teignmouth
TIA/2 Manuscript lives and biographies
TIA/3 Extracts from burial register
TIB/C/1 Necrologies and books of anniversary

Essex Record Office, Chelmsford [ERO]

D/Du 1056/8 Proposed new cemetery, Chelmsford, 1866
D/DU 1597/19/1 Extracts from Evelyn's visit to New Hall, 1656
D/G 3/4/1 Contracts for new cemetery 1854–94
D/G 3/5/4 Contracts for new cemetery 1854–5
D/HS/45 Bundle of docs from Southend Board of Health re application from Sr Mary Rudolph to convert ground into burial ground, 1887
D/K 4/1/1 Records of the Roman Catholic Church of the Holy Family, Withal: Baptisms 1774–1837 and Confirmations 1776–1830
D/P 29/8/2 Boreham vestry minutes 1804–25
D/P 29/8/3 Boreham vestry minutes 1825–91
D/P 211/8/1 Springfield vestry minutes 1840–54
D/P 211/8/2 Springfield vestry minutes 1810–38
D/P 211/11/4 Springfield Parish rate book 1831–1840 and some vestry minutes 1833–40.
D/P 245/24/1 Papers relating to Colchester burial board establishment 1854–8
D/P 263/8/2–4 Ardleigh vestry minutes 1788–1866
D/P 263/28/9 Ardleigh Burial Board 1835–1900, including rules of Colchester Cemetery
Q/CR 3/2/10 Parliamentary returns of nonconformist congregations, September 1829
Q/RRo 1/43/2 Quarter Sessions Papists Roll, 1792–1815
Q/Ssb 474/60 Body of woman stolen from grave 1824
Q/SBb 529/105 Certificate of a building called St James Catholic Church in Colchester being a Roman Catholic Church, 1837
T/B 171/11 *The Chelmsford Chronicle*, 1798–1800
TM 396/1 Map of Boreham and Springfield c.1800
TM 397/1 Map of Boreham and Springfield, 1799
TM 406/1–2 Plan of New Hall, n.d. [late 17th century]
T/R 293/1 Death register of Our Lady Immaculate, 1848–1915

Stonyhurst College, Lancashire [SCA]

Ms A.II.29 A collection of letters and other documents relating to the history of the Jesuit College at Bruges, Liege and Stonyhurst
Ms A.III.22 'A short account of the chief events that took place before, and during, the migration, of the English College, or Academy, from Liège to Stonyhurst in the year 1794'.
MS C.II.4/A 'Fundatio Bavarica Collegii Angl. Leodiensis'
MS C.II.4/C Liege Affairs letters of Fr Nicolaus SJ and Fr Barrow SJ 1796–1814
Ms C.II.20 Burial Register 1795–1842

The National Archives, London [TNA]

PROB 11/683/336 Will of Dame Dorothy Goring, 2 July 1729 (proved 8 June 1737)
PROB/11/1534 Will of Reverend Francis Clifton, otherwise Fanning, 22 May 1812 (proved 6 June 1812)
PROB 11/1632 Will of Louisa Fermor, 3 June 1820 (proved 6 July 1820)
PROB 11/1691/ 202 Will of Simon Guillauime Van Ham, 19 February 1824 (proved 26 October 1824)

Ushaw College, Durham [UC]

[uncatalogued—Fr Vincent Smith's papers] Mss of the Nuns of Rouen
H 297a List of those buried in the cemetery in chronological order, Jan 1809–May 1893
UC/H 297a List of those buried in the cemetery by month, 1809–93
UC/P42/301 Letter from Chepstow, 24 December 1859
'Praeterita I', *Ushaw Magazine* (1920), pp. 89–98.

Westminster Diocesan Archives, London [WDA]

A66 Papers of Bishop William Pointer
VII Convents, 1812–26
IX (1) Political Activities 1812–16
E5603 AFS Bundle of correspondence relating to Provincial Synod 1855 and Provincial Synod 1858–63.
Ma 2/36/1 Manning correspondence, 1858–86
Z/72 Diary of Bishop Douglass Part 1, 1792–9
Z1 Diary of Bishop Douglas Part II, 1800–12

ONLINE RESOURCES

https://historyofwomenreligious.org/women-religious-bibliography.
Who were the Nuns? database, https://wwtn.history.qmul.ac.uk/about/convent-notes/ [*WWTN*]
Clifford family tree, as cited on *WWTN*
Stourton family tree, *WWTN*
Langdale family tree, *WWTN*
Geoffrey Scott, 'Catholic Committee (*act*. 1782–1792)', *Oxford Dictionary of National Biography* [*ODNB*], online edition.
Dom Aidan Bellenger, 'The Brussels Nuns at Winchester 1794–1897', *English Benedictine Congregation History Commission Symposium*, 1999
John Thornhill, *History of the Parish of Hampshire Downs* (published online, url: http://www.hampshire-downswinchester.org/wp-content/uploads/2013/11/Hampshire-Downs-Parish-history-timeline.pdf, 2013)
Caroline M. K. Bowden, 'Hawley, Susan (1622–1706)', *ODNB*
Caroline M. K. Bowden, 'Dennett, Mary (1730–1781)', *ODNB*

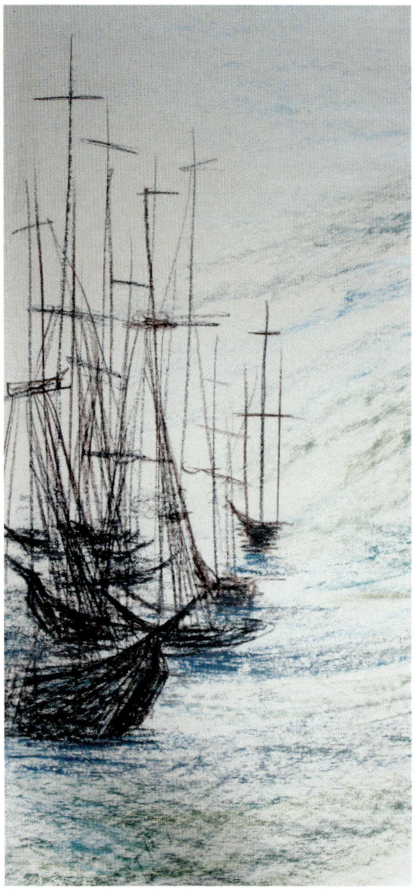

Index of Persons

The numbers are those of the graves.

Angier, Thomas 103
Archdeacon, Barbara 62
Archdeacon, Elizabeth 146

Bamford, Ann 279
Bampton, George 119
Barraud, Harriet 137
Barry, Margaret 142
Barwell, Elizabeth 184
Bateman, James 116
Beere, Noah Gabriel 295
Bellord, Alice 280
Beaumont, Margaret 179
Birmingham, Ethel Maud 305
Birmingham, Maurice John 305
Blake, Mary 53
Bleasdale, Ann 177
Bleasdale, Anne 175
Blount, Anna Maria 117
Boardman, Margaret 40
Boland, Margaret Frances 263
Brennfleck, Aloysia 222
Britten, Mary Antonia Josephine 227
Brown, Kathleen Kerenhappuch 259
Brown, Mary 200
Brownbill, James 130
Budd, Frances 18
Bunney, Mary 172
Burchal, Mary 48
Burke, Helen 29
Burke, Mary Josephine 78
Butler, Julia 133
Butler, Mary 26
Butler, Reuben 231

Caballero, Adelaide 136
Caddell, Paulina 114
Callow, Maureen Sylvia 292
Carey, Joy 260
Carpue, Teresa 198
Carter, Matilda 204
Champney, Bridget 69

Chaplin, Mary 314
Chapon, Stephen 98
Clancy, Elizabeth Ann 247
Clancy, Ellen 246
Clarke, David 308
Clement, Christina 50
Cleverly, Alice 192
Clifford, Anna Maria 35
Clifford, Anne 123
Clifford, Charlotte 39
Clough, Bridget M. A. 93
Coleman, Louisa 199
Coles, Elizabeth 181
Cooke, Emma Catherine Frances 282
Cooke, Nancy 283
Cooper, Maud 242
Corney, Caroline 118
Cortes, Francisca Fuster 236
Costello, Anne 57
Coupe, Jane 27
Coventry, Isabella 148
Coverdale, Beatrice Mary 268
Craven, Mary 178
Crewse, Alice Mary 243
Crispin, Catherine 195
Cronin, Maria 138
Cross/Tristram, Joseph 125
Cross/Tristram, Margaret 8
Cross/Tristram, Mary 37
Crowther, Kate 313
Crowther, Pauline Mary 278
Crowther, Reginald 313

Daly, Joseph 224
Daly, Julia 55
Daly, Mildred 244
Davies, Miriam 274
de Burgh Atkinson, Elizabeth 228
Delraye, Mary 21
Dennett, Elizabeth 97
Dennett, Margaret 96
Desombres, Blanche 254

Devine, Elizabeth 258
Dickinson, Madeline 209
Dignan, Clare 197
Doherty, Anthony 319
Dolan, Agnes 90
Dolan, Winifred Mary 230
Donohue, Catherine 208
Dubois, Harold Leslie 312
Dufrene/Freeman, Emilia 13

Eagar, Frances 284
Earle, Madeleine Constance 277
Ellison, Frances Clare 171
Ellison, Rose 20
Emery, Sarah Ann 54
Engel, Amalia Hertha 272
Engel, Ruth Margot 272
Errington, Louisa 135
Evans, Trevor John 306
Evens, Elizabeth Winefred 14
Ewers, Emma Anne 269

Falkiner, Naomi E. M. 265
Falls, Elizabeth 161
Falls, Mildred 67
Fermor, Henrietta 71
Fermor, Louisa 9
Finn, Mary 167
Fitzgerald, Mary 145
Fitzpatrick, Anne 2
Fitzpatrick, Clara Maud 225
Flavin, Dorothy Minchin 261
Fontenay, Hermione de 143
Ford, Geoffrey William 311
Forrester, Charles H. Henry 94
Freeman/Dufrene, Emilia 13
Freeman, Emma 151
Fullwood, Elizabeth 68
Furze, John Arnold (Jack) 289

Gallwey, Lucy 139
Gandolfi, Anna Maria 126
Gandolfi, Dorothy 100
Gandolfi, Louisa Maria 159
Gandolfi, Mary 147
Genin, Gervais 43
Gerard, Elizabeth 124
Gillow, Teresa 25
Grehan, Jane 120

Hacking, Ann 193

Hague, Nora 241
Hales, Ann 70
Hall, Jean Margaret 286
Hall, Catherine [Jemima] 182
Hall, William Ernest 286
Haly, Lelia 173
Ham, Martha Van 202
Hammond, Bernard L. 188
Hargitt, Mary 41
Harwood, Grace 134
Head, Mary Ann 60
Heery, Edward 112
Henry, Camille 82
Henson, Mary 166
Higgins, Catherine 165
Hill, Frances 33
Hilliard, Lydia M. 191
Hogg, Margaret Mary 262
Howard, Mary Susanna 66
Hubbard, Frances 154
Hughes, Emily 217

Jackson, Diana Irving Pauline (Margot) 290
Jarrett, Catherine 215
Jerningham, Paulina 174
Jones, Teresa 88
Jordan, Sarah 129

Kelly, Mary Eliza 1
Kemper, Herman 92
Kendal, Agnes 213
Kendal, Agnes Mary Aloysia James 113
Kendal, Cecilia 121
Kendal, Etheldreda 64
Kendal, Mary 155
Kendal, Mary Josephine 189
Kendal, Ursula Mary 226
Kennedy, Barry James 303
Kennedy, Nicola 302
Keogh, Mary Ellen 111
King, Matilda 127
King, Mike 238
King, Sarah 186
Kirby, Doris 315
Kirk, Margaret Eileen 234
Kitchen, Gertrude 291
Kitchen, Harold Herbert 291
Knight, Elizabeth 214

Lacey, Henry 212
Lane, Ellen 221

Index of Persons

Laurenson, Catherine 101
Laurenson, Martha 102
Laurenson, Mary 144
Lawrenson, Laura 149
Lawrenson, Mary 76
Lilly, Mary 176
Lloyd-Thomas, Muriel 218
Loughnan, Georgiana 30
Loughnan, Maria 132
Lucas, Mary 163
Lynch, Anna Maria 128

McEvoy, Ann Mary 61
Madden, Margaret 3
Marsh, Catharine 56
Marshall, Mary 12
Maskell, Virginia Shakerley 281
Mason, Margaret 206
Mason, Rosina 108
Mathews, Anne 85
McCartney, Sarah 249
McLeod-Jones, Ian 235
McLeod-Jones, Shaun 235
McConville, Elizabeth 15
McDermott, Jane M. A. 267
McGhee, James 298
McSwiney, Anne 169
Merrells, Joan 273
Merrells, Teresa 229
Mescher, Mary Anne 162
Mitchel, Mary 31
Moers, Mary Jane 183
Molliet, Angelique 51
Morris, Gwyneth Rosalind 288
Morris, John William Talwin 288
Mortlock, Louisa 187
Mullarkey, James 296
Mutter, Elizabeth 185
Murray, Margaret 318
Myerscough, Mary 256

Nadit, Euphrasine 6
Nangle, Catharine 34
Nangle, Elizabeth 86
Newsham, Elizabeth 194
Newton, Jan 317
Nicholson, James 95
Norris, Elizabeth 4

O'Brien, Peter 28
O'Byrne, Blanche 32

O'Connell, Edith 251
O Connor, Barbara 105
O'Connor, Mary Dorothy Bridget 275
O'Connor, Daniel Michael 316
O'Donohue, Catherine 208
Osmond, Rose 152

Palmer, Ernie 300
Parkinson, Alice 104
Parkinson, Ann 49
[Parry], Bette 297
Parsons, Annabel 294
Parsons, Tho[ma]s 321
Pearson, Dory 307
Pearson, Eric 307
Pearson, Jean 307
Pereira, Delphine 79
Pereira, Georgina 84
Perrin, Catherine 63
Petre, Gertrude 74
Phillipson, William Abraham 211
Plowden, Minnie 207
Poisman, Elizabeth 19
Poole, Barbara 196
Poole/Stevenson, Elizabeth 17
Porter, Elizabeth 158
Porter, Isabella 157
Porter, Jane 5
Power, Evelyn 24
Power, Mary 253
Pratt, Elizabeth 52
Price, Elizabeth Mary 23
Purcell, Andalusia 160

Reeks, Elizabeth 44
Regina, Pauline Capece Galeota 109
Reynolds, Jane [Joan] 16
Reynolds, Rhoda Clare 270
Richards, Mary 205
Riddell, Mary 190
Roberts, Colin Edward Geoffrey 309
Roberts, Guilia 310
Roffey, Frances Nairne 264
Rorke, Catherine 153
Rorke, Margaret 99
Roskell, Rose 110
Rowland, Joyce Elizabeth 271
Rushbrooke, Victoria 168
Russell, Agnes Mary 170
Russell, Etheldreda 255
Russell, Frances 252

Rutherford, Williamina 156
Ryan, Catharine 77

Schmidt, Rosie 304
Scoles, Agnes 210
Scoles, Winefride Mary 58
Semmes, Clare 46
Seymore, Mary 11
Simmons, Barbara 201
Smith, Elizabeth 91
Smith, Mary 65
Smithers, Gertrude 45
Souza, Marshall Dominic de 293
Standish, Elizabeth 87
Steel, Elizabeth 180
Steuart, Isabella 80
Stevenson/Poole, Elizabeth 17
Stokes, Dorothy Mary 301
Stourton, Anna Maria 24
Stowrton, Mary 122
Straffen, Elizabeth 42
Strickland, Diana 22
Stutter, Elizabeth 73
Swallow, Gladys 245
Sygrove, Edith Joyce 233
Sygrove, Percy 233

Talbot, Elizabeth 75
Taylor, Sarah Ann 81
Ternan, Kathleen Isobel 232
Terney, Margaret May 276
Thomas, Teresa 141
Thunder, Charlotte 164
Trant, Sarah (S. Francis Xaveria) 72
Trant, Sarah (S. Mary Christina) 89

Trappes-Lomax, Catherine 220
Trappes-Lomax, Frances 219
Trappes-Lomax, Helen 320
Travers, Mary Helen 216
Tristram/Cross, Joseph 125
Tristram/Cross, Margaret 8
Tristram/Cross, Mary 37
Turner, Emily 240

Van Ham, Martha 202

Wadden, Bridget 83
Waite, Penelope 237
Warrington, Elizabeth Gertrude 285
Warrington, Monica Mary 250
Watts, Maria 107
Waud Waud, Margaret Ann 239
Weaver, Mary Ann 36
Webbe, Bridget 38
Weld, Angela 150
Weld, Eleonora 131
Whateley, Rosamond 287
Whattolley, Harriet 59
Wheble, Maria 115
Whelan, Katherine 223
Whiteside, Jane 140
Wickwar, Anne 7
Williams, Anna 106
Williams, Edna May 299
Wilson, Norah 257
Winnard, Elizabeth 10
Wright, Anna 47
Wright, Mary Ann 203

Young, Elsie 266

New Cemetery

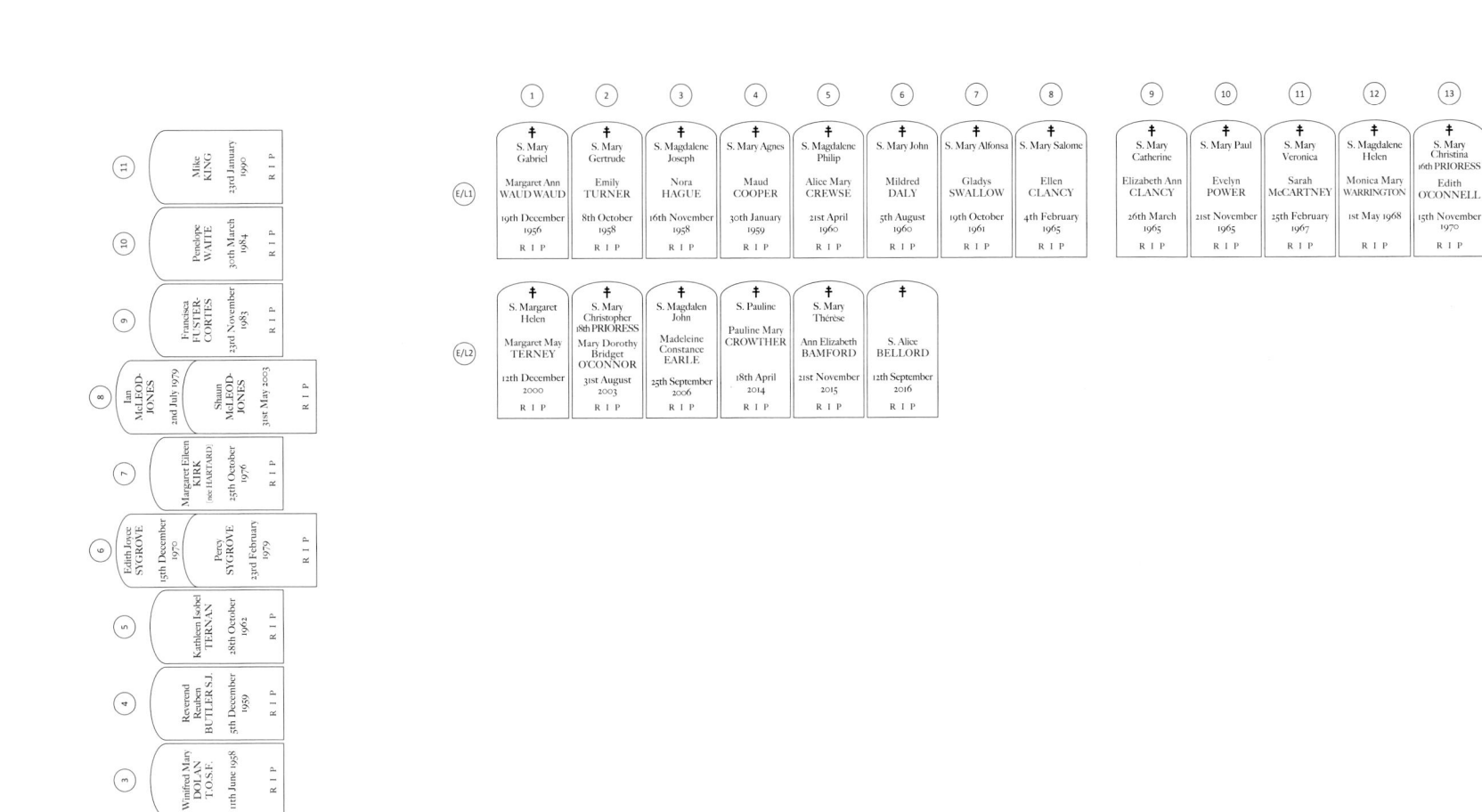

Row E/L1

#	Name	Secular Name	Date	
1	S. Mary Gabriel	Margaret Ann WAUD WAUD	19th December 1956	R I P
2	S. Mary Gertrude	Emily TURNER	8th October 1958	R I P
3	S. Magdalene Joseph	Nora HAGUE	16th November 1958	R I P
4	S. Mary Agnes	Maud COOPER	30th January 1959	R I P
5	S. Magdalene Philip	Alice Mary CREWSE	21st April 1960	R I P
6	S. Mary John	Mildred DALY	5th August 1960	R I P
7	S. Mary Alfonsa	Gladys SWALLOW	19th October 1961	R I P
8	S. Mary Salome	Ellen CLANCY	4th February 1965	R I P
9	S. Mary Catherine	Elizabeth Ann CLANCY	26th March 1965	R I P
10	S. Mary Paul	Evelyn POWER	21st November 1965	R I P
11	S. Mary Veronica	Sarah McCARTNEY	25th February 1967	R I P
12	S. Magdalene Helen	Monica Mary WARRINGTON	1st May 1968	R I P
13	S. Mary Christina 16th PRIORESS	Edith O'CONNELL	15th November 1970	R I P
14	S. Antony Magdalene	Frances RUSSELL	30th December 1972	R I P
15	S. Mary Genevieve	Mary POWER	12th January 1973	R I P
16	S. Mary Berchmans	Blanche DESOMBRES	6th August 1973	R I P
17	S. Ma... Berna...	Etheldre... RUSSE...	27th Decem... 1974	R I P

Row E/L2

Name	Secular Name	Date	
S. Margaret Helen	Margaret May TERNEY	12th December 2000	R I P
S. Mary Christopher 18th PRIORESS	Mary Dorothy Bridget O'CONNOR	31st August 2003	R I P
S. Magdalen John	Madeleine Constance EARLE	25th September 2006	R I P
S. Pauline	Pauline Mary CROWTHER	18th April 2014	R I P
S. Mary Thérèse	Ann Elizabeth BAMFORD	21st November 2015	R I P
S. Alice	S. Alice BELLORD	12th September 2016	R I P

Original Cemetery

1	Elizabeth Pascuala de BURGH ATKINSON	25th November 1956	R I P
2	Teresa MERRELLS	6th July 1957	R I P
3	Winifred Mary DOLAN T.O.S.F.	11th June 1958	R I P
4	Reverend Reuben BUTLER S.J.	5th December 1959	R I P
5	Kathleen Isobel TERNAN	28th October 1962	R I P
6	Edith Joyce SYGROVE (15th December 1970); Percy SYGROVE (23rd February 1979)		R I P
7	Margaret Eileen KIRK (née HARVARD)	25th October 1976	R I P
8	Ian McLEOD-JONES (2nd July 1979); Shaun McLEOD-JONES (31st May 2003)		R I P
9	Francesca FUSTER CORTES	23rd November 1983	R I P
10	Penelope WAITE	30th March 1984	R I P
11	Mike KING	23rd January 1990	R I P

20	Anthony Francis DOHERTY [TONY]	1939 – 2016	R I P
21	Margaret Helen ...GRAY	...August 2015	R I P

Cemetery Map

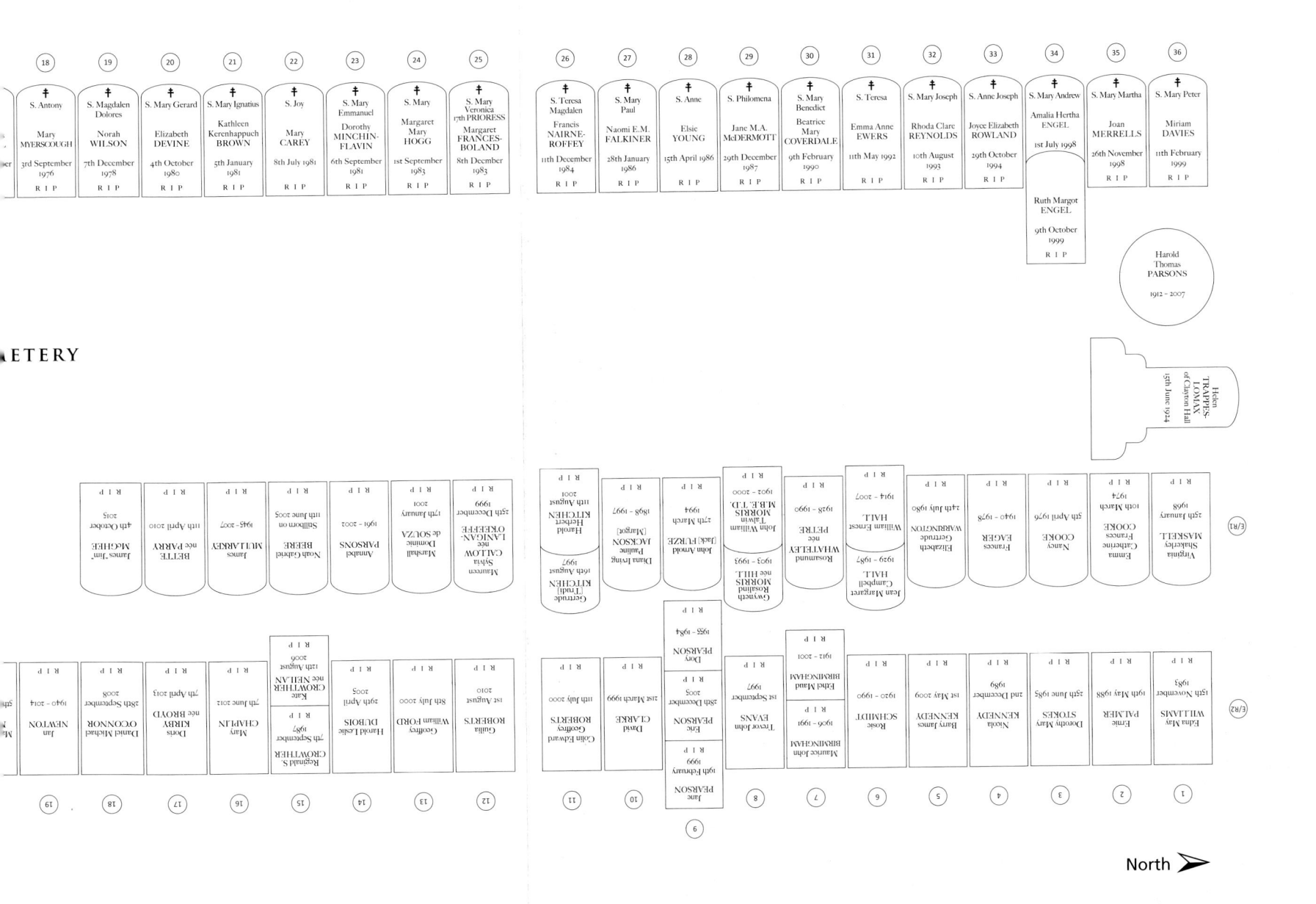

Top row (graves 18–25, 26–36) — upright headstones

#	Religious Name	Name	Date	
18	S. Antony	Mary MYERSCOUGH	3rd September 1976	R I P
19	S. Magdalen Dolores	Norah WILSON	7th December 1978	R I P
20	S. Mary Gerard	Elizabeth DEVINE	4th October 1980	R I P
21	S. Mary Ignatius	Kathleen Kerenhappuch BROWN	5th January 1981	R I P
22	S. Joy	Mary CAREY	8th July 1981	R I P
23	S. Mary Emmanuel	Dorothy MINCHIN-FLAVIN	6th September 1981	R I P
24	S. Mary	Margaret Mary HOGG	1st September 1983	R I P
25	S. Mary Veronica 17th PRIORESS	Margaret FRANCES-BOLAND	8th December 1983	R I P
26	S. Teresa Magdalen	Francis NAIRNE-ROFFEY	11th December 1984	R I P
27	S. Mary Paul	Naomi E.M. FALKINER	28th January 1986	R I P
28	S. Anne	Elsie YOUNG	15th April 1986	R I P
29	S. Philomena	Jane M.A. McDERMOTT	29th December 1987	R I P
30	S. Mary Benedict	Beatrice Mary COVERDALE	9th February 1990	R I P
31	S. Teresa	Emma Anne EWERS	11th May 1992	R I P
32	S. Mary Joseph	Rhoda Clare REYNOLDS	10th August 1993	R I P
33	S. Anne Joseph	Joyce Elizabeth ROWLAND	29th October 1994	R I P
34	S. Mary Andrew	Amalia Hertha ENGEL	1st July 1998	
		Ruth Margot ENGEL	9th October 1999	R I P
35	S. Mary Martha	Joan MERRELLS	26th November 1998	R I P
36	S. Mary Peter	Miriam DAVIES	11th February 1999	R I P

Harold Thomas PARSONS
1912 – 2007

Helen TRAPPES-LOMAX of Clayton Hall
15th June 1924

Middle row

- Maureen McGHEE — 4th October 2015 — R I P
- James "Jim" BETTE née PARRY — 11th April 2010 — R I P
- James MULLARKEY — 1945 – 2007 — R I P
- Noah Gabriel BEEBE — Stillborn on 11th June 2005 — R I P
- Annabel PARSONS — 1961 – 2002 — R I P
- Marshall Dominic de SOUZA — 17th January 2001 — R I P
- Sylvia CALLOW née LANIGAN-O'KEEFFE — 25th December 1999 — R I P
- Gertrude Trudi KITCHEN [Margot] — 16th August 1997 — R I P
- Herbert KITCHEN — 11th August 2001 — R I P
- Diana Irving Pauline JACKSON — 17th March 1994 — R I P
- John William Tawm FENZIE — 1898 – 1997 — R I P
- John Arnold MORRIS M.B.E. T.D. — 1903 – 1993 — R I P
- Gwyneth Rosalind MORRIS née HILL — 1902 – 2001 — R I P
- Rosamund PETRIE — 1925 – 2000 — R I P
- Jean Margaret Campbell HALL — 1926 – 1987 — R I P
- William Ernest HALL — 1914 – 2007 — R I P
- Elizabeth Gertrude WARRINGTON — 24th July 1980 — R I P
- Frances EAGER — 1940 – 1978 — R I P
- Nancy COOKE — 5th April 1976 — R I P
- Emma Catherine Frances COOKE — 10th March 1974 — R I P
- Virginia Shakerley MASKELL — 25th January 1968 — R I P

Bottom row (plots 1–19)

1	Edna May WILLIAMS	15th November 1983
2	Ernie PALMER	19th May 1988
3	Dorothy Mary STOKES	15th June 1985
4	Nicola KENNEDY	1989
5	Barry James KENNEDY	2nd December 1989
6	Rosie SCHMIDT	1st May 2009
7	Maurice John BRODRINGHAM	1906 – 1991
8	Ethel Maud BRODRINGHAM	1920 – 1990
9	Trevor John EVANS	1st September 1997
10	Eric PEARSON	28th December 2005
11	Jane PEARSON	19th February 1999
	Davy PEARSON	1955 – 1984
	David CLARKE	1st March 1999
	Colin Edward Geoffrey ROBERTS	11th July 2000
12	Guilia DUBOIS	8th July 2000
13	Harold Leslie ROBERTS	1st August 2010
14	Geoffrey William FORD	19th April 2005
15	Reginald S. CROWTHER — 7th September 2006 / Kate CROWTHER née NEILAN — 12th August 2006	
16	Mary CHAPLIN	7th June 2012
17	Doris KIRBY née BROYD	7th April 2013
18	Daniel Michael O'CONNOR	28th September 2008
19	Jan NEWTON	1940 – 2014

North ➤

Cemetery Map

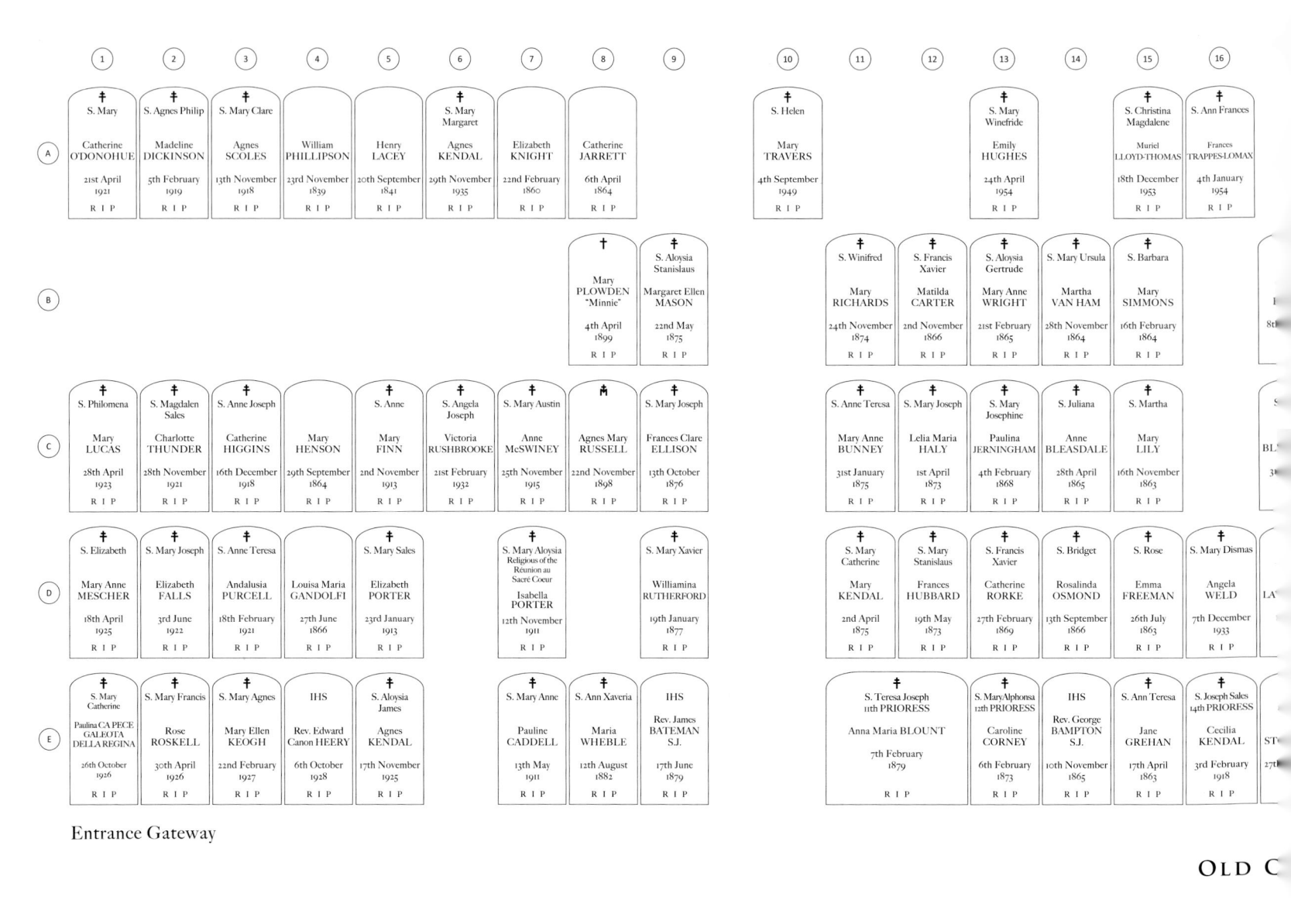

Upper Section (Rows A–E, Columns 1–16)

Row A
#	Religious Name	Name	Date
1	S. Mary Catherine	O'DONOHUE	21st April 1921
2	S. Agnes Philip	Madeline DICKINSON	5th February 1919
3	S. Mary Clare	Agnes SCOLES	13th November 1918
4		William PHILLIPSON	23rd November 1839
5		Henry LACEY	20th September 1841
6	S. Mary Margaret	Agnes KENDAL	29th November 1935
7		Elizabeth KNIGHT	22nd February 1860
8		Catherine JARRETT	6th April 1864
10	S. Helen	Mary TRAVERS	4th September 1949
13	S. Mary Winefride	Emily HUGHES	24th April 1954
15	S. Christina Magdalene	Muriel LLOYD-THOMAS	18th December 1953
16	S. Ann Frances	Frances TRAPPES-LOMAX	4th January 1954

Row B
#	Religious Name	Name	Date
8		Mary PLOWDEN "Minnie"	4th April 1899
9	S. Aloysia Stanislaus	Margaret Ellen MASON	22nd May 1875
11	S. Winifred	Mary RICHARDS	24th November 1874
12	S. Francis Xavier	Matilda CARTER	2nd November 1866
13	S. Aloysia Gertrude	Mary Anne WRIGHT	21st February 1865
14	S. Mary Ursula	Martha VAN HAM	28th November 1864
15	S. Barbara	Mary SIMMONS	16th February 1864

Row C
#	Religious Name	Name	Date
1	S. Philomena	Mary LUCAS	28th April 1923
2	S. Magdalen Sales	Charlotte THUNDER	28th November 1921
3	S. Anne Joseph	Catherine HIGGINS	16th December 1918
4	S. Anne	Mary HENSON	29th September 1864
5	S. Angela Joseph	Mary FINN	2nd November 1913
6		Victoria RUSHBROOKE	21st February 1932
7	S. Mary Austin	Anne McSWINEY	25th November 1915
8		Agnes Mary RUSSELL	22nd November 1898
9	S. Mary Joseph	Frances Clare ELLISON	13th October 1876
11	S. Anne Teresa	Mary Anne BUNNEY	31st January 1875
12	S. Mary Joseph	Lelia Maria HALY	1st April 1873
13	S. Mary Josephine	Paulina JERNINGHAM	4th February 1868
14	S. Juliana	Anne BLEASDALE	28th April 1865
15	S. Martha	Mary LILY	16th November 1863

Row D
#	Religious Name	Name	Date
1	S. Elizabeth	Mary Anne MESCHER	18th April 1925
2	S. Mary Joseph	Elizabeth FALLS	3rd June 1922
3	S. Anne Teresa	Andalusia PURCELL	18th February 1921
4		Louisa Maria GANDOLFI	27th June 1866
5	S. Mary Sales	Elizabeth PORTER	23rd January 1913
6	S. Mary Aloysia, Religious of the Réunion au Sacré Cœur	Isabella PORTER	12th November 1911
8	S. Mary Xavier	Williamina RUTHERFORD	19th January 1877
11	S. Mary Catherine	Mary KENDAL	2nd April 1875
12	S. Mary Stanislaus	Frances HUBBARD	19th May 1873
13	S. Francis Xavier	Catherine RORKE	27th February 1869
14	S. Bridget	Rosalinda OSMOND	13th September 1866
15	S. Rose	Emma FREEMAN	26th July 1863
16	S. Mary Dismas	Angela WELD	7th December 1933

Row E
#	Religious Name	Name	Date
1	S. Mary Catherine	Paulina CA PECE GALEOTA DELLA REGINA	26th October 1926
2	S. Mary Francis	Rose ROSKELL	30th April 1926
3	S. Mary Agnes	Mary Ellen KEOGH	22nd November 1927
4	IHS	Rev. Edward Canon HEERY	6th October 1928
5	S. Aloysia James	Agnes KENDAL	17th November 1925
7	S. Mary Anne	Pauline CADDELL	13th May 1911
8	S. Ann Xaveria	Maria WHEBLE	12th August 1882
9	IHS	Rev. James BATEMAN S.J.	17th June 1879
11	S. Teresa Joseph, 11th PRIORESS	Anna Maria BLOUNT	7th February 1879
13	S. Mary Alphonsa, 12th PRIORESS	Caroline CORNEY	6th February 1873
14	IHS	Rev. George BAMPTON S.J.	10th November 1865
15	S. Ann Teresa	Jane GREHAN	17th April 1863
16	S. Joseph Sales, 14th PRIORESS	Cecilia KENDAL	3rd February 1918

Entrance Gateway

OLD C[EMETERY]

Lower Section (Rows A–D, Columns 20–35)

Row A
#	Religious Name	Name	Date
20	S. Mary Clare	Elizabeth EVENS	13th July 1799
21	S. Barbara	Emelia FREEMAN	14th July 1799
22	S. Cleophae	Mary MARSHALL	3rd May 1803
23	S. Loyola	Mary SEYMORE	28th October 1820
25	S. Baptist	Miss Louisa WINNARD	8th May 1820
26		Elizabeth FERRIOR	23rd January 1837
27	S. Francis Borgia	Margaret CROSS	13th May 1840
28	S. Teresa Austin	Euphrasia NADIT	1st April 1817
29	S. Winifred	Jane PORTER	26th March 1831
30	S. Catherine	Elizabeth NORRIS	29th April 1837
31	S. Agatha	Margaret MADDEN	11th April 1897
32	S. Magdalen Stanislaus	Anne FITZPATRICK	14th November 1897
33	S. Catherine Joseph	Mary Eliza KELLY	14th July 1898

Row B
#	Religious Name	Name	Date
20	S. Magdalen	Mary HARGITT	23rd January 1837
21	S. Anne Xaveria	Elizabeth STRAPPEN	19th March 1805
22	IHS	Rev. Mr. Gervais GENN S.J.	1st October 1800
23	S. Martha	Gertrude REEKS	21st February 1805
24	S. Ursula	Clare SEMJES	19th March 1820
25	S. Mary Ursula	Mary Anne WRIGHT	17th October 1940
26	S. Aloysia Gonzaga	Elizabeth SMITHERS	7th April 1819
27	S. Magdalen	Mary BURCHAL	31st October 1831
28	S. Salome	Ann PARKINSON	13th November 1833
29	S. Mary Euphrasia	Mrs. Angélique Christina CLEMENT	14th March 1837
30		Madelle Angélique MOLLIET	30th April 1831
31	S. Winefride	Mary Elizabeth PRATT	14th February 1831
32	S. Winifred	Mary BLAKE	17th December 1899
33	S. Salome	Sarah Ann EMERY	1st April 1906
34	S. Monica	Julia DALY	9th November 1900

Row C
#	Religious Name	Name	Date
20	IHS	Rev. Peter O'BRIEN S.J.	28th February 1807
21	S. Mary Juliana	Anne HALES	21st May 1811
22	S. Mary Magdalen	Bridget CHAMPNEY	5th April 1813
23	S. Mary Magdalen	Elizabeth FULLWOOD	7th September 1947
24	S. Paul	Mildred FALLS	22nd December 1813
25	S. Mary Magdalen	Mary Louise HOWARD	24th June 1817
26	S. Bertmans	Susanna SMITH	14th May 1819
27	S. Mary Philip	Eufrieda PERRIN	9th November 1940
28	S. Mary Rose	Catherine KENDAL	12th May 1833
29	S. Aloysia	Barbara ARCHDEACON	3rd February 1836
30	S. Mary Ann	Mary NEVOY	13th January 1836
31	S. Mary Stanislaus	Harriet HEAD	26th May 1837
32	S. Frances Xavier	Mary Winifride WHATTOLEY	31st January 1900
33	S. Aloysia Joseph	Ann COSTELLO	16th August 1907
34	S. Flaviana	Catherine MARSH	24th July 1909

Row D
#	Religious Name	Name	Date
20		Rev. James NICHOLSON	7th November 1934
21	IHS	Elizabeth DENNETT	6th April 1816
22	S. Stephen	Rev. Stephen RORKE	19th July 1825
23	S. Christina	Margaret CHAPSON	17th July 1856
24	S. Mary Clare	Dorothy GANDOLFI	aged 21 years 2nd August 1856
25	S. Teresa Austin	Dorothy GANDOLFI	26th March 1834
28		Catherine LAURENSON	4th August 1831
29	IHS	Rev. Thomas ANGLES S.J.	18th January 1837
30	S. Lucy	Alice PARKINSON	8th February 1837
31	S. Mary Clementina	Barbara O'CONNOR	22nd May 1837
32	S. Mary Josephine	Anna WILLIAMS	5th March 1941
33	S. Mary Gonzaga	Maria WATTS	17th October 1906
34	S. Ignatia Frances	Rosina MASON	21st February 1909

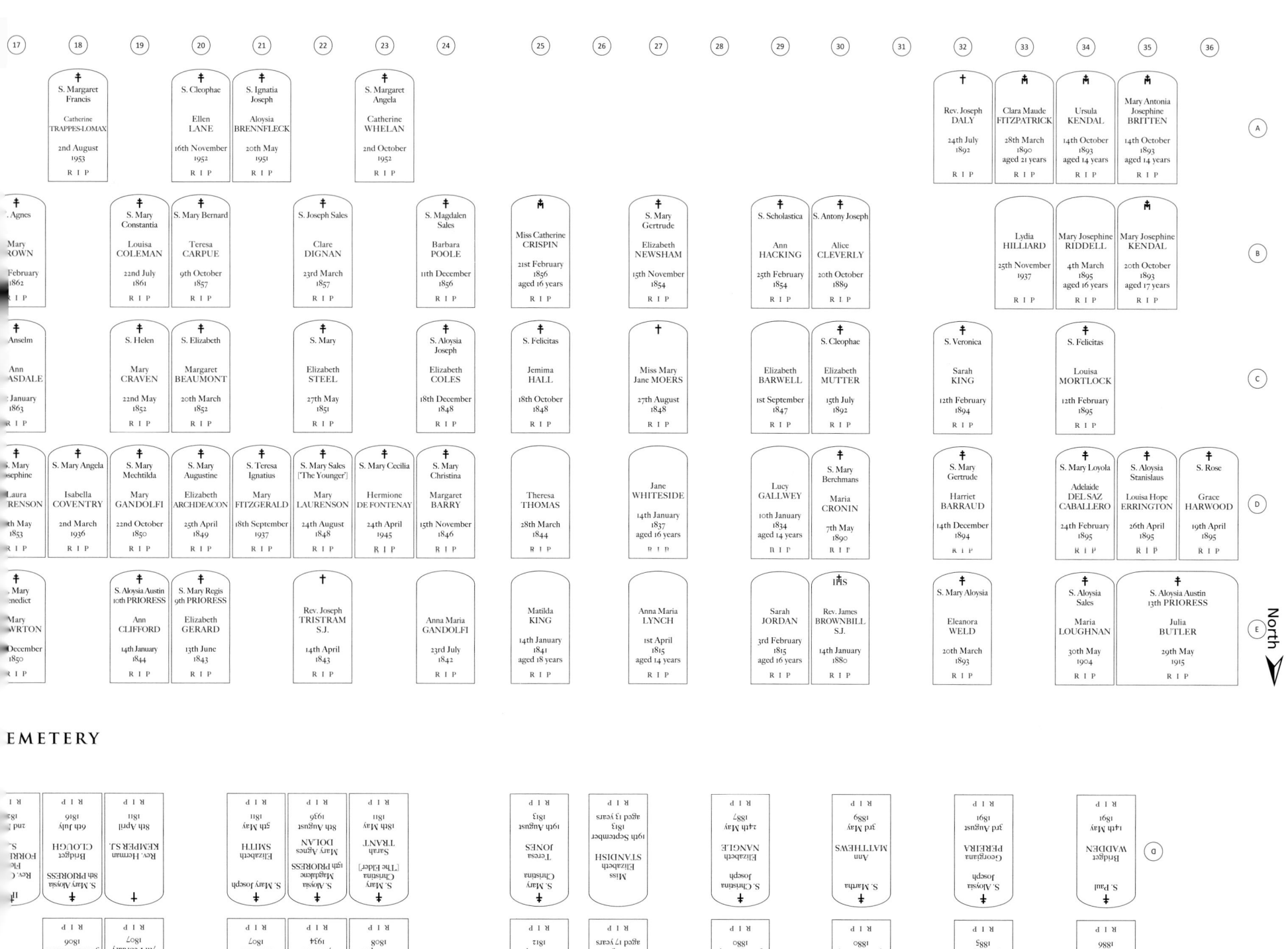

Cemetery Map

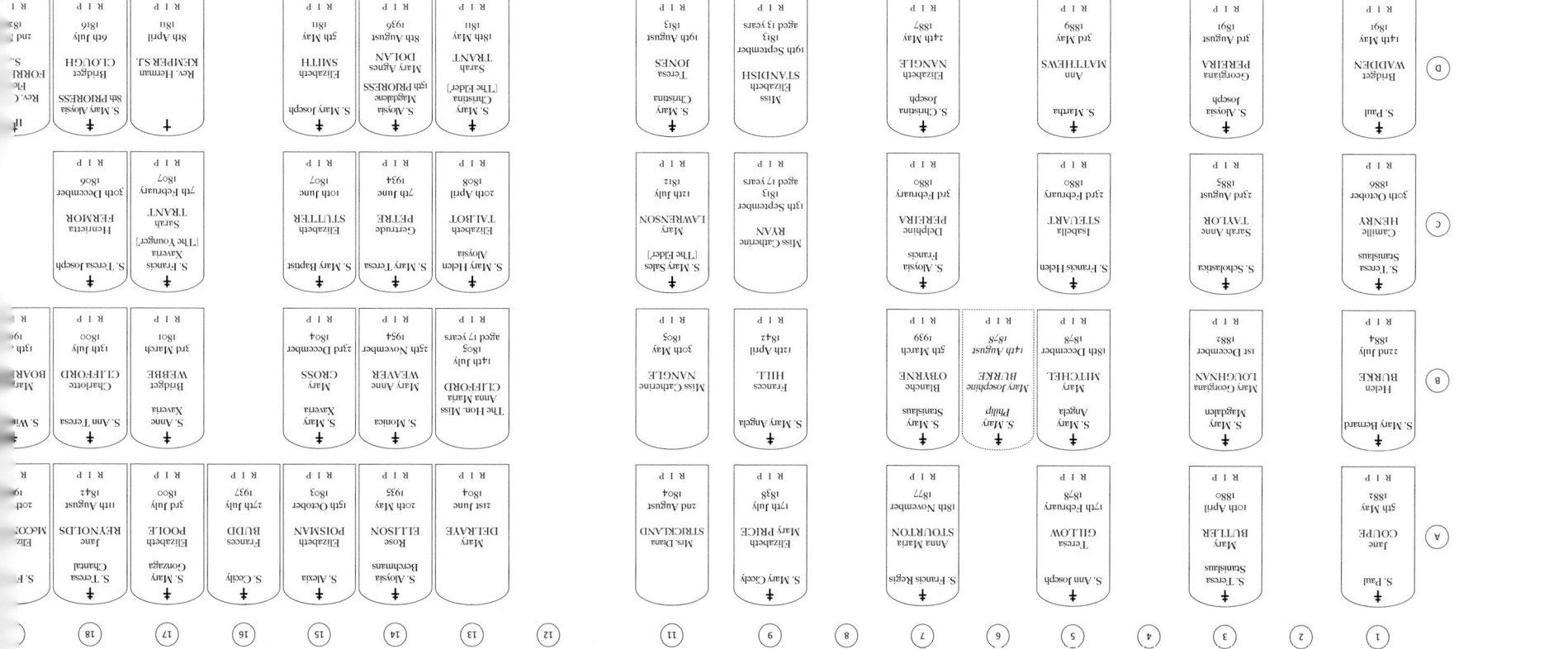

North ↑

Row A (North section)

Col	Name	Religious Name	Date	Age
18	Catherine TRAPPES-LOMAX	S. Margaret Francis	2nd August 1953	
20	Ellen LANE	S. Cleophae	16th November 1952	
21	Aloysia BRENNFLECK	S. Ignatia Joseph	20th May 1951	
23	Catherine WHELAN	S. Margaret Angela	2nd October 1952	
32	Rev. Joseph DALY		24th July 1892	
33	Clara Maude FITZPATRICK		28th March 1890	aged 21 years
34	Ursula KENDAL		14th March 1893	aged 14 years
35	Mary Antonia Josephine BRITTEN		14th October 1893	aged 14 years

Row B

Col	Name	Religious Name	Date	Age
17	Mary BROWN	S. Agnes	February 1862	
19	Louisa COLEMAN	S. Mary Constantia	22nd July 1861	
20	Teresa CARPUE	S. Mary Bernard	9th October 1857	
22	Clare DIGNAN	S. Joseph Sales	23rd March 1857	
24	Barbara POOLE	S. Magdalen Sales	11th December 1856	
25	Miss Catherine CRISPIN		21st February 1856	aged 16 years
27	Elizabeth NEWSHAM	S. Mary Gertrude	15th November 1854	
29	Ann HACKING	S. Scholastica	25th February 1854	
30	Alice CLEVERLY	S. Antony Joseph	20th October 1889	
32	Lydia HILLIARD		25th November 1937	
33	Mary Josephine RIDDELL		4th March 1895	aged 16 years
34	Mary Josephine KENDAL		20th October 1893	aged 17 years

Row C

Col	Name	Religious Name	Date	Age
17	Ann LASDALE	S. Anselm	January 1863	
19	Mary CRAVEN	S. Helen	22nd May 1852	
20	Margaret BEAUMONT	S. Elizabeth	20th March 1852	
22	Elizabeth STEEL	S. Mary	27th May 1851	
24	Elizabeth COLES	S. Aloysia Joseph	18th December 1848	
25	Jemima HALL	S. Felicitas	18th October 1848	
27	Miss Mary Jane MOERS		27th August 1848	
29	Elizabeth BARWELL		1st September 1847	
30	Elizabeth MUTTER	S. Cleophae	15th July 1892	
32	Sarah KING	S. Veronica	12th February 1894	
34	Louisa MORTLOCK	S. Felicitas	12th February 1895	

Row D

Col	Name	Religious Name	Date	Age
17	Laura RENSON	S. Mary Josephine	8th May 1853	
18	Isabella COVENTRY	S. Mary Angela	2nd March 1936	
19	Mary GANDOLFI	S. Mary Mechtilda	22nd October 1850	
20	Elizabeth ARCHDEACON	S. Mary Augustine	25th April 1849	
21	Mary FITZGERALD	S. Teresa Ignatius	18th September 1937	
22	Mary LAURENSON	S. Mary Sales ['The Younger']	24th August 1848	
23	Hermione DE FONTENAY	S. Mary Cecilia	24th April 1945	
24	Margaret BARRY	S. Mary Christina	15th November 1846	
25	Theresa THOMAS		28th March 1844	
27	Jane WHITESIDE		14th January 1837	aged 16 years
29	Lucy GALLWEY	S. Mary Berchmans	10th January 1834	aged 14 years
30	Maria CRONIN		7th May 1890	
32	Harriet BARRAUD	S. Mary Gertrude	14th December 1894	
33	Adelaide DEL SAZ CABALLERO	S. Mary Loyola	24th February 1895	
34	Louisa Hope ERRINGTON	S. Aloysia Stanislaus	26th April 1895	
35	Grace HARWOOD	S. Rose	19th April 1895	

Row E

Col	Name	Religious Name	Date	Age
17	Mary LAWRTON	S. Mary Benedict	December 1850	
18	Ann CLIFFORD	S. Aloysia Austin, 10th PRIORESS	14th January 1844	
19	Elizabeth GERARD	S. Mary Regis, 9th PRIORESS	13th June 1843	
21	Rev. Joseph TRISTRAM S.J.		14th April 1843	
23	Anna Maria GANDOLFI		23rd July 1842	
25	Matilda KING		14th January 1841	aged 18 years
27	Anna Maria LYNCH		1st April 1815	
29	Sarah JORDAN		3rd February 1815	aged 16 years
30	Rev. James BROWNBILL S.J.	IHS	14th January 1880	
32	Eleanora WELD	S. Mary Aloysia	20th March 1893	
33	Maria LOUGHNAN	S. Aloysia Sales	30th May 1904	
34	Julia BUTLER	S. Aloysia Austin, 13th PRIORESS	29th May 1915	

CEMETERY (South section)

Row A

Col	Name	Religious Name	Date
1	Jane COUPE	S. Paul	5th May 1882
2	Mary BUTLER	S. Teresa Stanislaus	10th April 1880
3	Teresa GILLOW	S. Ann Joseph	17th February 1878
5	Anna Maria STOURTON	S. Francis Regis	18th November 1877
7	Elizabeth HILL	S. Mary Angela	17th July 1842
8	Mrs Diana STRICKLAND		2nd August 1804
13	Mary DELRAVE		21st June 1804
14	Rose NOSMAN [POSMAN?]	S. Aloysia Berchmans	20th May 1803
15	Elizabeth POOLE	S. Alexia	17th October 1927
16	Frances BUDD	S. Cecily	3rd July 1800
17	Jane REYNOLDS	S. Mary Gonzaga	11th August 1843
18	Eliz. McCOURT	S. Teresa Chantal	20th May	

Row B

Col	Name	Religious Name	Date
1	Helen BURKE	S. Mary Bernard	22nd July 1884
2	Mary Georgiana LOUGHNAN	S. Mary Magdalen	1st December 1883
3	Mary MITCHEL	S. Mary Angela	18th December 1878
4	Blanche Mary Josephine O'BYRNE	S. Mary Philip	14th August 1878
5	Frances BURKE	S. Mary Stanislaus	5th March 1939
7	Miss Catherine HILL		30th May 1805
13	The Hon. Miss Anna Maria CLIFFORD	S. Monica	14th July 1805 aged 17 years
14	Mary Anne WEAVER	S. Mary Teresa	15th November 1954
15	Mary CROSS	S. Mary Xaveria	23rd December 1805
16	Bridget WEBBE	S. Anne Xaveria	3rd March 1801
17	Charlotte CLIFFORD	S. Ann Teresa	13th July 1800
18	Mary BOARD	S. Weld		

Row C

Col	Name	Religious Name	Date
1	Camille HENRY	S. Teresa Stanislaus	30th October 1885
2	Sarah Anne TAYLOR	S. Scholastica	23rd August 1885
3	Isabella STEUART	S. Francis Hem	23rd February 1885
4	Delphine PEREIRA	S. Aloysia Francis	3rd February 1880
5	Mary LAWRENSON	Miss Catherine RYAN	S. Mary Sales ['The Elder']	13th September 1813 aged 17 years / 12th July 1812
15	Elizabeth PETRE	S. Mary Baptist	7th June 1807
16	Gertrude PETRE	S. Mary Teresa	10th June 1807
17	Sarah TALBOT	S. Francis Xaveria ['The Younger']	7th February 1807
18	Henrietta FERMOR	S. Teresa Joseph	30th December 1806

Row D

Col	Name	Religious Name	Date
1	Bridget MADDEN	S. Paul	14th May 1891
2	Georgiana PEREIRA	S. Aloysia Joseph	3rd August 1889
3	Ann MATTHEWS	S. Martha	3rd May 1889
4	Georgie NANGLE	S. Joseph	14th May 1887
6	Miss Elizabeth STANDISH	S. Christina	19th September 1813 aged 13 years
7	Teresa JONES	S. Mary Christina	19th August 1811
14	Sarah TRANT	S. Mary Magdalene, 11th PRIORESS	18th May 1811
15	Mary Agnes DOLAN	S. Aloysia	8th August 1936
16	Elizabeth SMITH	S. Mary Joseph	5th May 1807
17	Rev. Herman KEMPER S.J.		8th April 1816
18	Bridget CLOUGH	S. Mary Aloysia, 8th PRIORESS	6th July 1816